Front cover:
Marlon Brando as
Emiliano Zapata, ca. 1952.

See Rewriting revolution: the origins,
production and reception of *Viva Zapata!*
(page 115).

This issue:
THE 1950S AND BEYOND

Edited by John Belton

Editorial office:

Richard Koszarski
American Museum of the Moving Image
36-01 35th Avenue
Astoria, NY 11106
USA

Publishing office:

John Libbey & Company Pty Ltd
Level 10, 15–17 Young Street
Sydney, NSW 2000
Australia
Telephone: +61 (0)2 9251 4099
Fax: +61 (0)2 9251 4428

© 1996 John Libbey & Company Pty Ltd

Other offices:

John Libbey & Company Ltd
13 Smiths Yard, Summerley Street
London SW18 4HR, UK
Telephone: +44 (0)181-947 2777
Fax: +44 (0)1-947 2664

John Libbey Eurotext Ltd, Montrouge, France
John Libbey - CIC s.r.l., Rome, Italy

Printed in Australia by
Gillingham Printers Pty Ltd, South Australia

FII
HI

CW00496058

An International Journal

Volume 8, Number 2, 1996

The *Canadian Journal of Film Studies / Revue canadienne d'études cinématographiques* is available to all members of the *Film Studies Association of Canada / Association canadienne d'études cinématographiques*. The Journal can also be obtained through individual subscriptions at the cost of $35.00 per volume in Canada, and US $35.00 in all other countries. Postage is included. Back issues are available at $15.00 per volume.

Don't miss the upcoming issue of the

Canadian Journal of Film Studies
Revue canadienne d'études cinématographiques

On the
CENTENARY OF CINEMA IN CANADA
(vol. 5 no. 2, Fall 1996)

This issue of the *Canadian Journal of Film Studies / Revue canadienne d'études cinématographiques* will include:

"Querying or Queering the Nation: the Lesbian Postmodern and Women's Cinema," by **Jean Bruce**; "Exile on Hastings & Main Streets: The Vancouver Films of Larry Kent," by **Dave Douglas**; "The Introduction of the Lumière Cinematograph in Canada," by **André Gaudreault and Germain Lacasse**, translation by Madeleine Beaudry; "Alterity and Nation: Screening Race, Sex, Gender and Ethnicity in *Back to God's Country*," by **Christopher Gittings**; "Cinema, Theater and Red Gushing Blood in Jean Beaudin's *Being at Home with Claude*," by **André Loiselle**; "The Crisis of Naming in Canadian Film Studies," by **Brenda Longfellow**; "The Challenge for Change in the Alternative Public Sphere," by **Scott MacKenzie**; and "Hags, Nags, Witches and Crones: Reframing Age in *Company of Strangers* by **Angela Stukator**. Also "J. Booth Scott, A Personal History (1966)," introduced by **Blaine Allan**. Plus *Book Reviews* by Gene Walz and Lianne McLarty.

For subscription information and complimentary issues and to order back issues and single copies, please contact the Editorial Office:

SCHOOL FOR STUDIES IN ART AND CULTURE:
FILM STUDIES
Carleton University
1125 Colonel By Drive Ottawa, Ont. K1S 5B6
Tel. (613) 520-2600 Ext. 6693 Fax (613) 520-3575

Film History, Volume 8, pp. 107–108, 1996. Copyright © John Libbey & Company
ISSN: 0892-2160. Printed in Australia

The 1950s and Beyond

John Belton

This issue of *Film History* contains a special section on the 1950s, one of the most turbulent and exciting periods in the history of the cinema. It also looks beyond this period, back to American cinema of the 1920s, 1930s and 1940s, as well as forward to the 1990s.

The post-war era witnessed a dramatic transformation of the cinema in response to social, political, economic and technological change. Internationally, filmmakers in England, France, Italy, Japan and elsewhere attempted to rebuild their national cinemas in the wake of the war and the threat of post-war American domination. Within the United States, the film industry was forced to redefine itself in reponse to a changing political climate (McCarthyism and anti-communism), a shifting socio-sexual reality ('mature' themes and sexual controversy) and changes in the patterns of leisure-time activities brought about by new technologies, such as television.

In this issue, Jonathan Schoenwald documents the pre-production history of John Steinbeck's and Elia Kazan's *Viva Zapata!* (1952). He views the development of the project in terms of Steinbeck's and Kazan's attempts to negotiate the political problems related to telling the story of a revolutionary hero in a period in which radical activities (in Hollywood and elsewhere) were regarded with suspicion. Zapata's rejection of totalitarian temptation (he is offered a dictatorship but refuses) in favour of democratic ideals emphasises his status as a Populist leader and undermines any notion that he might be a peasant committed to a communist overthrow of the government. Schoenwald's discussion of the reception of the film situates popular criticism of its historical inaccuracies in relation to the ideological demands of 1950s America.

In the wake of post-war American efforts to dominate British screens, England sought to stimulate domestic production and to compete in the world market by subsidising the creation of a new state agency, dedicated to film production, known as Group Three. Simon Popple examines this experiment, which brought together the creative talents of Michael Balcon, John Grierson and others. Designed, in part, as an alternative to the films made by the Rank Organisation, Group Three films looked back to the pre-war documentry tradition and were influenced by post-war Ealing comedies. As Popple demonstrates, the failure of Group Three provides a valuable lesson in the virtues and limitations of state intervention in film production.

Resistance to Hollywood films came in other forms as well, most significantly in the post-wr success of foreign films in American theatres known as art houses. Barbara Wilinsky reviews the debates and discourses surrounding the rise of foreign film distribution and exhibition in the 1950s, relating this new market to the economic problems brought about by the Paramount Case and to the interest on the part of certain sectors of the post-war American audience in adult entertainment. The advent of this new market raises questions about the status of these films – are they art or are they exploitation? Wilinsky explores their dual nature as 'adult' entertainment, viewing them as 'adult' in both senses of the word. They are sophisticated, difficult and artistically challenging, yet they are also 'adult' in terms of their sexual content.

The interest of 1950s audiences in sexually controversial material motivates Twentieth Century-Fox's production of *The Girl on the Red Velvet Swing* (1955), a CinemaScope and DeLuxe colour spectacle that has as its basis the notorious Thaw-White scandal that took place almost fifty years earlier. Drawing on files from the Motion Picture Producers

Association, documents from the Twentieth Century-Fox's legal department, motion picture trade journals and newspapers and magazine articles, Stephanie Savage situates the 1955 film within contemporary discourses about sexuality and the female body. At the centre of the original scandal of 1906 was Evelyn Nesbit. In retelling her story, Fox relied extensively on Nesbit, who was still alive in 1955, to promote the film. Savage traces the history of the media's fascination with Nesbit from 1906 to her death in 1967, documenting its transformation of her into sexual spectacle.

New technology, in the form of television, forced Hollywood to rethink the way it made films and the kind of films it made. Jerome Delamater places the production history of Warner Bros.' Western *Yellowstone Kelly* (1959) within the context of the studio's own televsion series, *Warner Bros. Presents*. Using the Warner Bros. archives at the University of Southern California, Delamater investigates the studio's efforts to tailor its motion picture productions to the changing entertainment marketplace. In *Yellowstone Kelly*, the classic motion picture western is reconceived in terms of the 1950s television western. The film thus reflects the contradictory forces competing within the film industry itself.

The second half of this issue covers a variety of topics, from Charles Chaplin to black audiences in Atlanta and spans several decades, from the 1920s to the 1990s. Jeffrey Vance reconstructs the circumstances surrounding Chaplin's production of *The Circus*. Though beset by a series of professional and personal obstacles, ranging from a fire that destroyed the film's set to divorce proceedings that froze his assets (including the film), Chaplin succeeded in making a film that is clearly a masterpiece. Vance also explores the autobiographical aspects of the film and provides a detailed account of three of the film's major sequences.

Using Mary Carbine's work on black movie-going in Chicago in the 1920s as a model, Randy Gue explores the exhibition strategy of a black movie theatre in Atlanta in the mid-1930s. Gue discovers a pattern of progrmming at Atlanta's 81 Theatre that specifically addresses the needs of black audiences for black entertainment. Thus Hollywood films featuring white stars would regularly be accompanied by live stage shows starring black performers. On other occasions, the theatre would screen 'race' films directed by Oscar Micheaux and others.

Atlanta hosted the premiere of Walt Disney's *Song of the South* in 1946. As Matthew Bernstein points out in his analysis of the film's reception, the film's controversial portrait of plantation life in the Old South was viewed as racially offensive by the northern press. However, the only black newspaper in Atlanta took a different tack, viewing the film ambivalently rather than simply condemning it. Bernstein situates this reponse in the context of the city's troubled race relations in the mid-1940s. He compares the coverage of the film in the black press with that in the city's two leading 'white' newspapers. What emerges is a complex portrait of the different responses to the film that is shaped by the unique nature of the needs and interests of the black and white communities in Atlanta. Both Gue and Bernstein demonstrate the importance of local reception studies which often reveal unpredictable results.

Independent filmmaker Kevin Smith has completed two films, *Clerks* (1994) and *Mallrats* (1995). In an interview with Clinton Duritz, Jr., Smith talks about film-going in New Jersey, film school in Vancouver, film theory, the Sundance Film Festival and low-budget filmmaking. The interview provides a snapshot of state-of-the-art independent filmmaking in the 1990s.

Special thanks to Matthew Bernstein, Scott Curtis, the late William K. Everson and Karla Fuller for their help in the preparation of this issue.❖

John Belton
Associate Editor

Film History, Volume 8, pp. 109–130, 1996. Copyright © John Libbey & Company
ISSN: 0892-2160. Printed in Australia

Rewriting revolution: the origins, production and reception of Viva Zapata!

Jonathan M. Schoenwald

n early 1952, the Cold War was a fact of life for most Americans. Fought primarily as a political contest of ideology and rhetoric, the standoff grew to affect the lives of average and not-so-average Americans. In Korea, where the Cold War had become a life-and-death matter, the date of 2 February denoted when American commitment to the 'police action' surpassed the level of involvement in World War I.[1] Domestically, the ideological battle touched institutions the public heretofore had perceived of as apolitical. The film industry became one of the most contested fronts, where politics, economics and popular culture all collided with rarely predictable results. For example, that same week in February, a film producer named Sidney Buchman was cited for contempt for refusing to testify before the House Un-American Activities Committee (HUAC).[2] And in Dallas, Texas, the censor board's decision to ban the well- known director Elia Kazan's Pinky (1949) was upheld by the Court of Criminal Appeals.[3] Coincidentally, the following week saw the release of Kazan's latest film, Viva Zapata! (1952), about an agrarian revolutionary during the Mexican Revolution. The film came out of a Hollywood which faced a triple threat: declining box-offices due to changes in leisure-time entertainment habits and television, worries about increased censorship and

governmental control and heightened public awareness about 'subversive' stories which could potentially derail a picture. Many in the industry had hopes that 1952 would be a banner year, a time when Hollywood reasserted its preeminence in the American entertainment industry. But as was often the case with Hollywood productions, the 1952 they envisaged bore little resemblance to what actually transpired.

In June 1952, John Steinbeck wrote from Rome to his friend and screenwriting collaborator Jules Buck. Steinbeck was enjoying an extended honeymoon with his wife Elaine and was in no hurry to return to hectic New York. Unlike his previous letters, however, Steinbeck did not recount the sights of Europe to Buck. This time his tone was more urgent and concerned:

> I talked with Gadge [Elia Kazan] this morning on the phone. He said he was going to see you tomorrow I believe. He sounded fine on the telephone and I am glad because he has taken

Jonathan M. Schoenwald is pursuing his doctorate in American history at Stanford University. Please address correspondence to Department of History, Stanford University, Stanford, CA 94305-2024, USA. e-mail: jonathan@leland.stanford.edu

a terrible beating. But he'll come through it. He is a great guy. And he will do better work than he has ever done. This must be a great weight off him in one way.[4]

Steinbeck was referring to two events to which he, Buck and Kazan were all related: the release and subsequent box-office failure of *Viva Zapata!*, and Kazan's testimony in April in front of HUAC. The film was relatively expensive for Twentieth Century-Fox (Marlon Brando alone was paid $100,000[5]) and Kazan's decision to 'name names' at the hearings excommunicated him from much of the Hollywood community.[6] *Viva Zapata!*, however, was not another trivial Hollywood genre picture. In many ways, *Zapata!* was a microcosm of the upheaval that resulted from clashing ideologies and the economic and social consequences of those collisions.

In the forty years since its release much has been written about *Zapata!*. Some authors have advanced historical perspectives that cast new light on the representations in the film within a Cold War context.[7] Most research and writing about the film, however, focuses on the question of whether or not the movie was anti-revolutionary, and if it was whether that means it was historically inaccurate. While these studies are surely important and enlightening, they fail to place the film within the context of American society and Hollywood society (two different but intersecting cultures). Some authors have scrutinised the script and Kazan's direction. Others have concentrated solely on the finished product, since that is what audiences saw. Still others have examined the studio's role in the production and how Hollywood fears and priorities shaped the film. But only by examining the entire project within the context of Hollywood and the politics that pervaded Hollywood can the film be properly evaluated. More specifically, the contributions of Steinbeck, Kazan and Buck must be explored; they wrote what was filmed. What is potentially most revealing is *why* Steinbeck, Kazan and Buck conceived of Zapata in the ways that they

Fig. 1. A shift in the political winds? Anthony Quinn, Brando, and Lou Gilbert confront Harold Gordon's Madero after the fall of Díaz. [Photo courtesy of Twentieth Century-Fox.]

did. By uncovering their ideas about Zapata and 1950s politics and integrating them into an analysis of the film as an entire project, the hidden meanings of the film, as well as what it meant politically and culturally in 1952 and after, may at last begin to reveal themselves.

Origins

In 1910, at the beginning of the Mexican Revolution, Emiliano Zapata emerged as an agrarian leader in the sugar-producing state of Morelos. Zapata's story is the stuff of high drama – it is not surprising that the rebels in Chiapas, Mexico in 1994 adopted the name *Zapatistas*. Born probably in 1879, Zapata came from a family of farmers which, in the late nineteenth century, was forced off their land by sugar plantations. By the end of the first decade of the twentieth century, the horse-trainer Zapata was involved in grass-roots politics. He was made president of his village council in 1909, and he rose steadily in power as he marshalled the agrarian masses against the land-robbing *haciendas*. After the outbreak of the Revolution in 1910, launched by Francisco Madero and supported by Pancho Villa and Zapata, Zapata acted as one of a handful of major players in the long struggle, leading men against the federal soldiers.[8] By 1911 Madero, Villa and Zapata had forced the dictator Porfirio Díaz to resign, and Madero was elected President (see Fig. 1). In 1913, however, Madero fell to General Victoriano Huerta, a Díaz supporter, who immediately began demobilising Zapata's forces in Morelos. Zapata, however, was rightly suspicious of Huerta, and he and Villa continued their struggle to win land and representation for the people. By mid-1914, Huerta resigned when faced with the advancing forces of Villa, Alvaro Obregón and Venustiano Carranza. In yet another turn of events, however, Carranza soon turned on Villa and Zapata, and in the end was elected President, having Zapata killed in 1919.[9]

The story of Zapata is a good one – perhaps too good. It is difficult to get a clear account of his life; the temptation for authors and storytellers to exaggerate seems hard to pass up. Not long after his death in 1919 when he was ambushed by government soldiers in a one-sided battle[10], ideas began circulating for books and perhaps films about Zapata's life. An ex-Zapatista (a soldier of Zapata's) wrote a two-volume biography of Zapata, part of which was translated and adapted by an American, Edgcomb Pinchon, in the early 1930s.[11] From these writings came *Viva Villa!* (1933).[12] While most critics writing from a historical perspective credit *Viva Villa!* with influencing Steinbeck's script, neither Steinbeck nor Kazan ever mention the film or the writings of that time. In fact, there are three possibilities for the origins of the idea for *Viva Zapata!*: *Viva Villa!* and the subsequent projects undertaken by Metro-Goldwyn-Mayer; Steinbeck's own fascinations; and Kazan's own motives.

The most credible story (due to its extensive documentation) is that MGM, which had produced *Viva Villa!*, was convinced by Pinchon to make the film about Zapata depicting a Mexican fight for a kind of American democracy, very much unlike what actually took place during Zapata's struggles.[13] But research by MGM screenwriters uncovered just how revolutionary Zapata's ideas about land reform really were. Zapata wanted the government to have the ability to regulate and, if need be, nationalise private property – including that which was owned by foreigners.[14] Such power drew obvious comparisons to Soviet communism. Additionally, the outbreak of World War II forced MGM to concentrate on more timely subjects and the project was quickly shelved. In 1946 MGM returned to the subject, fully intending to produce the film. But by late 1948, with much of the preliminary work completed, MGM sold the property to Twentieth Century-Fox. The reasons for this are well-documented: MGM's fears of a too-revolutionary central character and story, combined with the first round of the HUAC hearings in 1947, convinced them to drop the project.

Steinbeck, however, always claimed to be interested in the film since having taken trips to Mexico in the 1930s and 1940s. Writing to a friend from Cuernavaca, Mexico, in the summer of 1945, Steinbeck said:

> I was approached the other day by an outfit that calls itself Pan-American Films with the proposition that I do a film on the life of Emiliano Zapata. Now there is no other story I would rather do. But there are certain things

that are in the way. ... There are still men living and in power who helped to trick and murder Zapata. I would only make it straight. I would require gov't assurance that it could be made straight historically. This will have to be an iron bound agreement because Zapata could be one of the great films of all time as by a twist or a concession it could be a complete double cross of the things Zapata lived and died for.[15]

Whether Pan-American Films had any knowledge of Pinchon's or MGM's earlier efforts is not known. Two weeks later Steinbeck wrote to Clemente Internacional Films in Mexico, insisting that:

> ... the picture follow the true life of Zapata unadulterated by the political or artistic distortions which have characterised such films as 'Viva Villa', 'Juarez' and 'Maximiliano', that it, in a word, be an authentic historical document.[16]

The fact that Steinbeck foresaw the political symbolism contained in Zapata provides some insight into how the writer saw the revolutionary as the world entered the Cold War era. Furthermore, it is entirely possible and believable that Steinbeck had no knowledge of Pinchon's and MGM's work.[17] If this is true, Steinbeck's work must be seen as a personal project with only his own sensibilities to guide the first draft of his script. While Steinbeck did do extensive research in Mexico, his perceptions as a novelist were different from those of an historian or political analyst. Thus, in the debate about historical accuracy, if this theory is accepted, Steinbeck's composition must be seen as the work of a fiction writer and not a historical biographer.

Finally, Kazan often claimed that the film was his idea alone: 'various things started Zapata, but it was my idea'.[18] It is possible that Kazan as well as Steinbeck had no knowledge of MGM's designs before 1944. Kazan, however, has offered conflicting dates attesting to when he became involved with the project: 'I'd had the idea of making a film on Zapata since 1935 when I took a trip to Mexico and heard about him'.[19] Kazan, however, also claims that he had:

> ... started making notes on a film about Emiliano Zapata in 1944. It's the first film I made

from an idea that attracted me – a revolutionist fights a bloody war, gains power, then walks away – one I started and saw through to the end. I'd made three trips to Mexico, knew every stone in the province of Morelos, done years of research and study, followed by bursts of frustration and doubt.[20]

While it might be naïve to think that Kazan and Steinbeck did not know of the extensive work which predated their own, it seems that they collaborated closely from the beginning. Whatever the case, Steinbeck and Kazan relied primarily on their own knowledge and deductions to craft *Zapata!*.

Kazan's and Steinbeck's inspiration for making a film about Zapata stemmed from their fascination with the legendary story of the man. After the movie had been released, Kazan responded to a bad review in the *Saturday Review*, mostly defending their historical interpretations and their controversial decision for Zapata to abdicate the Presidency. While Kazan obviously wrote for a specific audience and within a week of the letter's publication he testified before HUAC, the letter's basic premise was important: 'It is human character, above all, which concerns a director, writer, producer [Darryl Zanuck] and it was the character of Zapata which intrigued us all'.[21] It is difficult to know how deliberately Steinbeck and Kazan fashioned their other writing and directing projects as anti-communist *before* the first HUAC hearings in 1947. But by 1948–49 they, the studio executives (most importantly Zanuck and Spyros Skouras, president of Twentieth Century-Fox) and the critics all quickly came to associate both Zapata and the film as symbolic of the Cold War. In essence, the question had boiled down to what kind of Mexican revolution did Zapata lead: American or Russian?

No matter how great the story was, however, the movie had to have box-office potential. The combination of revolutionaries and the upcoming HUAC hearings had been enough to scare away MGM. Twentieth Century-Fox saw the film as a moneymaker through its appeal to American-style democracy and a Western setting. Moreover, Darryl Zanuck was famous for picking winning films. He knew the formulas that worked best with an audience the studio still perceived to be homogeneous. Kazan and Steinbeck knew Zanuck's methods; no matter how good a script they could produce, Zanuck judged a film by its money-making capacity. For example, in 1950 while Steinbeck and Kazan were in Mexico attempting to secure a location for filming, they realised (as Kazan later recounted) that Mexican communists were reading the script. Steinbeck questioned Kazan about people other than Zanuck reading the script in Hollywood:

> 'Aren't there people reading our script in California and criticising it to Zanuck?' John asked. 'Sure', I said, 'but we don't have to do what they say. Only what Zanuck says.' 'Is that better?' John asked. 'I prefer it', I said, 'for the simple reason that Darryl is geared to company profits'. 'You may regret that expression of choice', John said.[22]

The film was doubtlessly created for various ideological reasons, but ultimately the decision to make it depended on its ability to earn money. Zanuck knew what would sell. Critics who faulted the film for its historical inaccuracy were (and are), in a sense, attacking a set of economic guidelines determined by the intersection of public demand and Hollywood's desire (and need) to provide for them. While Kazan and Steinbeck insisted on the film's historical accuracy, the confines in which they were forced to work limited how accurate the film could ever become. When writing the script, Steinbeck cared less about what would make the movie sell, but he did consider contemporary politics. And Kazan would know that making a pro-revolutionary film with communist overtones would be the equivalent of economic (and professional) suicide. While the embedded contemporary politics are difficult to uncover, in their correspondence Steinbeck and Jules Buck did hint at how their historical and political ideals created their archetypal leader.

The script

Even after returning from a trip to Mexico in 1948, Steinbeck did not know whether he would actually write a script about Zapata. Corresponding with a friend that May, he sounded more unsure than ever about what project to tackle next:

> ... As to the future, I don't know. I may do a

picture of the life of Emiliano Zapata if I can find someone to do it honestly. The great danger of Zanuck is that he writes and he can't but he thinks he can. I don't mean Zanuck, of course, I mean Selznick. They all sound alike. But Zanuck did a good picture for me in the *Grapes of Wrath* and [Lewis] Milestone did a good one in both the *Mice and Men* and the *Red Pony*.[23]

Steinbeck's worries about Zanuck's (or any producer's) tendency to corrupt his script had not disappeared. Zanuck liked to stay involved in his productions from beginning to end, although by his own admission he had little to contribute before a first draft existed. This fact, however, did not prevent him from offering advice to Steinbeck, urging him to write while keeping in mind how the final production might look:

> Of course a story of this sort depends almost entirely upon what we do with it or rather what you do with it. You can make a very dull, historical and enlightening version or it can be a powerful exciting and also worthwhile version, depending entirely on what *you* set out to do.[24]

Zanuck's binary world, where historically accurate pictures were dull, while pictures which took liberties with the events were exciting, brought additional tension to the already beleaguered writer.

In June 1948, however, having returned from Mexico where he had collected far more research material than could ever be used in one film alone, Steinbeck's attitude had changed dramatically:

> I am going to write a moving picture while I get on my feet. It is about one of the greatest men who ever lived. His name was Emiliano Zapata. It will be unbearably hard work and that will be a good thing. I have to do that. ... A certain amount of energy must be poured out from one fire or another and then it is done. This Zapata job is worth doing. It can be very fine.[25]

Steinbeck's first task was to condense the various stories into a cohesive narrative. Just after his return from Mexico, Steinbeck wrote to Oscar Danziggers, a friend in the Mexican film industry, asking him to investigate details ranging from whether Zapata's brother, Eufemio, was really dead, to whether his sister currently sold tortillas in a market in Cuernavaca, to how accurate Pinchon's book was: 'I want [three experts] to tell me in detail how much of this book is true and how much is the invention of Pinchon'.[26] Between his own research and that of friends like Danziggers, Steinbeck amassed details telling of Zapata's exploits on and off the field of battle.[27] A few days before he began writing, Steinbeck told a friend of the energy which pulsed through his body in anticipation of getting the story down on paper:

> My material for the Zapata script is all collected now and next Monday I will go to work on it with great energy, for I have great energy again. Whether there is any talent left I do not know nor care very much. But the churning joy in the guts that to me is the physical symptom of creation is there again.[28]

The ordeal was not an easy one for Steinbeck; long before he had the assistance of Buck or Kazan, he wrote to a friend:

> I've wondered whether it might be better to do this Zapata script down there with the sound of it in my ears. I am really having trouble with this one. It evades me. It is a wonderful story and I can't seem to get hold of it. Maybe I'm rushing it.[29]

At this point Steinbeck had been working on the script for six months. He realised it was too long to spend on the first draft of a film script; he also had novels and plays in different stages of development.[30]

By the fall of 1949, Steinbeck had completed enough of the script for Darryl Zanuck to assign a studio scriptwriter to help Steinbeck polish up the first draft. Jules Buck, one of innumerable, anonymous screenwriters in Hollywood (Buck was not credited in the film or in any related publications), went to Pacific Grove, California, to work closely with Steinbeck.[31] While no one involved in the film's production nor any film historian has paid much attention to Buck, he is important since his work with Steinbeck shaped much of the initial character conceptualisations in the movie.[32]

On 1 November 1949, Steinbeck wrote to Elaine Scott, his future wife, of the coming month:

'So the week starts. Jules Buck got in last night and we go to work today. Darling, it's going to be only notes for a while, I think. This month is going to be pure work'.[33] Buck and Steinbeck worked on the script for four weeks straight. At the end of November, Steinbeck wrote to a friend, 'Well we finished and I think it is good. Jules took it down and it is being mimeographed now'.[34] The first copies went out to Kazan and Zanuck. About a week later, Buck, Kazan and Zanuck exchanged letters, all written on the same day. Their correspondence reveals more than just their initial reactions to the 'First Draft Continuity'; it established the bases of their ideological designs for the picture. While Kazan's letter to Zanuck reveals little since he did not want to worry Zanuck about problems with developing the script, the letters from Buck to Zanuck, and Zanuck to Kazan shed new light on the story and particularly the character of Zapata.

Critics have questioned whether the real Zapata would have led the revolution in the manner of Steinbeck's and Kazan's Zapata, an opinion which depends as much on one's contemporary politics as historical evidence. Less mysterious is how the writers meant Zapata to be perceived. Buck's collaboration with Steinbeck shaped what would be very similar to the final screen depiction of Zapata. Buck told Zanuck that 'the major lack in this continuity is the failure to fully dramatise Zapata, the man. The man first – simple, typically indifferent to the dynamic events of his time and place – then, the leader, born out of those events and time'.[35] A truly revolutionary story would not be the story of one man, since a modern political revolution is, almost by definition, built on a movement of the masses. But Buck and Steinbeck knew that the film needed to focus on a central character and, in fact, Zapata had been a charismatic leader. Thus, even before the second draft was written and, arguably, out of Hollywood formulaic necessity, *Viva Zapata!* was not meant to be a truly accurate accounting of the Mexican Revolution.

Buck and Steinbeck were also influenced by an outline Kazan provided for them. After the film was released, Kazan repeatedly denied that Zapata was a communist or anything else except a type of American Jeffersonian. These assertions are substantiated by Buck's references to Kazan's desire to draw in his outline 'the parallel between

Fig. 2. Marlon Brando as Emiliano Zapata, ca. 1952.
[Photo courtesy of Twentieth Century-Fox.]

Zapata and Lincoln'.[36] But Buck clearly thought Kazan's rendition to be both hollow and unhistorical and he and Steinbeck added a great deal of complexity to Kazan's original visions. Instead of simply applying an idealised American convention to a Mexican, Buck saw a more intricate leader:

> ... we must remember that Lincoln was *not* a completely dedicated man at the time he signed the Emancipation Proclamation. Political necessity *after* [sic] he had committed himself to an unpopular course of action. The lives of most truly great men follow this course – the 'born' leaders have responsibility thrust upon them. And it would seem, as in Zapata's case, that these great men uniformly had first to die to be born.[37]

Buck's foresight saved the Zapata character from becoming even more American than he finally appeared. Buck, however, not unlike other screen-

writers, had a limited background about his current subject. He was not an expert on Mexican history. He relied on what Steinbeck told him to be the truth. So while Buck used his sense of what would work on the screen to depict Zapata's personality and character, he could not offer a more accurate vision of Zapata's actions than Steinbeck's or Kazan's.

Since Steinbeck was faced with the massive collection of material he had gathered over the years, and Kazan and Buck knew that for the story to work on the screen it had to focus on one man, they constructed the Zapata character more from their American sensibilities than from historical fact. Buck clearly stated his opinion to Zanuck, knowing full well that Zanuck would match up one of his formulas with Zapata:

> I am convinced that Zapata's story is and should remain a simple one against a background of oppression, violence and revolution. It should be the story of the growth of a man from conventional self-interest to that of responsibility – responsibility to himself and his people – the one being socially impossible without the other.[38]

Buck realised that for Zanuck to accept the script and more importantly, for American audiences to identify with Zapata without upsetting their cultural stereotypes of Mexicans, the character needed to behave the way the audience would *want* him to behave (see Fig. 2). The hero outlined above was one that Americans would admire, almost a Frank Capra-ish Mexican. Thus, while arguments about historical accuracy are important, they are restricted by the screenwriters's own limitations; their knowledge about Zapata, Mexico and what American audiences would watch determined what was written. Therefore, the criteria for evaluating the film and its characters must be found *within* Steinbeck's, Kazan's, Zanuck's and Buck's project.

After reading a draft of the script, Zanuck responded to Steinbeck and Kazan with a lengthy memo which, after acknowledging that *Zapata!* 'will make a tremendous and worth-while motion picture. It is exciting, dramatic and enlightening',[39] went on for seventeen pages to discuss problems in the script. Zanuck was extremely concerned with the writers' intentions of having a *Corrida* singer deliver the narration, rather than including relevant background information in the dialogue or in a standard voice-over. Zanuck was particularly worried about using Spanish; he had imagined that the actors would speak English with Spanish accents and that 'here and there we will employ certain Mexican phrases, such as "Adios", etc.'. Still, Zanuck believed, combining singing with a drama about Zapata might 'run the risk of having [the narration] sound like something out of Gilbert and Sullivan'.[40] Although Zanuck knew the power of novelty in show business, he was concerned that a project dealing with Mexico was already risky: 'Not many pictures about Mexico have been financially successful. As a matter of fact, the only really outstanding success was a terrible piece of hoke called *Viva Villa* starring Wallace Beery'. Furthermore, Zanuck knew the production costs for a script like the one he had just finished evaluating would be high:

> I realise that no matter how many corners we cut and how shrewd we are in designing the technical production, we are not by any means making an inexpensive picture. I am hopeful, however, that we all recognise the economic situation as it is today in the motion picture business and that we can design our physical production accordingly.[41]

One of Zanuck's first suggestions to save money was to stock the picture 'with a more or less "unknown" cast', a thought that was soon dropped.

Although Zanuck had a reputation among screenwriters and directors for watching the bottom line and little else, his penetrating insight often cut the Gordian knots which early drafts of screenplays had the tendency to become. Part of his response to Steinbeck's and Kazan's treatment was to emphasise the idea of leadership and how Zapata would act when faced with a situation where he might be called upon to serve his country:

> For some reason this idea [that a leader would rise out of 'an enlightened people'] has been eliminated. I think it is a serious loss. I think it was really the whole *answer* to the theme of the story. 'Give the people a voice and from them will come the leader'. This can be stated in the truest terms of democracy. As long as one man [Díaz] can hold off for 34 years and continue

to perpetuate himself, there is no democracy no matter what label you put on it.[42]

Like the writers, Zanuck was concerned with the political situation in Mexico and the United States. He knew that the message the movie sent would have to be pro-democratic and he took confidence in the fact that the Mexican government had a two-party system and was 'moving toward genuine democracy'. But even if the actual politics were never made obvious in the film, Zanuck believed that 'these are the things Zapata must have been thinking about or at least these are the conclusions we should have him reach at the end'.[43]

After Steinbeck and Buck had finished the first draft, they continued to correspond even though Buck was soon replaced by Kazan as the collaborative scriptwriter. Both thought they had produced an excellent script, and their egos often seemed to get the better of them: 'John, I know that *Zapata* can be one of the greatest motion pictures of all time and although much work remains, I know now that the road ahead is not a long one'. And a few days later:

> So, J.S., I will just say to you again what I have said before – this first draft of *Zapata* is a prodigious piece of work and when you go over it and finish it, it will become one of the few *great* screenplays in motion picture history. I dislike the use of adjectives but, in this case, adjectives are necessary.[44]

Perhaps Buck was simply in awe of Steinbeck, but they clearly thought the picture had potential to be a critically acclaimed film. The exchanges between Buck and Steinbeck point to another conclusion besides self-aggrandisement: the idea that they meant the film to be more than a shallow anti-communist polemic. Buck and Steinbeck wanted to make a great film, not a simplistic one. They knew that critics and more discriminating audiences would not hail a rendition of *I Was A Communist For The FBI* (1951) set during the Mexican Revolution. But no matter how much they might have tried to separate the film's content from contemporary political controversies, the very nature of Zapata's struggle invited easy and often damaging parallels. The first run-in between the film and 1950s politics occurred when Kazan and Steinbeck proposed to shoot the film in the Mexican state of Morelos.

```
COPY                                    FILE:  JOHN STEINBECK
                                  New York City
                                  February 9, 1950


Dear Jules:

I finished my book today -- last correction of last draft.  To-
morrow it goes in to the publisher and to Annie Laurie and I am
through with it.  If it is to be produced, that is Elaine's job
and one she loves.  I'm both glad and sorry to get it done.  I'll
have to start another very soon to keep the work rhythm.  I hate
to lose that.

Haven't heard from Gadg.  He is due in any day now.  He wants me
to go out with him the 7th or 8th.  But he will go by train and
I simply won't.  It's too much time.  I'll fly and meet him there.
I don't know how long I'll be there.  Not long, I hope.  I like
it too well here.  But then I suppose I'll have to get to work
on the final ZAPATA.  That should not take long now that the
story line is down.  That's the hardest.  But by now Zanuck may
have a whole new line.  I would probably do better just to stick
with my own work and let other people work with this.  But I'm
caught in this and it can be very good.  But I'll be glad to see
Gadg and to hear what his plans are, if any.

I think this play is pretty good.  I would like to send it to
you but I don't have any copies, only three, and they are needed
here.  I'll take a copy out, though, when I go.

Rain today -- lots of rain.  We needed it so we can bathe.  Had
dinner with Bogart last night and he keeps yauking about how he
wants CANNERY ROW.  I tell him -- just pay a lot of money and
give me control of the script.  That's very simple.  This seems
outrageous to him.  So he says he won't, so I say I won't.  That's
very simple, too.

I love Betty.  I think she is a wonderful girl.  We had a lot of
fun last night -- John and Belle O'Hara and Betty and Bogart and
Elaine and me.  Drank too much, of course, but it was a kind of
celebration on finishing.

Neale is going into the dry cleaning and pressing business.  It
is the business he really knows.  I'm setting him up with a down
payment on his machinery.  Now if he really works, he should make
a good thing of it.  He is awfully good at it.  And also my
responsibility disappears.  So all is happy there.

There isn't any more news here.  We have seen a little theatre
but not very much.

Guess I'll get a shower now and go down and take Elaine to dinner.

                              So long,

                                  John
```

Fig. 3. Before the May 1950 trip to Mexico. Steinbeck's and Kazan's (Gadg) encounter with communists in the Mexican film industry helped both to take a tougher line against communism. Although their experiences made *Viva Zapata!* slightly more anti-communist, the film's original pro-democracy ideology changed little. After the film's release, however, Kazan used the experience to defend himself against charges of un-Americanism. From *Correspondence Between John Steinbeck and Jules Buck*, Box 1, Folder M538/2, Stanford University Archives, Stanford California. [Reproduction courtesy of Stanford University Archives and McIntosh and Otis, Inc.]

Production

Since Kazan and Steinbeck wanted to convey the scope of Zapata's uprising through the characters' emotions rather than their politics, they both felt that filming the picture in the actual country of the Zapatistas would add a compelling but unscriptable aura to an already dynamic story. In addition, this would be Kazan's first attempt at making a picture that was not an adaptation of a play, and he would be faced with technical and creative problems he had never encountered (e.g. filming in the wide open spaces of Morelos). So, after Zanuck approved the initial re-writes of the script (the final shooting script would take another year to complete), Steinbeck and Kazan went to Mexico in May of 1950. While he was reluctant to leave New York, Steinbeck had high hopes for the trip (See Fig. 3). As he wrote to Buck, 'We [he and Elaine Steinbeck] will go directly to Cuernavaca and he [Kazan] will join us there. I will introduce him to [Gabriel] Figueroa and show him the locations I have thought of using. All in all it should be a good trip'.[45] Neither Steinbeck nor Buck realised, however, that on this scouting trip they would face the first political op-position to their historical characterisation of Za-pata. It would not be the last battle they or their Zapata would fight.

Because Steinbeck had made previous trips to Mexico and had worked on the screenplays for the documentary *The Forgotten Village* (1941) and the drama *The Pearl* (1947)[46], he had connections in the Mexican film industry, a business far less rigidly organised than the American studio system. Stein-beck was friends with Gabriel Figueroa, a well-known Mexican cinematographer (he was the cinematographer for *The Pearl*) who was also presi-dent of the Syndicate of Film Technicians and Workers.[47] Figueroa was taken aback when Stein-beck and Kazan told him that they wanted to make the film with an American actor and told them he needed some time to consider the script. According to Kazan, Figueroa returned to their hotel the next day accompanied by an unidentified man. Kazan did not admire Figueroa's cinematic style to begin with ('His work was full of filtered clouds and peas-ant madonnas, their heads covered with *rebozos*'[48]), so when Figueroa told them that the film could not be made in Mexico using the present form of the script, Kazan and Steinbeck immedi-ately perceived this refusal to be Communist Party-inspired. Whether or not communists were actually behind the rejection, Kazan and Steinbeck believed that they were. As Kazan recalled:

> They came back with an attack that left us reeling. The script was impossible! We listened ... But above all, they attacked with sarcastic fury our emphasis on his [Zapata's] refusal to take power ... John said, 'I smell the Party line'. I smelled it too.[49]

For Kazan and Steinbeck, the mysterious man who accompanied Figueroa embodied the logic and calculation of communism. It is not unimagin-able that Kazan used this figure to enliven the char-acter of Fernando Aguirre, the evil advisor to Zapata whose only loyalty was to power and ra-tionality.

Zanuck had no doubts about the origins of their troubles trying to produce the picture in Mexico. Unlike Kazan who used the meetings in Mexico as a defense when called before HUAC in 1952, Za-nuck made his opinion well known in 1950:

> ... we are of the unanimous opinion that the main trouble lies in the fact that the people he [Kazan] has been dealing with are definitely either Communists or leftwingers and that also they do not want to jeopardise their position by being associated with this historical story unless it definitely turns out to be proleft or procommunistic ... It is clearly obvious to me that there is something deeper behind all of this than the content of our script and I know that these people will not just sit by and let us go ahead unmolested. ... When they insist the character of Zapata was not divided at all and that our approach was cheap and we did not intend to tell the whole truth then it is obvious that they want us to make our story about an extreme leftwinger or Communist. They cer-tainly don't want us to make him a Republi-can.[50]

The pieces of the puzzle fit together so neatly that there could be no other answer for Zanuck. How could anyone refuse a partnership with Twentieth Century-Fox? After Kazan and Steinbeck had failed to strike a deal in Mexico, Zanuck decided that were the film to be made, it could only be shot in the United States, where democracy guaranteed their freedom to make the film they wanted to make.

While it is difficult to determine whether Kazan always believed the difficulties of a Mexican pro-duction were due to communist-inspired tactics, or that he introduced these political problems as a defence when some critics accused him of making a film based on communist ideology, Steinbeck himself believed communists were behind their problems. In letters to Buck, who had by this time dropped out of the project to work on other scripts, Steinbeck reiterated their fears that the film would never be made in the form they envisaged:

> The trip to Mexico was very interesting. I will tell you about it some day. The party line was everywhere. I do not want to be one of the fearful ones. And I am afraid of the other side, too. But if this film should be killed – it will be by the CP not the other side. For, it now seems to me that the communists are the real reaction-aries of the world. That is strange but it seems true.[51]

Buck knew exactly to what Steinbeck was referring. And while Buck did not see a world-wide conspiracy against the film, he did begin drawing comparisons to Cold War events in other parts of the world:

> I am very curious to know exactly what went on in Mexico, although I have a hunch that you ran into trouble with Communist-controlled unions about the characterisation of Zapata. It seems to me that the CP would want to glorify him as a party man, which would be damn good propaganda for them. Of course, this is only a theory of mine and you may have run into something entirely different, but I feel somehow or other that this must be it ... We have some very tough days ahead and only God knows what will develop from this Korean mess.[52]

While their exchange might lead one to argue that Kazan and Steinbeck saw the film as anti-communist from the beginning, a more likely explanation is that their dealings in Mexico and the direction of world events helped reinforce their ideas that the historical characterisation of Zapata would be most accurate – and best received by American audiences – if the revolutionary were portrayed as an exponent of American democracy. Steinbeck and Kazan, responding to Zanuck's 3 May 1950 evaluation of their script, said this outright:

> It is not our intention to write or produce a *historical* drama. But through this historical character and incident to highlight and perhaps explain the problems of the present day. This test is true of all surviving literature. In other words we were trying to say something about 1950 and Democracy, not about 1915 and Mexican History. We both hate historical dramas. They are almost always DULL! Our picture may be a little long, but not dull.[53]

While Steinbeck might not have felt this way when he constructed the first draft of the script, and perhaps the two men were trying to ingratiate themselves with Zanuck, their blunt admission that the picture was more about advocating democracy than accurately depicting the story of Zapata invites questions concerning whether the picture actively

condemned political ideologies – like communism – which opposed democracy.

The conception, writing and direction of *Zapata!* were not undertaken with the goal of attacking communism. In Steinbeck's original script and even in subsequent drafts, the writer placed his greatest emphasis on promoting American-style democracy. In fact, in the 'Introduction and Background' for the screenplay, Steinbeck mentioned politics only twice: first, he explained how Mexicans in the late nineteenth and early twentieth centuries lived: 'Communal it was in a pre-Marx sense, but communistic it was not. The system it most closely resembled was the early Greek city-state or city group'. Later, Steinbeck positioned Zapata as not only a leader, but as an anti-politician of sorts:

> Collectivisation can come from both directions – from the extreme left and the extreme right – and the life of Emiliano Zapata is a symbol of the individual standing out against collectivisation from either side. He is the strong, self-contained individual, which the whole world needs right now.[54]

Yet opposition to communism, while present in every stage of the writing as well as in the final print, was never more than a secondary or tertiary subtheme. Script changes made between 1949 and 1951 provide some of the best evidence for such an argument. While a few scenes that affected the political motivations or actions of characters were altered, the vast majority of changes concerned non-political matters, proving Steinbeck's and Kazan's pro-democratic themes were never subordinate to anti-communist doctrines.

Steinbeck's original script of 200 pages was shortened to only 128 for the 'Shooting Final' of 16 May 1951. Many of the cuts were to Steinbeck's elaborate battle scenes, where very early on Darryl Zanuck wrote to Kazan, 'The present script is about forty pages overlength and most of this deals with repetitive battle sequences. There isn't enough blood in Mexico to make up for what is spilled in this script and there isn't enough money at Fort Knox to pay for producing it, but I am certain we can be clever enough to keep only the battle sequences that are dramatically essential'.[55] Of course, Steinbeck's original research and attempts at scripts were much more detailed than Kazan's final production, so more than just battle sequences were simplified. Steinbeck's characters were necessary agglomerations; while he wanted to represent many points of view, he did not have the temporal space to develop the intricacies of each.[56] These characters could also be interpreted as oversimplified to a degree where their political ideologies were simply one-dimensional and unrealistic. The best example of this problem is seen in the character of Fernando Aguirre, the evil advisor who first aids Madero, then Zapata, then General Huerta, finally counselling Carranza, under whom Zapata was murdered.[57] After the movie had been released and Kazan had been attacked on the grounds of misrepresenting history, the director responded to accusations that Aguirre never existed and he had therefore changed the story of Zapata. Kazan defended his decisions almost solely on political and not filmic grounds; he *could* have included someone other than Aguirre who was less stridently polemic. Instead, Kazan and Steinbeck decided that:

> ... there is such a thing as a Communist mentality. We created a figure of this complexion in Fernando, whom the audience identify as 'the man with the typewriter'. He typifies the men who use the just grievances of the people for their own ends, who shift and twist their course, betray any friend or principle or promise to get power and keep it.[58]

Kazan wrote these words, however, after the film had been released and when he knew that he would testify in front of HUAC, facts which change why he made such statements. Kazan and Steinbeck certainly wrote anti-communist lines in their interpretations of Zapata and the Mexican Revolution. Opponents of democracy, however, do not necessarily represent communism – they might believe anything which denied an individual his or her rights or the collective of individuals representation in the government, where people like themselves would make decisions.[59] And for all of the critical outcry against Aguirre, he was not responsible for Zapata's downfall. Kazan and Steinbeck hinted at the constant plotting of others, whether Aguirre was involved or not. For example, General Huerta and the others who killed Madero and eventually Zapata seemed to have little ideology beyond capturing and retaining power, doctrines which Aguirre

did not instil in them. While this could be seen as totalitarian and thus Stalinist, a more likely explanation is that they were idealised dictators who were power-hungry and thus un-American. And when Zapata meets Pancho Villa, Villa complains 'Someone took a shot at me today. Someone I don't even know!', eliciting a knowing smirk from Aguirre and insinuating that there was deadly competition for capturing leadership or simply commenting on the anarchical state of the Revolution. Aguirre does add to the suspense of what will happen to Zapata and Joseph Wiseman plays the role with gleefully evil intent. But in the end, had Aguirre not existed, the pro-democratic themes (and thus pro-American visions) still would have proved to be more prevalent (and powerful) than existed during the time of Zapata.[60]

Many of the changes that Kazan made between the 'Shooting Final' and the final print made little difference when interpreting the movie's politics. For example, two or three scenes relating to a woman jealous of Josefa, Zapata's eventual wife, were cut, as were scenes concerning a woman who was with Pablo, Zapata's dear friend whom he is forced to execute for conspiring with the enemy. A few scenes that were removed, however, added complexity to the political story. In these, not only were the middle- and upper-class's views explored, but they were not all united against Zapata (as might be expected in a straight anti-communist diatribe). In one scene, Don Nacio, a wealthy horse rancher and Zapata's patron, defended Zapata's goals to other wealthy men when discussing the future of the elite classes like themselves. This, however, is the exception to the rule. Most of what was removed or changed did little to further the political story. Kazan altered scenes he, Steinbeck and Buck had written that affected the story through the characters's personalities, not their politics.[62]

Reception

Many thematic interpretations of the film have been offered over the last forty years.[63] Equally revealing and more relevant in a historical way, however, were the critic's thoughts on the film when it first appeared and the ensuing debates over the film's historical validity. The controversy which immediately arose not only reflected the contested figure

Zapata had become, but also the political tenor of 1952.

Steinbeck and Kazan had opposing reactions to the final product – a prescient representation of the popular reviews. Just before the film was released, Steinbeck wrote to Buck:

'Went out to Skouras last Sunday and saw *Zapata*. Delighted with it. I think it is a fine picture – one of the very best. It may make some history. That Gadg [sic] is something – gets you right in the stomach'.[64] Kazan, on the other hand, recalled, 'I'd seen *Viva Zapata!* and been disappointed. I thought it another "almost"; I had to do better'.[65]

The reviewers' split paralleled Steinbeck's and Kazan's thoughts almost perfectly. Half thought the film was stirring and powerful, while the others thought it to be shallow and misguided. Bosley Crowther wrote in *The New York Times*, 'certainly this ardent portrait of him [Zapata] throbs with a rare vitality and a masterful picture of a nation in revolutionary torment has been got by Director Elia Kazan'.[66] Philip T. Hartnung, writing in *The Commonweal*, complained of the film's bad editing and Kazan's failure 'to keep his lengthy scenes or connecting footage within legitimate bounds'. Yet Hartnung still recommended the film: 'In spite of these technical weaknesses, however and of a certain intellectual coldness that pervades "Viva Zapata!" this film deserves to be seen'.[67]

Other reviews, however, dismissed the film for being too similar to other Steinbeck scripts or Marlon Brando films. *The New Republic* thought that as a biography the movie fell short, although with a little more attention to the romance and horse action, 'it could have been a good period horse opera instead of a slightly presumptuous biography'.[68] *The New Yorker* reviewer also found the film misguided, saying, 'What 'Viva Zapata!' really adds up to is an old-fashioned Western and taken as that it's quite entertaining. As a matter of fact, if Mr. Steinbeck's murky views on revolution and Mr. Kazan's art-for-art's-sake shots were played down a bit, there wouldn't be any room for complaint about the picture at all'.[69]

The trade journal *Variety* thought that while the film's formula should have been a winning one, the 'Picture misses in that the ideas and ideals with which it deals come over the top too symbolically and it lacks the humanness and heart that could have clinched popular appeal'.[70] Moreover, their reviewer added, 'Elia Kazan's direction strives for a personal intimacy but neither he nor the John Steinbeck scripting achieves in enough measure to generate the kind of sympathy an audience should have for the characters'. Such reviews had the potential to sink the film, since owners of independent and chain theatres read them as economic forecasts, a fact which *Variety* and other trade papers took into consideration. In fact, *Variety* was forthrightly pessimistic about *Zapata!*'s chances at the box office: 'It is generously supplied with exploitation angles that can give it the selling push usually accorded a Zanuck effort, so strong grosses can result in individual top key bookings. Outlook in general release, however, is less assured and the going is likely to be spotty.' In 1952 Zanuck's reputation proceeded him, but even with an all-star production team and cast, nothing was guaranteed in the economically-strapped Hollywood of the early 1950s. Most interesting, however, was the analysis in the popular press concerning whether the film was pro- or anti-communist. *The New Yorker* reviewer only alluded to the question (as did other reviewers), but in *The Saturday Review* a full-fledged debate took place lasting a number of months.

Hollis Alpert fired the first salvo of the campaign in his negative review of 9 February 1952. Alpert wished that Kazan had simply stuck with a standard Western, but he also criticised Kazan's interpretation of Zapata and the creation of Aguirre.[71] Kazan responded to both Alpert and a defence of the film written three weeks later by another *Saturday Review* writer, Laura Hobson.[72] Kazan's 5 April rejoinder to Alpert focused almost solely on political symbolism and the possible interpretations audiences could formulate after seeing his story of Zapata. For Kazan, the biggest question was Zapata's use of power: would he accept the Presidency from Pancho Villa and become corrupted as leaders had before him, or would he refuse power and return to his people, theoretically leaving power to reside with the people themselves. Kazan defended the decision he and Steinbeck (and Buck) came to, where Zapata abdicated the throne in favour of returning power to its proper

Fig. 4. After refusing to sit in the President's chair, a dour Zapata poses with Alan Reed's Pancho Villa as Mexico celebrates the Revolution. [Photo courtesy of Twentieth Century-Fox.]

place: with the people. In the film, Zapata tells his followers, 'There are no leaders but yourselves'. Kazan told *The Saturday Review*'s readers, 'In his moment of decision, this taciturn, untaught leader must have felt freshly and deeply, the impact of the ancient law: power corrupts. And so he refused power'.[73] Kazan wanted his interpretations of Zapata's actions to be grounded in the conscience of an individual who could not allow himself either to become corrupt or to use power for ignoble purposes. What was not mentioned in the letter, however, was the fact that only five days later Kazan would testify in front of HUAC, where he would 'name names' of friends who were associated with the American Communist Party.[74] Reading the letter as a defence of Kazan's film as *anti*-communist places it in an entirely different light.

Instead of offering specific rebuttals to Alpert's criticisms, Kazan spent almost all of his energy summarising the evidence that led Steinbeck and him to depict Zapata as a reluctant leader rather than a traditional commander who, first and last, desired power. Kazan recalled their meeting with Figueroa (without naming names), stating at least twice that, 'No Communist, no totalitarian, ever refused power'.[75] When read with the HUAC hearings in mind, the way Kazan must have originally written the letter, Kazan's response was more a defence of himself and his anti-communism than a defence of the film. In fact, one week later Kazan's famous advertisement in *The New York Times* appeared as a counter to criticism leveled by his Broadway and Hollywood colleagues. The ad, titled 'A Statement', obliquely referred to *Viva Zapata!* when he recalled that firsthand experience of dictatorship, 'left me with an abiding hatred of Communist philosophy and methods and the conviction that these must be resisted always'.[76] Kazan's Zapata underwent a similar experience, seeing how power corrupts and quickly realising it must always be resisted, even by the most principled individuals. As a further defence, Kazan also cited his creation of Aguirre,

Fig. 5. Zanuck the salesman – publicity for *Viva Zapata!*, 1952.
[Photo courtesy of Twentieth Century-Fox.]

employing the amalgamation to illustrate that he not only did not make a pro-communist movie, but that he consciously made an anti-communist movie.[77] Kazan's post-release comments are an excellent example of a director putting 'spin' on his own work as a bulwark against political or artistic criticism.

If Zapata's character is substituted for Kazan's experience, it becomes clear that Zapata is as much an extension of Kazan as he is the 'real' Zapata. Moreover, Kazan's artistic license went beyond any

of Steinbeck's and Buck's various charac-terisations, further explaining any subtle shift of Za-pata from pro-democracy to anti-communist. In many ways, then, it was Kazan's post-release inter-pretations of *Zapata!* that created the controversy that has surrounded it ever since.

Kazan's letter, testimony and advertisement did not, however, end the debate in *The Saturday Review* or elsewhere. Nearly two months later, an-other exchange took place, this time between an academic, Carleton Beals and Kazan. Beals took Kazan to task for caricaturing nearly every character in the film. Focusing on such factual errors as Zapata's supposed renunciation of power and the fictional Aguirre, Beals cited his own experiences of knowing Zapata's men and having spent time among the ex-Zapatistas: 'I have ridden with the men of Morelos for months on end, slept on their straw mats, eaten their tortillas and chilli and know the stuff of which they are made'.[78] Beals, however, also set himself up as the American 'expert' who truly 'knows' the Mexicans. The picture he painted of himself was, in this sense, no better than that of Kazan, just politically different.

Kazan's response (published in the same issue) used Steinbeck's research and the overwhelming number of 'experts' on Zapata in both the United States and Mexico to refute Beals's assertions. The most curious dimension of the letter is the fact that Kazan responded on creative and not political grounds. Steinbeck, wrote Kazan, had to make choices, 'and he made them with an eye to implementing his interpretation'.[79] Now this certainly could be taken as an 'interpretation' of pro-American democracy and anti-communism, but Kazan never moved the argument in that direction. In fact, Kazan only once mentioned communism (when referring to a comparison between Alpert's review and one in the communist publication *The Worker*). Kazan, then, controlled the argument from a defensive posture, a difficult task when attacked from the political right and left. The upshot of this controversy, however, was not a wave of interest at the box office. Instead, the public lost interest in a film which they perceived required a fair amount of background on the Mexican Revolution, and the patience to grapple with ambiguous political meanings. Nevertheless, the economic and political legacies of *Viva Zapata!* resonated far beyond the picture's closing.[80]

Legacies

Debates over the critical success or failure of a film, while important, often are secondary to its economic success or failure. In no other case was this more true than *Zapata!*. Zanuck and Skouras had high hopes for their picture, but the market was tight and the competition keen – released around that same time were *The African Queen* (1952), *Quo Vadis* (1952) and even a re-issue of *Snow White* (1937). However, if one traces *Zapata!*'s box office receipts through its first eight weeks (the time it played in New York City), a curious phenomenon emerges. Reports in *Variety* place *Zapata!* among the high earners; in its first week it was the top opening film, grossing $68,000 in New York alone[81] (see Fig. 5). After three weeks *Variety* could report that, '"Viva Zapata!" is maintaining its strong pace at the Rivoli with $38,000 likely for second stanza, particularly pleasing in view of sluggish tone at most house the middle of last week'. One month after its premiere, *Zapata!* was in fifth place in national receipts, although in New York it had fallen to about $21,000 for the week's end.[83] One week later the film had slipped to seventh place, although *Variety*'s evaluation was still upbeat and sure enough, on the strength of its national showing, it moved back up to fifth place by its eighth week. One week later *Zapata!* had dropped off of *Variety*'s 'National Boxoffice Survey', but most observers agreed that the picture had defied the odds, lasting far longer than many analysts expected. Why, then, was Zanuck so disappointed with *Zapata!*'s performance?

Zapata! was not an inexpensive picture to produce and Twentieth Century-Fox had a lot riding on it. The days of making large numbers of quick, cheap films were largely over. In the first quarter of 1949, for example, only 22 pictures – half the normal number – were in production in all of Hollywood.[84] Each film that was produced, then, bore additional economic weight; if one expensive film out of only a few released failed, the impact on the studio would be far greater – a state of affairs which has lasted to the present day. Moreover, the advent of television and the realisation that the audience was not a homogeneous mass which would flock to whatever the studios produced, forced the companies to turn to technical gimmicks such as 3-D or CinemaScope to offer audiences something which could not be seen on TV. Additionally, McCarthyism and the Cold War severely limited what films producers felt safe in undertaking. *Zapata!* was not easily recognisable by audiences due to its historical subject, political overtones and non-American setting. For all of these reasons, *Zapata!* became symbolic of a risky film species which at best promised only moderate pecuniary rewards. While its legacies were debated and lasted within the film critic's world, its most immediate impact was within the studio.

The aftermath of *Zapata!* within Twentieth Century-Fox has been little explored. For nearly three years after its release, Darryl Zanuck used *Zapata!* as an example of the differences between the domestic and foreign markets for the studio. Since Twentieth Century-Fox was going through financial difficulties, it was up to Zanuck to figure out how to get the most out of every picture in every market. This meant coordinating subject matter with culture and being particularly careful about what might offend domestic *or* foreign audiences. Accordingly, about a year and a half after the release of *Zapata!*, Zanuck issued a confidential memo to all executives, producers and directors, his urgent tone reflecting his concern over the decisions about which movies would be produced next: 'The purpose of this note is not an effort on my part to be critical although there is certainly plenty of room for criticism – the idea is to acquaint you with the facts so we may be guided in the selection of subject matter for the future'.[85] Zanuck was being critical; in other memos he proposed to Spyros Skouras salary cuts for everyone and new ways to keeps the studio moving ahead in the tough economic times. In reviewing *Zapata!* and other films, Zanuck focused on their ability to redeem themselves in the foreign markets after terrible domestic showings. His evaluation of *Zapata!* shows the priority of receipts for both himself and the studio:

> *Viva Zapata!* – This one will probably break even on the world market. Domestically it grossed about $250,000 less than *Lure of the Wilderness* (1951). But in the foreign market and South America it shows a little more strength – once again a case of a selection of stupid subject matter. Most people thought Zapata was the name of a new hair tonic. It received four stars and international critical acclaim but you cannot pay the rent with acclaim and there is no prestige in ever making an artistic flop.[86]

While the film did receive some international acclaim, most critics did not think it was a four-star picture. Additionally, Zanuck did not address the quality and amount of publicity given to the film. Nevertheless, the bottom line was that it was a financial failure.

About a year later, Zanuck wrote another confidential memo to all producers and directors, again comparing domestic and foreign markets, while trying to reach some general conclusions about the relationship between content, culture and profits. Zanuck was typically blunt about his beliefs: 'With but few exceptions typical American stories dealing with American sports, school life, etc. are absolutely worthless outside of the United States'.[87] Since the studio had been producing fewer and fewer films, Zanuck hoped to find pictures that could cross over to the foreign market and gain important extra profits. *Zapata!* might have been one of those films had it been received better in the United States, but as Zanuck noted:

> *Viva Zapata!* – Unsuccessful in the United States and England, yet managed to roll up in the foreign field $1,120,000.[88]

Had the United States income been proportional to its foreign receipts, *Zapata!* might be remembered as a very different film. The controversy generated by Kazan's HUAC hearings, the depiction of Zapata, and expensive, big-name stars such as Brando, Jean Peters and Steinbeck did not help the film's cause within the studio. Only its foreign receipts saved it from a complete financial failure, and Zanuck and others knew they could not rely on foreign markets to guarantee their studio's health.

The meanings of *Viva Zapata!* would be disputed for the next forty years, reminding critics involved in recent debates over historical interpretations in film that appropriations of characters and ideologies have gone on since the early days of narrative pictures.[89] It appears, however, that *Zapata!* helped to lead Twentieth Century-Fox further away from movies that could be interpreted as questioning American values, or perhaps better suited to non-American audiences. The studios rarely took risks and during hard times they were even more conservative. While the subject extends beyond the scope of this essay, one might argue that films that failed in the early 1950s like *Zapata!* pushed the studios toward more bland and conservative films, making risky standouts such as *The Wild One* (1953) all the more acclaimed because they were so *unlike* the majority of films studios produced in light of past mistakes and fears of the future.

In the end, though, Kazan would go on to make, among other films, *On the Waterfront* (1954) and *East of Eden* (1955), escaping the 1950s with little real damage. John Steinbeck would continue writing fiction, having four more films made from his books. And in 1963, Steinbeck asked Kazan to persuade Skouras to re-release *Zapata!*; unlike 1952, Steinbeck was now willing to use his film to achieve political aims, namely the education of the Cuban people now living under Castro's communist rule. Skouras and Twentieth Century-Fox, however, wanted nothing more to do with the film.[90] And Jules Buck would remain in obscurity, gaining none of the public notoriety of his collaborators. Yet his creation lived on, one more example of a time when Hollywood's ideological agenda prescribed how history had happened.❖

Notes

1.   *Facts on File*, Vol. 7, No. 588, 1 February – 7 February, 1952, 52.

2.   On the 1947 HUAC hearings about Hollywood, see M.J. Heale, *American Anticommunism* (Baltimore: Johns Hopkins Press, 1991), 139 and Richard M. Fried, *Nightmare in Red* (New York: Oxford University Press, 1990), 73–80.

3.   *Facts on File*, Vol 7, No. 588, 1 February – 7 February, 1952, 41,43. The Censor Board deemed *Pinky*'s treatment of race too controversial. For more on *Pinky*, see 'Asks MPAA Join Burstyn High Ct. Film Censor Test', *Variety*, 6 February 1952, 3 and 16.

4.   John Steinbeck to Jules Buck, 17 June 1952, *Correspondence Between John Steinbeck and Jules Buck*, Box 1, Folder M538/4, labelled '1951–1953', Stanford University Archives, Stanford, California. See also Steinbeck to Pat Covici, 18 April 1952, in Elaine Steinbeck and Robert Wallsten, eds., *Steinbeck: A Life in Letters* (New York: The Viking Press, 1975), 443.

5.   Cobbett S. Steinberg, *Film Facts* (New York: Facts on File, Inc., 1980), 67.

6.   While much has been written on the 1952 HUAC hearings, the best work about Hollywood is Victor S. Navasky's *Naming Names* (New York: The Viking Press, 1980).

7.   See, for example, Peter Biskind, 'Ripping Off Zapata: Revolution Hollywood Style', *Cineaste 7*, No. 2 (Fall, 1976), 10–15 and Paul J. Vanderwood, 'An American Cold Warrior: *Viva Zapata!*' in *American History/American Film*, ed. John E. O'Connor and Martin A. Jackson, (New York: The Ungar Publishing Company, 1988), 183–203. Perhaps the most wide-ranging and insightful analysis, however, comes from Richard Slotkin, *Gunfighter Nation*, (New York: Atheneum, 1992), 418–433.

8.   Roger Parkinson, *Zapata* (New York: Stein and Day, 1975), 20–38.

9.   For an interesting summary of the Mexican Revolution, see Ronald Atkin, *Revolution!: Mexico, 1910–29* (New York: The John Day Company, 1969).

10. See John Womack, Jr., *Zapata and the Mexican Revolution* (New York: Vintage Books, 1968), 326.

11. The American's name is variously described as Edgcomb Pinchon, Edgcumb Pinchon, Thomas Pinchon, Thomas Pynchon and Edgecumb Pinchon. See Vanderwood, *American History/American Film*, 185; Robert E. Morsberger, ed., *Viva Zapata!: The Original Screenplay by John Steinbeck* (New York: The Viking Press, 1975), 133; Thomas H. Pauly, *An American Odyssey* (Philadelphia: Temple University Press, 1983), 145; and Lester Cole, *Hollywood Red* (Palo Alto: Ramparts Press, 1981), 260.

12. For an insightful analysis of *Viva Villa!*, see Slotkin, *Gunfighter Nation*, 413–415.

13. See Vanderwood, 185. Lester Cole, one of the Hollywood Ten, recounts in his autobiography that in 1947 Jack Cummings, a producer at MGM, told him that MGM had bought Pinchon's novel along with *Viva Villa!* 'a dozen years ago'. Cole worked up a treatment he called *Zapata, the Unconquerable*, after which he and Cummings flew to Mexico where they made a deal with Mexican President Miguel Aleman to have their government subsidise the film's production in Mexico. Cummings and Cole convinced Eddie Mannix, MGM General Manager, that the film was almost guaranteed to show a profit since the studio's investment would be minimal. Mannix agreed, but two days later Cole was subpoenaed by HUAC, thus starting his life as one of the Hollywood Ten. While Cole adds credence to the theory that MGM initiated the project, his story must be taken with a grain of salt. In trying to explain how a Marxist could rationalise earning $1000 per week in the 1940s, Cole often seems to seek forgiveness from his readers. His power of recall is astounding (and probably selective), recounting conversations verbatim which, in

Cole's rendering, always illustrate his unfailingly correct political and social consciousness when those about him struggle for money and power. See Cole, *Hollywood Red*, 259–265, 288, 352.

14. The revolutionary constitution, drafted in early 1917, included Article 27, which called for government control over land distribution. This, of course, did not make American business interests happy. See John A. Britton, *Revolution and Ideology: Images of the Mexican Revolution in the United States* (Lexington: The University Press of Kentucky, 1995), 5–6.

15. John Steinbeck to Annie Laurie Williams, 26 June 1945, in Steinbeck and Wallsten, eds., *Steinbeck: A Life in Letters*, 282.

16. John Steinbeck to Francisco Z. Clemente, 13 July 1945, in MA 3659, 'Letters, documents, memoranda, telegrams, clippings, printed matter and maps concerning the planning and production of the film', [hereafter MA 3659], Autograph Manuscript Collection, Pierpont Morgan Library, New York, New York. Curiously, however, Steinbeck must have forgotten this pledge when he undertook his first draft. In an effort to bypass the political problems he knew a movie on Zapata would surely raise, Steinbeck proposed avoiding the use of full names: 'The President ... will simply in my script be the Presidente. Zapata himself will be, in his early youth, Emiliano and later he will be El Chefe or The Chief and later The General and his name will not be used, except, possibly, once in the very last of the film'. The writer thought this would alleviate any controversy since without the use of full names, the film would be 'a matter of folklore'. See MA 3657, '"Introduction and Background" for Preliminary Version of the Screenplay, Here Entitled "Zapata"', [hereafter MA 3657], Autograph Manuscript Collection, Pierpont Morgan Library.

17. For an attempt at an explanation of this controversy, see Millichap, footnote 2, 123 and 188.

18. Michel Ciment, *Kazan on Kazan* (New York: The Viking Press, 1974), 88.

19. Ibid.

20. Elia Kazan, *A Life* (New York: Alfred A. Knopf, 1988), 427. See also Morsberger, 132, for another version of Kazan as the originator of the initial idea.

21. Elia Kazan, 'Elia Kazan on "Zapata"', *Saturday Review*, 5 April 1952, 22.

22. Elia Kazan, *A Life*, 399.

23. John Steinbeck to Bo Beskow, 22 May 1948, in Steinbeck and Wallsten, eds., *Steinbeck: A Life in Letters*, 312.

24. Darryl Zanuck to John Steinbeck, 21 June 1948, MA 3659, Autograph Manuscript Collection, Pierpont Morgan Library.

25. John Steinbeck to Bo Beskow, 19 June 1948, in Steinbeck and Wallsten, eds., *Steinbeck: A Life in Letters*, 317. See also Steinbeck to Bo Beskow, 24 June 1948, in ibid., 318.

26. John Steinbeck to Oscar Danziggers, 22 and 29 June 1948, in MA 3659, Autograph Manuscript Collection, Pierpont Morgan Library.

27. Steinbeck's research told him, among other things, that Zapata was a fierce and often cruel warrior, who was not above torturing his enemies or even his own men. He was also a womaniser, although perhaps no more so than other men of his stature. Steinbeck's first try at a script reflected these findings, where his Zapata executes disloyal soldiers and carries on an extramarital affair with 'the Blonde'. See MA 3658, 'Typescripts of Research Materials in English and Spanish', [hereafter MA 3658], Autograph Manuscript Collection, Pierpont Morgan Library.

28. John Steinbeck to Bo Beskow, 19 November 1948, in Steinbeck and Wallsten, eds., *Steinbeck: A Life in Letters*, 342.

29. John Steinbeck to Elizabeth Otis, 13 January 1949, *John Steinbeck Manuscript Collection*, Box 2, Folder 4 labelled 'JS to Elizabeth Otis, 1946–1950', Stanford University Archives, Stanford, California.

30. Jay Parini's biography of Steinbeck offers the most thorough description of how Steinbeck wrote *Zapata!*. See Jay Parini, *John Steinbeck: A Biography* (London: Heinemann Publishers, 1994), 355, 392 and 395–397.

31. Buck later worked as a producer on such films as *Operation Snatch* (1962), *The Party's Over* (1966) and *Great Catherine* (1968). See Richard P. Krafsur, executive editor, *The American Film Institute Catalog of Motion Pictures* (New York: R. R. Bowker, Co., 1976), 809, 827 and 426. Kazan did eventually acknowledge Buck, but then only obliquely: 'Zanuck had assigned one of his assistants to work with John and prepare the script ...'. See Kazan, *A Life*, 395.

32. Only Jay Parini directly addresses Buck's role in developing the script. Parini recounts how Steinbeck and Buck collaborated in the fall of 1949: Steinbeck would dictate a scene into his Ediphone and then Buck would transcribe it, making changes as he typed. According to Parini, the pair produced twelve pages of script per day. See Parini, 406–407.

33. John Steinbeck to Elaine Scott, 1 November 1949, in Steinbeck and Wallsten, eds., *Steinbeck: A Life in Letters*, 382–383.

34. John Steinbeck to Jack Wagner, ca. November 1949, *John Steinbeck Collection*, Box 4, Folder 9 labelled 'JS to Max and Jack Wagner, 1949–1966', Stanford University Archives, Stanford, California.

35. Jules Buck to Darryl Zanuck, 5 December 1949, *Correspondence Between John Steinbeck and Jules Buck*, Box 1, Folder M538/1, labelled 'Studio Correspondence, 1949', Stanford University Archives, Stanford, California.

36. Ibid.

37. Ibid.

38. Ibid.

39. Darryl Zanuck to John Steinbeck and Elia Kazan, 3 May 1950, MA 3659, Autograph Manuscript Collection, Pierpont Morgan Library.

40. Ibid.

41. Ibid.

42. Ibid.

43. Ibid. Kazan was, however, never very impressed with Zanuck's comments: 'I'm very much afraid of Darryl's speed. He's a great man for fast solutions. He's always' amazed when he finds he has very quickly and easily solved something but the reason he has solved it so quickly and easily is that he has seen it somewhere before in some other picture and you know how deadly this would be'. Elia Kazan to John Steinbeck, 18 May 1949, MA 3659, Autograph Manuscript Collection, Pierpont Morgan Library.

44. Jules Buck to John Steinbeck, 7 December 1949 and 30 December 1949, *Correspondence Between John Steinbeck and Jules Buck*, Box 1, Folder labelled '1949', Stanford University Archives, Stanford, California. Steinbeck knew that Kazan felt similarly. Writing about revisions he proposed, Steinbeck told Kazan, 'You said once you would like this to be a kind of monument. By the same token I would like it to be as tight and terse as possible. It is awfully good but it can be better'. Some reviewers, however, took Steinbeck to task for an overly-tight and terse script. John Steinbeck to Elia Kazan, late summer 1950, in Steinbeck and Wallsten, eds., *Steinbeck: A Life in Letters*, 407.

45. John Steinbeck to Jules Buck, 15 May 1950, *Correspondence Between John Steinbeck and Jules Buck*, Box 1, Folder M538/3, labelled '1950, May-Dec.', Stanford University Archives, Stanford, California.

46. See Morsberger, 124–125. For an analysis of *The Forgotten Village*, see Britton, *Revolution and Ideology*, 173–174.

47. Steinbeck was not unaware of the Figueroa's usefulness in their political difficulties: '[He] would eliminate about 80 per cent of the difficulties arising from anti-gringoism and so forth'. John Steinbeck to Darryl Zanuck, 9 December 1949, in MA 3659, Autograph Manuscript Collection, Pierpont Morgan Library.

48. Kazan, *A Life*, 398.

49. Elia Kazan, 'Elia Kazan on "Zapata"', *Saturday Review*, 5 April 1952, 22. For a more complete description by Kazan, see *A Life*, 397–401 and *Kazan on Kazan*, 89–90.

50. Darryl Zanuck to Joseph Moshowitz, 7 June 1950, MA 3659, Autograph Manuscript Collection, Pierpont Morgan Library.

51. John Steinbeck to Jules Buck, 19 June 1950, *Correspondence Between John Steinbeck and Jules Buck*, Box 1, Folder M538/3, labelled '1950, May-Dec', Stanford University Archives, Stanford, California.

52. Jules Buck to John Steinbeck, 20 July 1950, in ibid.

53. John Steinbeck and Elia Kazan to Darryl Zanuck, n.d., MA 3659, Autograph Manuscript Collection, Pierpont Morgan Library.

54. See MA 3656, 'Introduction and Background' for Preliminary Version of the Screenplay, here Entitled 'Zapata', [hereafter MA 3656], Autograph Manuscript Collection, Pierpont Morgan Library.

55. Darryl F. Zanuck to Elia Kazan, 5 December 1949, *Correspondence Between John Steinbeck and Jules Buck*, Box 1, Folder M538/1 labelled 'Studio Correspondence, 1949', Stanford University Archives, Stanford, California.

56. One example of such condensation was the ever-decreasing role Eufemio, Zapata's brother, played in the script. Eufemio dominated the first thirty pages of the first draft of the screenplay, and throughout the script Emiliano deferred to his brother as head of the household. See MA 3657 and MA 3656, 'Zapata' (The Little Tiger), 13 May 1949, [hereafter MA 3656], Pierpont Morgan Library.

57. Aguirre did not exist until late in the screenwriting process, although his origins can be found in a character named 'Bicho', who Zanuck thought would support a 'strong Mexico' rather than the people. 'He is just the kind of a guy who believes in a dictatorship'. Darryl Zanuck to John Steinbeck, 10 August 1950, in MA 3659, Autograph Manuscript Collection, Pierpont Morgan Library.

58. Elia Kazan, 'Elia Kazan on "Zapata"', 22.

59. In early versions of the screenplay, the class-based struggle between the landed *haciendados* and the farmers was much more richly illustrated. In one scene, for example, a sugar planter brings his French guests to a village festival where they start a riot, resulting in the deaths of many farmers. See MA 3657 and 3656, Autograph Manuscript Collection, Pierpont Morgan Library.

60. The historian Richard Slotkin offers a similar analysis: 'It is more accurate to see *Viva Zapata!* as an attempt to make a positive political statement that would distinguish the essential values of American liberalism from both Stalinist Marxism and right-wing conservatism and that would claim for those values a "revolutionary" or liberating world mission'. See *Gunfighter Nation*, 421.

61. For a complete inventory of what was removed, see Morsberger, ed., *Viva Zapata!: The Original Screenplay by John Steinbeck*.

62. The major creative contribution of Darryl Zanuck was the use of a white horse ('Blanco') throughout the movie, suggesting that it appear symbolically in the mountains at the end. See *A Life*, 396 and *Kazan on Kazan*, 97. In an otherwise accurate analysis of the film, historian Richard Slotkin writes, 'At the end, the white horse which has escaped to the mountains, becomes the symbol of Zapata's spirit – a symbol which Steinbeck and Kazan intended seriously but which is strongly reminiscent of the "B"-Western hero's preference for his horse over "the girl"'. Slotkin was more correct than he knew. See *Gunfighter Nation*, 423.

63. See, for example, Lloyd Michaels, *Elia Kazan: A Guide To References And Resources* (Boston: G.K. Hall & Co., 1985), 27–28, Thomas H. Pauly, *An American Odyssey: Elia Kazan and American Culture* (Philadelphia: Temple University Press, 1983), 146–156, Peter Biskind and Dan Georgakas, 'Viva Zapata! Pro and Con', *Cineaste* Vol. 7, No. 2 (Fall, 1976), 10–17 and Morsberger, ed., *Viva Zapata!: The Original Screenplay by John Steinbeck*, xv-xxxiii.

64. John Steinbeck to Jules Buck, 12 January 1952, *Correspondence Between John Steinbeck and Jules Buck*, Box 1, Folder M538/4, labelled '1951–1953', Stanford University Archives, Stanford, California.

65. Kazan, *A Life*, 448.

66. Bosley Crowther, *The New York Times*, 8 February 1952,19. Crowther later pronounced *Zapata!* one of the ten best pictures of 1952. See 'The Year's Best', *New York Times*, 28 December 1952, Sect. II, 1.

67. Philip T. Hartnung, 'Viva Higher Standards', *The Commonweal*, 29 February 1952, 517. For other positive reviews see also *Newsweek*, 4 February 1952, 78 and *Time*, 11 February 1952, 92.

68. Robert Hatch, 'Hue and Cry', *The New Republic*, 25 February 1952, 21.

69. John McCarten, 'Wool From the West', *The New Yorker*, 16 February 1952, 95.

70. Brog., 'Viva Zapata!', *Variety* 6 February 1952, 6. Based on its Academy Award nominations for Best Picture, Best Actor and Best Screenplay and Anthony Quinn's Best Supporting Actor award, historian Richard Slotkin claims the film was 'a commercial and critical success ...'. See *Gunfighter Nation*, 732, footnote 38.

71. Hollis Alpert, 'Kazan and Brando Outdoors', *Saturday Review*, 9 February 1952, 25–26.

72. Laura Hobson, 'Trade Winds', *Saturday Review*, 1 March 1952, 6.

73. Elia Kazan, 'Elia Kazan on "Zapata"', *Saturday Review*, 5 April 1952, 22.

74. For an interesting summary of Kazan's decision to name names, see Stephen J. Whitfield, *The Culture of the Cold War* (Baltimore: Johns Hopkins University Press, 1991), 107–117. Surprisingly, Whitfield never mentions *Zapata!*.

75. Ibid.

76. Elia Kazan, 'A Statement', reprinted in Victor S. Navasky, *Naming Names* (New York: The Viking Press, 1980), 205. Also reprinted under the title 'Where I Stand', *Reader's Digest* Vol. 61, No. 363 (July 1952), 45–46.

77. See Kazan, *A Life*, 448.

78. Carleton Beals, 'Zapata Again', *Saturday Review*, 24 May 1952, 28.

79. Elia Kazan, *Saturday Review*, 24 May 1952, 28.

80. Zanuck also did his share of defending the film against critics who thought it glorified Communism. Before the film was released Zanuck tried to quell any controversy when the head of the Catholic War Veterans wrote him with the accusation that '3 players in this motion picture have records of affiliation with organisations deemed as subversive or Communist by recognised Government Agencies'. Dodging the charges, Zanuck replied that 'Zapata was a complete individualist. His idol was Abraham Lincoln and he fought violently against the tyranny

of dictatorship and control of the people by the state'. See John J. Coughlin to Darryl Zanuck, 21 January 1952 and reply, 24 January 1952, both in MA 3659, Autograph Manuscript Collection, Pierpont Morgan Library. Later, responding to a column Frank Conniff wrote in the New York *Journal-American*, Zanuck said, '... careful study of Mexican history with research experts revealed to me that everything about Zapata's political life was anti-Communistic and anti-dictatorship. He desisted "state control" of everything and anything'. Darryl Zanuck to Frank Conniff, 14 February 1952, in ibid.

81. See 'B'Way Spurts; "Zapata" Top Newcomer, Sock $68,000, "Worlds" Neat 31G, "Trees" 12G; "Show" 5th Smash 143G, "Sailor" 56G', *Variety* 13 February 1952, 9.

82. See 'B'Way Spotty; "Girl" – Vaude Good 59G, Garland Reissue Fine $16,000, "Zapata!" Holds Up at 38G in 2d Week', *Variety* 20 February 1952, 9.

83. See 'National Boxoffice Survey', *Variety* 5 March 1952, 3. For New York receipts, see 'Snowstorm Nips B'Way; "This Woman" Plus Vaude Fair $56,000, Show Off to 104G in 8th, Other HO's Hit', 9. By this time, however, *Zapata!* had opened across the country and seemed to be doing quite well. A headline in the same issue of *Variety* said it all: '"Zapata!" Sockeroo $25,000 Philly', 9. As Steinbeck related to a friend, however, Kazan, unlike Zanuck, was ecstatic about the film's receipt's: 'He told me that Zapata has already grossed three million dollars. He wants to work out some kind of deal where we own a chunk of the picture and can share in the profits.' See Steinbeck to Annie Laurie Williams, 17 June 1952, in *Steinbeck: A Life in Letters*, 450.

84. See David A. Cook, *A History of Narrative Film*, 2nd Edition, (New York: W.W. Norton and Company, 1990), 478.

85. Memo from Darryl Zanuck to Executives, Producers, Directors, 9 June 1953, *Spyros P. Skouras Papers*, Box 37, Folder labelled 'Production heads of Studio – Zanuck, Darryl F 1949 to 1954', Stanford University Archives, Stanford, California.

86. Ibid.

87. Memo from Darryl Zanuck to Producers and Directors, 22 October 1954, *Spyros P. Skouras Papers*, Box 37, Folder labelled 'Production Heads of Studio – Zanuck, Darryl F. 1949 to 1954', Stanford University Archives, Stanford, California.

88. Ibid. Parini, however, calls *Zapata!* a 'commercial success', since it earned 'over three million dollars in less than one month'. See Parini, 431. Parini, however, probably took Kazan at his word – see footnote 83 above.

89. For relevant examples, see American Historical Review *Forum*: 'JFK and the Culture of Violence', *American Historical Review* 97, No. 2 (April 1992), 486–511, as well as the many writings about Spike Lee's *Malcolm X*.

90. See Morsberger, 141–142. Apparently, Steinbeck never forgot Zapata's heroism. Writing to Adlai Stevenson in 1961, Steinbeck mused, 'Once Emiliano Zapata, the Mexican Revolutionary, said on being warned that he would be assassinated – "Then that's the way it must be and perhaps better, for some men find their real and permanent strength there, I think ..."'. See Steinbeck to Adlai Stevenson, 23 September 1961, in Steinbeck and Wallsten, eds., *Steinbeck: A Life in Letters*, 716.

Film History, Volume 8, pp. 131–142, 1996. Copyright © John Libbey & Company
ISSN: 0892-2160. Printed in Australia

Group Three – a lesson in state intervention?

Simon Popple

Group 3 existed as a film company between March 1951 and February 1956, producing low budget films for the commercial cinema in Britain. Its position as the first British government sponsored commercial film company has assured it an important place in the history of British cinema. The political and aesthetic issues raised by its establishment have framed particular perspectives through which state intervention in the film industry has subsequently been viewed. This has been accompanied by a tendency to regard Group 3 as a symbolic rather than an actual working concern, as a hobbyhorse for particular political and aesthetic arguments and approaches. While Group 3 does represent much that is of relevance to the present age and political climate, it needs to be set firmly into the context of its creation and operation.

The Group Scheme, of which Group 3 is the best known example, emerged as a part of the Labour administration's package of aid to an ailing and internationally uncompetitive post-war film industry. The industry emerged from the Second World War under the shadow of a debate about 'Monopolies', externally in the form of Hollywood and internally in the guise of Rank and the Associated British Picture Corporation. Previous attempts at government intervention, such as the formation of the British Film League in 1921 and the quota system implemented by the Cinematograph Film Act of 1927 to stem the flow of American films had limited success. While the balance of market share shifted in favour of British producers[1], the wholly artificial conditions of the quota period masked the

deep structural problems within the industry. Despite the temporary boost given by Alexander Korda and the threatened colonisation of America by British films, it would take a World War for the British industry to find its feet, but again within highly artificial conditions. Even then, when the broad popularity of British wartime cinema appeared especially relevant, audiences were still overwhelmingly exposed to American films.[2]

There was also a strongly perceived preference for American films among British audiences. James Agate, writing in 1946 drew attention to the failures of the British film compared with its American counterpart:

> American: Vapid, nauseating, improbable, technically brilliant and nearly always exciting. British: fatuous, inane, feeble and dull almost to incoherence ... I know that when in the cinema I feel as though I were sitting in a bucket of tepid white-wash drinking flat champagne the picture I am looking at is a British one.[3]

Lack of regulated investment meant that the development of the British industry tended to be on a fragmentary, small scale basis. It functioned at the

Simon Popple is Lecturer in the History of Film and Visual Media at Manchester Metropolitan University, UK. He is joint author of the forthcoming *In The Kingdom of Shadows: A Companion to Early Cinema*, published by Cygnus Arts in Spring 1996. He is currently working on a collection of early British film Catalogues. Correspondence c/o Dept. of History of Art and Design Manchester Metropolitan University Righton Building, Cavendish Street, Manchester M15 6BG. UK.

Fig. 1. J. Arthur Rank (1888–1972), seen here at California's Pebble Beach Golf Course, expanded his film interests so greatly during the war that many feared he would dominate the entire British motion picture industry. [All photos, Museum of Modern Art Film Stills Archive.]

studio space requisitioned and ceased film production for the duration of the war. The British Government's intention was to keep the two strong, particularly the Rank organisation, so that it could 'remain' effective for meeting and possibly dealing with American competition.[4]

This patronage of Rank and post-war resurgence of ABPC was not universally approved.

They were seen as not only preventing independent filmmakers from functioning, but as forestalling any attempted response which might have been mounted to counter the aesthetic sterility of the British film. Again these charges were not totally fair as Rank was supporting a roster of independent producers such as Michael Powell and Emeric Pressburger and bankrolling the Ealing Company. But the fears were realised when Rank embarked on its disastrous foray into the American market in 1948, incurring losses of £3,400,000 in 1949 and with an overdraft of £12,000,000.[5]

Action to counter the perceived problem of the twin monopolies had begun during wartime. Hugh Dalton, as President of the Board of Trade constituted a committee in December 1943 to look at the problem. The so-called Palache Report, submitted in July 1944 considered the primary areas in which monopoly control of the industry was apparent; in the distribution of films, the ownership of studio space, the executive control of exhibition and the restrictive practices by both companies and unions. In response to these problems that the committee had highlighted they made a number of recommendations to reduce the power of the individual companies and to try and ensure, 'reasonable access both to the means of production of films and to screen time and freedom from restrictive practices in the field of film distribution'.[6] Among the recommendations to limit the growth of monopolies, control distribution and exhibition, was expressed the wish that the Board of Trade

level of numerous independent companies and producers working on single productions, renting rather than owning their facilities. There were naturally exceptions to this pattern, most notably after the war in the form of Rank and ABPC whose relative size and breadth of interests soon earned them the tag of monopolies. While not totally deserved, this perception was heightened by government policy towards the industry during the war, a factor recognised by Sir Stafford Cripps in 1945:

> The war brought prosperity to Britain's film duopoly, the J. Arthur Rank Organisation and the associated British Picture Corporation. Rank grew tremendously in all parts of the industry during the war, whilst ABPC had all its

would set up and administer a Film Bank to provide resources to encourage independent production.

The report was obviously contentious as it implied a level of state intervention in the British film industry never before contemplated. Only the unions fully supported the proposals and the eventual consequences of the report were a weak set of self regulatory controls.

With the Labour victory of July 1945 it seemed for a while that the opportunity to implement the major recommendations of the Palache Report might be at hand, especially as Dalton was replaced by Stafford Cripps as President of the Board of Trade. As well as receiving his civil servant's reports on the committee's findings, he also commissioned Paul Rotha, a well known supporter of state intervention and a leading independent filmmaker, to prepare a memorandum for his own use on the Government and the film industry.

His report began with an analysis of the industry that mirrored very closely the one presented in the Palache Report, but he also treated the problem not as a purely economic one, but as a problem with very important aesthetic and cultural implications. In this sense the two reports at the disposal of Sir Stafford Cripps both stressed the multifaceted nature of the film industry and argued that any resulting solutions could not be achieved by the manipulation of market forces alone. As Rotha put it:

> In these twenty-five years of haphazard existence, the production of British films has done less than justice to the reflection of British ideas and thought to people overseas. In most markets, including the commonwealth, the Hollywood film has had precedence. The qualities of the cinema as a great instrument of public education have been ignored by the industry's exponents.[7]

Rotha issued a long series of proposals centred on the notion that the Government should not only regulate the commercial industry, but establish and finance small units of independent film producers and provide guaranteed distribution and exhibition for their films.

In embryo, he proposed the National Film Finance Corporation and the Group Production scheme. As far as Cripps and the Board of Trade were concerned the possibility of the Government

directly running the industry, which had been accepted as the best method for the major utilities, was out of the question. The administration had more pressing concerns.

More positive headway was made after Harold Wilson took over the presidency of the Board of Trade in September 1947, Cripps becoming Chancellor. Wilson commissioned a series of reports under the chairmanship of Sir Henry Gater into the film industry. The first, published in November 1948, cautiously advocated the need for the state provision of finance and facilities:

> Unless free-lance producers form a co-operative production society, it would be hazardous for the Government to provide additional space in any form. If Independent producers formed a co-operative organisation the Government would buy and own a studio for it and the management of the Government's studio should be entrusted to a limited company ... in conclusion we feel bound to emphasise that in the event of free-lance producers failing to achieve an efficient organisation it would be hazardous for the government to embark upon the provision of additional studio space in any form.[8]

The second Gater Report considered wastage in the film industry, the third finance. These findings precipitated the Plant enquiry into the overall finances of the industry, which whilst supporting the need to establish help for the independent sector, ruled out nationalisation as a solution.

> For our part we are unanimously of the view that film production which requires the free exercise and development of individual enterprise, skill and craftsmanship is among the businesses least appropriate for state ownership and operation.[9]

The evidence contained in these reports all tended to point to the need for some form of action in favour of independent filmmakers which would reduce monopoly control and stimulate production, but within a commercial rather than collectivist framework. The pressure was increased by the acute capitalisation difficulties encountered by two major film concerns, British Lion and Pilgrim Films. Both companies were unable to finance their future

production schedules. Korda's British Lion had ex-
pended most of its resources since the end of the
war attempting to compete with Rank in increasing
production and distribution facilities.

Harold Wilson had pressed the Treasury for a
loan to establish the long vaunted State Film Bank,
the National Film Finance Corporation.

The decision was officially announced at the
end of July 1948 and as an interim measure a
temporary agency was established to provide loans
with an initial capital of £2,500,000, half the
promised capital of £5,000,000. The Cinematograph Film Production (Special loans) Act was
passed in March 1949 and the NFFC was officially
launched in April 1949 under the control of Lord
Reith, ex Director-general of the BBC. Reith's first
act was to dispose of three fifths of the NFFC's entire
budget to the ailing British Lion Company. This was
seen as a direct betrayal of independent interests
and seemed to confirm the Government's preference for existing companies, rather than encouraging new ones.

The British film industry was thrown deeper into
crisis following the disastrous effects of the imposi-
tion of the Dalton Levy in August 1947. The government placed an import levy of 75 per cent on all
American films, ostensibly to relieve the flow of
dollars from the British economy. The American film
industry retaliated by imposing a boycott on all new
films.

The failure of the major British companies, particularly Rank, to respond to the American embargo
of 1948 forced a drastic change of approach from
government, partially triggering the provision of aid
to new independent companies and the Group Production schemes. It was seen as a desperate
measure as the industry seemed on the verge of total
collapse, a perception reflected in Harold Wilson's
account:

> After the conclusion of hostilities, the re-expan-
> sion of film production to peace-time levels pro-
> ceeded without interruption ... It is true that the
> costs were rising steadily, but attendances in
> the cinema were still maintained at wartime
> levels and there was a general optimism not
> only in the industry itself, but also among those
> who provided it with finance ... It was at this
> point that, as one of the measures to meet the

Dollar crisis, an import duty was imposed on
foreign films designed to absorb 75 per cent
of their earnings in the United Kingdom. The
results of this action were most unfortunate for
our producers. The American industry chose to
regard the import duty as an act of war against
themselves. They ceased to import new films
and settled down to make as much as possible
from films already in store here. As a corollary
to this policy they ceased practically all participation in United Kingdom production and offers of screentime on the other side of the
Atlantic which had already been made to the
Rank organisation were withdrawn.[10]

With the remainder of the money left in the
coffers of the NFFC, in February 1950 Lord Reith
proposed providing direct finance to the industry
through an independent set of producers who
would act as brokers for the NFFC's money.[11]

This initial idea was followed up in June of the
same year advocating, in far more detail a whole
new series of executive functions being sought by
the NFFC.[12]

Reith sought:

(1) Group production.
(2) A new distribution company for the UK.
(3) A new distribution company for overseas.
(4) Training facilities for film personnel.
(5) The ability to own studios.

Also instrumental in the establishment of the
groups was Sir Wilfred Eady, head of the Treasury,
who acted as broker between the Treasury, the
Board of Trade and the NFFC.

He was also at the heart of canvassing opinion
from those within the industry whom he considered
vital for the running of the groups, most notably the
head of Ealing, Sir Michael Balcon and the father
of documentary John Grierson, as this letter from
Balcon to Eady indicates;

> John Grierson (who I believe has been talking
> to Lawrie) wants to see me next week. From a
> very casual conversation with Grierson, it
> seems that he has some ideas that might well
> dovetail in some way with the project you have
> in mind. I cannot say for certain until I have
> talked to him in more detail, although one must
> assume that Grierson is thinking of some devel-

Fig. 2. John Grierson (1898–1972) attempted to transfer the spirit of Britain's pre-war documentary
movement to the post-war commercial cinema.

opment of Crown Film activities and the use of their facilities and personnel.[13]

Both Eady's and Grierson's initial intentions centred on the desire to resurrect the spirit and methodology of the documentary movement of the 1930s within existing financial provisions made for the NFFC. Eady's memorandum[14] gave a brief outline of prospective costs and the possible use of Italian neo-realist techniques such as location work and the use of non-professional actors to reduce costs even further. The scheme envisaged a single unit with modest intentions. Grierson shared this initial premise, motivated by a desire to pick up the pieces of the soon to be disbanded Crown Film Unit by their absorption into a new commercial film unit to pursue a blend of documentary and fiction which Grierson called 'story documentary'. His initial, rather modest proposals, were to continue the work of the Crown Film Unit under commercial conditions which would produce second feature documentaries with a very strong story line to make them a

reasonable financial proposition. Costs would be kept to a minimum, between £20–35,000 and distribution would be through the major combines. There was no intention to compete with major producers but rather to make films similar to *Western Approaches* and *Target for Tonight*.

> I see a widening gap growing between the sponsored documentary film and entertainment supply. In the past there has been a middle world of second features, often honourably occupied – from *Drifters* and *North Sea* through *Target for Tonight* and *Western Approaches* to *Children On Trial* and *Daybreak In Udi*. The prospect in this area of production is now dimming to vanishing point.[15]

Following several months of horse-trading[16], the Group Production schemes were announced in January 1951:

> The Proposals made by the National Film Finance Corporation for the creation of three Brit-

ish film Production Groups were announced yesterday.

The plan is outlined in a letter sent by Lord Reith, Chairman of the corporation, to the President of the Board of trade, Mr Harold Wilson, on 12 January. In his acknowledgement, dated last Tuesday, Mr Wilson conveys the approval of the chancellor of the exchequer and himself for the proposals and their good wishes for success.[17]

Group 3 was officially registered as a company on 31 March 1951 and operated until May 1956 when it was sold off by the NFFC to become Beaconsfield Films Ltd. In this short period it produced over twenty largely undistinguished films and lost nearly half a million pounds of government money, although this should be set against total NFFC losses of £3,600,993 between 1950 and 1957. On the face of things it was an unmitigated disaster, yet considering the odds it faced it was arguably better than many of its commercial counterparts. It was staffed by many experienced personnel drawn from all areas of the industry, its board of management boasting such luminaries as Sir Michael Balcon, John Grierson, John Baxter and James Lawrie. Whilst its production history is fairly well documented[18] the reasons for its apparent failure demand closer attention, relating to commercial as well aesthetic concerns. The quality of the films produced in its short history[19] perhaps offer some explanation for Group 3's failure, but also demonstrate the impossible situation in which the company was operating.

Group 3's first two films went into production in May and June 1951 at the recently leased Southall studios and were both completed within their initial production schedules, for a projected budget of around £50,000. Interestingly both also made wide use of documentary style exterior work allowing the company to achieve what was of vital importance, a continuous production schedule. However, if the approach to documentary technique was to be utilised fully it followed that the material must also be of a complementary nature, adding to the overall effect of the film rather than just enabling everything to be done on the cheap. This was sadly the case with *Judgement*

Deferred and *Brandy for the Parson*. The latter in particular could have been a much stronger film, being centred on the smuggling of brandy by innocent holiday makers from France in which boy scouts became the willing accomplices to the villain, the rather suave and unbelievable Kenneth More. Press reception was tepid, but not wholly dismissive:

> This agreeable comedy is an altogether more hopeful introduction to the work of Group 3 than its first effort *Judgement Deferred*. Unlike the latter, it was produced under the supervision of John Grierson and its accent is on young talent both in direction and playing. In style the comedy derives from the Ealing genre and though not particularly original it has wholesome freshness and intimacy. One would have liked a script with more wit and direction, with more humour.[20]

Stylistically distinctive within the context of British cinema, Group 3 continued to produce films in exactly the same sub-Ealing vein, with progressively worse results. Their fourth film *You're Only Young Twice* received terrible notices:

> It is incomprehensible, it is badly acted, badly directed and badly lit, it is a fiasco and a tragedy. Since Mr Grierson defends this filmed charade and proposes to film such plays for Group 3, there being, according to him, a dearth of young writers and directors, the formation of Group 4 would seem an urgent matter.[21]

Their breakthrough, certainly in terms of press reception came with what is commonly regarded as the one film which fully expressed Grierson's hopes for the docu-drama, *The Brave Don't Cry*. It was Grierson's favourite film, being scripted by him and co-produced with Philip Leacock. It stands out amongst Group 3's other films because of its perfect marriage of theme and style, a documentary realist approach to a mining disaster. Not only did it utilise as far as possible location footage and realistic settings recreated in the studio, but also a largely unknown, non-professional cast drawn from the Glasgow Citizen's Theatre. The film was selected to open the 1952 Edinburgh Film Festival, where it won universal acclaim.

Fig. 3. *The Brave Don't Cry* (1952), directed by Philip Leacock, utilised non-professional actors from Glasgow's Citizen's Theatre and involved a considerable amount of location filming.

Yet despite its profile the film performed poorly at the box office. Tied to a commercial distributor, Associated British Film Distributors, it only received a second circuit release in London. The problem of effective distribution and exhibition dogged the company and prevented badly needed income from being ploughed back into the venture. When a film which did excite critical acclaim, such as *The Brave Don't Cry* emerged it was almost doomed to commercial failure. Despite other highpoints, such as the widely praised *Conquest of Everest*, Group 3 was dogged by reliance on its competitors for exposure. When Group 3 folded in 1956 its loss went almost without notice; Balcon, Grierson and Lawrie had long since departed[22] and the experiment in state intervention in the industry seemed closed.

Yet it was hardly an experiment at all, but an underfunded and fudged attempt by the ailing Labour administration to breathe new life into the British film industry. As the product of centralised socialist state policy it was a sickly child and one ignored for the most part by all including the new Conservative government in 1951. They were content to permit its continuation due no doubt to a dearth of ideas on their own part as to how to attempt to deal with the film industry. Under these circumstances how should one attempt to assess its impact and what, if anything, remains as its legacy?

Despite the accepted need to provide finance for the independent sector, the NFFC's funds were initially channelled into propping up existing major film companies, swallowing up the majority of their £5,000,000 holdings. Such a start, for the NFFC never secured a return of its investment in British Lion, ensured that the NFFC would never again be trusted with such a relatively large sum. As a result subsequent projects, including Group 3 were starved of adequate resources. The subsequent moves towards establishing the group schemes represented a small-scale exercise in political compromise, with only one of the groups coming to enjoy an acceptable degree of autonomy. Even though Group 3 was to be divorced from other major companies in terms of its production capabilities, it was to remain reliant on established distribution and exhibition networks. Group 3 was also regarded as the cheapest option for providing aid to independent filmmakers by Harold Wilson. Initial funding of £250,000 compared ominously with that available elsewhere. Rank alone had a production budget of £12,000,000 in 1949. The Board of Trade itself was well aware that a realistic plan to develop the independent sector required high level, long term investment.

> If the public considers it desirable for political, cultural or economic reasons that British films should be produced then it must be prepared for the Government not only to protect the industry indefinitely, but also to aid it financially as far ahead as can be seen.[23]

The report came too late to influence the outgoing Labour administration, but highlighted the total inadequacy of the NFFC. It was further evidence of the failure of the Government to act on advice widely proffered, not only from interested parties and informed observers but from its own committees of enquiry. Instead it had produced a fatally flawed scheme, creating an enterprise with objectives totally beyond its economic capability. What resulted was a financially impotent company, tied to the goodwill of its major competitors in a period of crisis for the industry as a whole.

The inherent problems of Group 3 were further compounded by the productions undertaken by its directors. Many commentators, such as Paul Rotha and Harry Watt argued that the aesthetic decisions made by the company were the main reason for its failure. This evaluation rests heavily upon the premise that Group 3 was never in a position where the artistic freedoms Rotha and Watt assumed did in fact exist. Their own preferences for a documentary cinema within a commercial context was raised by the recruitment of Grierson and other ex-Crown personnel such as Donald Taylor and Terry Bishop. Watt in particular regarded Group 3's chosen course as a betrayal of the documentary ideal.

Dramatised documentary got one last chance through private enterprise, when in 1951 the NFFC set up Group 3 ... It is obviously leading with my chin to say now that Group 3 was a disaster, but the trade, that first arbiter of things cinematic, will confirm it. The films were notably old fashioned, snobbish and second-rate.[24]

Whilst this attack is rather sweeping and no one could accuse *The Brave Don't Cry* of snobbery, it does raise the question of Group 3's portrayal of class and class orientated subjects. Watt's criticism of Group 3's films in general appears partly justified. Some of the films do however deal with social issues of the day, such as divorce in *Background* and the problems of old age in *End Of The Road*. As far as snobbishness is concerned, here Watt is correct in identifying a broadly middle class tone, although the exception, *The Brave Don't Cry*, was a powerful exception indeed. It could be argued that Group 3 simply had to reflect the general trends within the market and one particularly apparent within comedy. The strongly working class music hall comedies of the 1930s and the war years had given way to the more middle class orientated comedies of Ealing Studios.

Coupled to these class sensibilities was the question of realism. Both Watt and Rotha were committed to a realist commercial cinema linked strongly to the documentary school of which they were both leading exponents. Rotha had already financed and made two feature films in this genre, the most notable being *No Resting Place* in 1951, demonstrating just what could be achieved in the independent sector if the will was there. In his view Group 3 presented the ideal opportunity and enjoyed far more support than he had ever received. The extension of documentary values into the commercial sector during and immediately following the war fired the hopes of Rotha and his contemporaries. It had really taken a hold in the midst of the war when documentarists like Humphrey Jennings had directed films such as *Fires Were Started* which had integrated the documentary approach within the fictional format. Films like *Fires Were Started* and *Western Approaches* were not merely peculiar to wartime Britain or for that matter concerned with the conflict. In Italy the forerunner of the neo-realist

Fig. 4. Paul Rotha (1907–84), an early proponent of government intervention in the British film industry, thought Group 3 had failed to live up to its potential.

movement, Luchino Visconti's *Ossessione*, produced in 1942, was a remarkable product of Mussolini's fascist cinema. Vittorio De Sica's *Bicycle Thief* released in 1948 won world wide acclaim and in Britain it was voted the best film ever made in *Sight and Sound* in 1952.

Hollywood had also begun to assimilate certain facets of this realistic approach, the use of genuine locations and a growing tendency towards social commentary. John Ford's 1940 production of *The Grapes Of Wrath* gave some early indicators which were to be developed by Jules Dassin's *The Naked City* in 1948. These films gave respectability to the genre and in their own right proved commercially viable. Audience surveys of the period also began to uncover a recognition of realism within the cinema-going public, an example of which can be found in J.P.Mayer's sociological survey of audiences in 1948:

... by now of course I had linked up films with

reality and I despised the futile attempts to portray life, so showily, gaudily and synthetically. But in the last few wartime years I have encountered with delight good British films, no gags or cracks as the Americans put it, but definite British wit.[25]

Rotha mirrored the general sentiments about the need for greater realism in the cinema and pointed out the failure of the industry to develop trends begun during the war years:

The British feature film was beyond question at its best during the war years ... Such films as *Squadron 992*, *Coastal Command*, *Fires Were Started*, *Western Approaches* and many more succeeded in expressing in terms that could be understood by all something of the real character of the British people ... Mr John Grierson at his Group 3, with resources provided by the NFFC has only made one film out of five which develops the realist principle. *The Brave Don't Cry* is a notable effort, but even it suffered from being anchored to the studio with which the group is burdened, where floorspace must be kept filled and overheads paid, when, maybe, the very stories it should be making do not need the artificial make-up of studio contriving.[26]

In this light it is possible to see Group 3 as the last stage in the development of the 1930s documentary movement, failing to perform the role of its so-called ancestors the Empire Marketing Board, General Post Office and Crown Film Units.

Grierson saw things somewhat differently. The demise of the Crown Film Unit, the last in the line of government sponsored documentary units, marked the end of the old documentary tradition within British cinema, a fact which Grierson was quick to point out, stating that 'The Government sponsorship has reached, for the present, its logical limit'.[27]

He also recognised the position in which it placed a great many skilled and gifted filmmakers. This does not however mean that Grierson sought in any way to create a new Crown Unit, despite its demise being his initial interest in the schemes. Grierson had ambitions outside the documentary arena, he wanted to dabble in the commercial sector, a point which his close friend H. Forsyth Hardy makes:

> I do not think Grierson had any intention of integrating the documentary idea or approach and story films for the cinema. He was at the time disillusioned about the government commitment to documentary and saw no way forward through the COI (Central Office of Information) … Grierson would like to have seen more films like *The Brave Don't Cry* but he would never have thought they should be the staple output. He loved fun and Group 3 films gave him the opportunity to have this.[28]

This, coupled with the chronic investment situation meant that the development of a consistent Group 3 style as there was in Ealing pictures never materialised. The company, being reliant on recouping as large a percentage of its cost as possible became locked into trying to emulate current vogues, such as light comedy, rather than forging a new agenda. Group 3 was also tied to a rigid production output, which on the one hand ensured a continuous production schedule, a stated aim of the group, but, on the other, left little or no room for experimentation.

The changes in personnel within the company also militated against stability, but just how much they contributed to the failure of the group is hard to determine. Grierson's illness and the loss of Sir Michael Balcon and James Lawrie from the board appear as heavy blows. Their individual impact, on the other hand, was not vital to the running of the group. Grierson was in reality inexperienced in the area of the commercial cinema. His withdrawal from executive involvement in the company in 1954 and quick return to the documentary arena, albeit on television, perhaps reflect a sense of disillusionment and frustration at the obstacles Group 3 faced.

The collective nature of Group 3 is also an important factor in examining the extent to which Grierson or anyone else may bear a personal responsibility for its policies. Projects were often in the hands of individuals outside the board and overall decisions were made through monthly gatherings.

As others sought to diversify within the film industry, Group 3 was constrained by its meagre circumstances. To meet the appeal of new leisure markets such as television, new forms of cinematic gimmickry were explored in the form of 3-D and CinemaScope. Group 3's belated use of colour was their main riposte, as they felt under more and more pressure to compete with the likes of Rank. Grierson's papers reveal that various projects were explored, including the possibility of filming a circus project in 3-D [29] and a cartoon version of *The Tempest*.[30]

Where Group 3 did contribute was in the field of training for the industry as a whole. As this had been at the core of the Group's concerns much weight may be given to their claims concerning this 'training school' function. An internal list of personnel was issued by Group 3 as part of the 1955 policy statement submitted to the NFFC.

Above all else Group 3 stands as a testimony not to the failure of state intervention but to halfhearted intervention. It is sad that Group 3 has come to be regarded as some sort of yardstick by which state sponsorship should be measured. The circumstances under which it was forced to operate and the lack of government support ensured that it would never achieve anything like its true potential.❖

Notes

1. Almost 30 per cent by the mid-1930s.

2. The American share of the market was 90 per cent in 1945. Dispatch 21682, 14 March 1945. From the *Cultural Attache*, US Embassy, London. 1.

3. James Agate, 'What's all the fuss about British Films?', *British Film Year Book*. 1947, 43–44,

4. PRO:BT 64/2426. Sir Stafford Cripps, Film Memorandum, 19 November 1945. While ABPC's Elstree studios were commandeered by The Royal Ordinance Corps in 1939, their own productions were transferred to other facilities, including the Welwyn Studios.

5. Ann McNeil, Films in 1951 – The Festival of Britain.

6. HMSO, *Tendencies to Monopoly in the Cinematograph Industry:* Report of a committee appointed by the Cinematograph Films Council. 1944.

7. Paul Rotha, 'The Government and the Film Industry', 1945. in *Rotha on Film*, London, 1978, 261–262.

8. Published in *Kinematograph Weekly*, 25 November 1948.

9. Cmnd 7;8337, *Report on the Distribution and exhibition of cinematograph films*, 38.

10. PRO:BT 65/45165, Memorandum by Harold Wilson, 'Present State of the Film Industry', 15 March 1949.

11. By way of example, the corporation, instead of financing many separate producers, should as quickly as it can, directly or indirectly, encourage the establishment of two or three new groups of producers working in company and under direction, as in the Ealing concern. PRO:BT64/4519, Lord Reith's memorandum to Harold Wilson, 9 February 1950.

12. As to group production: a word of encouragement from the president would put NFFC on to planning for speedy implementation of what it has long felt essential. It is quite possible that there might be two branches of this; one for first features, the other a combination of suggestions made by Eady and Grierson, aiming at employing some of the best documentary people on producing second features and shorts. These two branches would be closely linked; it might be desirable to plan the production of complete programmes. PRO:BT 64/4519, Reith memorandum to Wilson, 26 June 1950, para.7.

13. PRO:T 228/272 127580. Letter from Balcon to Eady, 31 May 1950

14. PRO:T 228/272 127580 Sir Wilfred Eady, The Film Industry, 31 May 1950.

15. Grierson's plans were received by Eady in the form of a detailed plan entitled 'A Project for the Production of a series of Story Documentaries'. PRO:T 228/273 127580, 8 June 1950.

16. For a detailed account see S.Popple. *Group 3: An Examination Of The Impact Of State Intervention Upon The Independent and Documentary Cinema, And Its Relationship With The Commercial Sector.* M.A Thesis. University of Leeds, 1988.

17. *The Times*, 26 January 1951.

18. Richard Dyer MacCann, 'Subsidy for the Screen', *Sight and Sound*, Summer 1977.

19. Group 3 Filmography

    1952 February *Judgement Deferred* (b.w.) Directed John Baxter

    1952 February *Brandy for the Parson* (b.w.) Directed John Eldridge

    1952 July *Time Gentleman Please* (b.w.) Directed Lewis Gilbert

    1952 July *You're Only Young Twice* (b.w.) Directed Terry Bishop

    1952 August *The Brave Don't Cry* (b.w.) Directed Philip Leacock

    1952 December *Miss Robbin Hood* (b.w.) Directed John Guillermin

    1953 March *The Oracle* (b.w.) Directed Pennington-Richards

    1953 April *Laxdale Hall* (b.w.) Directed John Eldridge

    1953 August *Background* (b.w.) Directed Daniel Birt

    1953 October *Conquest of Everest* (b.w.) directed Thomas Stobart

    1954 March *Devil On Horseback* (b.w.) Directed Cyril Frankel

    1954 April *Conflict of Wings* (col.) Directed John Eldridge

    1954 August *Man of Africa* (col.) Directed Cyril Frankel

1954 September *The Angel Who Pawned Her Harp* (b.w.) Directed A.Bromley

1954 October *The End of The Road* (b.w.) Directed Wolf Rilla

954 October *Orders are Orders* (b.w.) Directed David Paltenghi

1954 October *Child's Play* (b.w.) Directed Margaret Thompson

1954 December *Make Me An Offer* (col.) Directed Cyril Frankel

1955 February *The Love Match* (b.w.) Directed David Paltenghi

1955 June *John and Julie* (col.) Directed William Fairchild

1955 November *The Blue Peter* (col.) Directed Wolf Rilla

1956 February *Double Cross* (col.) Directed Anthony Squire

20. D.Powell, Review, *The Sunday Times*, 25 May 1952.

21. R.Winnington, Review, *News Chronicle*, 19 July 1952.

22. All three resigned from the Board in 1954, Grierson as a result of being diagnosed as tubercular.

23. Political and Economic planning, The British Film Industry 1952, PEP, 1952.

24. Harry Watt. *Don't Look at the Camera*, London. 1974, 191.

25. Commentary from unidentified 19 year old, J.P.Mayer, *British Cinemas and Their Audiences*. London, 1948, 70.

26. Paul Rotha, 'Forgotten Lessons In Realism', *The Times*, 25 September 1952.

27. John Grierson,Op.cit.

28. H. Forsyth Hardy, Letter to author, 2 November 1987.

29. Letter from J.D. Relph, M.D. Stereo Techniques Ltd. 1953. G.38:39:294

30. Letter from John Halas, Halas and Batchelor Cartoon Films Ltd.

25. March 1955,G.38:3.

Film History, Volume 8, pp. 143–158, 1996. Copyright © John Libbey & Company
ISSN: 0892-2160. Printed in Australia

'A thinly disguised art veneer covering a filthy sex picture': Discourses on art houses in the 1950s

Barbara Wilinsky

n 1955 *Newsweek* magazine ran an article entitled 'How Do You See the Movies? As Entertainment and Offensive at Times or as Candid Art?' This question illustrates the post-war ambivalence resulting from a re-evaluation of the nature and purpose of films as entertainment and as a cultural form. It is directly related to the 1952 case of Burstyn v. Wilson, the Commissioner of Education of New York, in which the Supreme Court determined that '... it cannot be doubted that motion pictures are a significant medium for the communication of ideas'.[1] This ruling began a chain of court rulings throughout the 1950s and 1960s that extended protection under the first and fourteenth amendments to films. This shift from a long-standing 1915 court decision that deemed motion pictures '... a business pure and simple originated and conducted for profit',[2] did not begin and end with court rulings; rather, transformations in US society over time opened up questions and disputes regarding film's place in US culture.

A new site for the exhibition of 'alternative' films provided one reason for the new interest in film as an art form in the 1950s. The increased cultural capital ascribed to films can be tied to the rising popularity of art film theatres in the US after World War II. Although art theatres date back to the 'little cinema' movement of the 1920s, it is in the 1950s that the popularity of art film theatres came to the mass public's attention in the United States. These theatres, which showed many films produced outside of the Hollywood studio system, not only offered viewers films that were different from the Hollywood studio offerings, but also provided an alternative environment for post-World War II film-going designed to increase the prestige of the films and the theatres.

According to Pierre Bourdieu, the search for prestige is related to the desire for economic gain. He suggests that the promotion of a cultural object as art and the attempts to erase its economic elements – what he calls the 'disavowal of the economic' – serve the purpose of increasing the long

Barbara Wilinsky is currently working on her dissertation on art houses in the late 1940s at Northwestern University. Please send correspondence to 1310 Chicago Avenue, #3F, Evanston, IL 60201, USA or to e-mail b-wilinsky@nwu.edu

Fig. 1. An art house in New York City: the Paris Theatre, at it's opening in 1948.
[Photo courtesy of the American Museum of the Moving Image.]

term potential for economic gain by increasing the longevity of the cultural object and the status of the producer.[3] Balancing the desire to enhance the long term economic potential of art films by increasing their prestige against the business need for immediate financial gain, filmmakers, producers, distributors, exhibitors and audiences (as well as more peripheral groups such as intellectuals and film censors) had different priorities in their negotiation of the cultural and economic potentials of art films often resulting in contradictory goals and inconsistent public rhetoric. The complexity – and perhaps impossibility – of disavowing the economics of the art film industry becomes even more clear when considering that the economic gains and expenditures of the film industry have consistently been a subject of public knowledge and discussion: indeed film companies themselves have used such information to prove a film's worth and encourage viewership.

The conflicting views of art houses as sites of prestigious culture and as camouflages for purely economic interests resulted in two radically different conceptions of these theatres: the art theatre as a source of cultural enlightenment, offering spectators films of a quality supposedly higher than Hollywood studio films and the art cinema as a place to go in order to see more off-colour films that could not be produced by mainstream Hollywood cinema still restricted by the Production Code. This association of the art theatre with 'sexy' and perhaps even 'perverse' films (most often foreign films) gave the theatres a risqué quality. Was this breaking of conventional mores in the service of artistic realism or conscious commercialism?

These two opposing images of the art theatre – as a place of high culture and a place of lower moral standards – generated various responses from critics and the general public. Looking at public discourse surrounding art houses and the films that they exhibited, this essay examines the possible reasons for the rise of this double-edged discourse surrounding art theatres in the US in the 1950s and the effects that these distinct discourses had on the development of the film industry in the postwar era. Exploring the ways in which art houses developed these two distinct reputations allows for an understanding of some of the shifts that occurred both in the US film industry at this time and in the popular reconsiderations about the status functions of motion pictures in society.

Art houses in the 1950s

The art film theatre phenomenon became commercially viable in the late 1940s/early 1950s. Art houses featured foreign films, documentaries, independent (not Hollywood studio) productions and classic (Hollywood) re-releases.[4] These theatres tended to be small, only showed single features, catered to mature (adult) audiences – sometimes even denying admission to children – and more likely sold coffee rather than popcorn.[5] Art houses also held films over for longer runs than most mainstream movie theatres. Generally, located in big cities and university towns, art theatres became more prevalent throughout the 1950s. Of the 12 art houses in the US in the late 1940s, half were located in New York City.[6] According to one report, between 1950 and 1952 the number of art theatres doubled to 470.[7] According to Douglas Gomery, by 1952 an additional 1,500 theatres, though not exclusively art houses, had some policy of booking 'art' films.[8] The meaning of 'sureseaters', the nickname given to art houses, even changed. At first the term mockingly referred to the viewer's certainty of finding a seat in art houses, but later this name suggested that all the seats in these theatres were certain to be filled.[9]

Studies showed that art house patrons were older, more educated and more up-scale than mainstream audiences. They were avid filmgoers who make more active use of other cultural products and are more likely to be influenced by reviews and word of mouth rather than advertising.[10] A variety of motives were offered for the art filmgoers' supposed search for higher quality films than those being produced by mainstream Hollywood studios.[11] World War II opened up an interest in more serious and socially critical forms of entertainment as well as an increased curiosity about foreign cultures. Additionally, with television in the home focusing on family fare, motion pictures attempted to offer adult audiences something different, something more mature, in order to motivate them to leave their homes.

There are several other reasons why exhibitors at this time searched outside the Hollywood studio system for film product. The Supreme Court's 1948 Paramount decision most strongly affected film exhibition. The ruling that vertical integration of the Hollywood studios violated anti-trust laws forced the studios to divorce production and distribution from exhibition. The process of divorcement continued throughout the 1950s. As this change took place, more and more theatres became independent, diminishing the control that the major studios exercised over exhibition by way of the Motion Picture Association of America (MPAA). Although in 1942 the MPAA eliminated fines and penalties against theatres (even those associated with the studios) which screened films without Production Code seals, the member companies still '... pledged to maintain in their theatres moral and policy standards as exemplified in the Production Code and accompanying regulations'.[12] Even as late as 1960 most theatres still required the films they exhibited to have the Production Code seal of approval; at that time only two films (*The Moon is Blue* and *The Man with the Golden Arm*) had received wide distribution without the seal.[13] However, despite the general trend to maintain the importance of the Production Code seal for exhibition, the Paramount decision, by favouring independent over studio-controlled exhibition, increased the possibility of exhibiting films that strayed from the Production Code's 'moral and policy standards'.[14]

Other industrial factors contributed to the rise of art film theatres. Between 1946 and 1956 the production of studio Hollywood films dropped approximately 28 per cent while the import of foreign films rose 132 per cent.[15] Theatres struggling to keep their screens filled often turned to independently produced Hollywood films, documentaries, or foreign films (which frequently did not receive the MPAA seal) in order to keep their theatres running. Decreased production within the major studios had several causes. The process of divorcement and impending divorcement meant that studios could no longer benefit from their cash cows – the theatres which had long provided the financial support for film production. Production,

Fig. 2. In *The Miracle* (1948), Anna Magnani (right) plays a simple-minded peasant girl who is seduced by a stranger (Federico Fellini) whom she believes to be St. Joseph. When she becomes pregnant, she thinks that she will be the mother of God. [Photo courtesy of Jerry Ohlinger.]

therefore, needed to be scaled back in order to be profitable in and of itself. The outlawing of block booking and blind bidding in the 1940s also led to decreased production. Since the studios could no longer rely on monopolistic practices to secure the rental of all their films, regardless of quality, the major film producers scaled back production to focus on A-pictures with enough appeal to guarantee rentals. Decreased production also resulted in a seller's market, driving up the rental prices for Hollywood films often beyond the means of many smaller, independent theatres. At the same time that the US film studios decreased production, the import of foreign films also began to rise. Using funds locked up in other countries following the war, the studios bought the American rights to foreign films.[16]

Although weakened by the Paramount decision and the increased numbers of independent exhibitors, the Production Code Administration continued to scrutinise the film industry, requiring that studio films meet certain moral standards in order to get a seal of approval. Independent and foreign films that did not seek PCA approval often found themselves the targets of local regulatory boards.[17] State and city censorship boards licensed films for public exhibition. *Business Week* reported in 1952 that seven states and approximately 90 cities still operated censorship boards. Perhaps the most vehement of the nationally-based moral watch dogs which assumed that motion pictures had a moral responsibility, was the Catholic Church's National Legion of Decency. Founded in 1934, the Legion rated films according to their acceptability (completely unacceptable films received a rating of 'C' for condemned) and also instituted a pledge which church-goers could (but were not required to) take once a year vowing not to attend any films condemned by the Legion.[18] It is important to note that the Legion did not represent all factions of the Church. For example, the Catholic magazine *Commonweal* frequently disagreed with the Legion regarding film censorship because 'The Legion of Decency ... operates on the principle of making only moral evaluations of movies, leaving to others all consideration of their artistic aspects. This sounds fine; the trouble is, it cannot be done ... Everything depends on what the artist does with his theme.'[19]

In the late 1940s, these interested parties thrust foreign films – which accounted for 80 per cent of some art house fare[20] – into the centre of the debate about the morality of motion pictures. At this time attention mostly focused on Italian neorealist films, such as Roberto Rossellini's *The Miracle*, partly because of the critical and popular success of these films and particularly because of their claims to 'realism': their attempts to capture and portray the 'real' world rather than a world that corresponded with a pre-approved production code. These Italian films generally did not get the MPAA seal of approval and so most theatres refused to exhibit them, limiting their exhibition to art houses. In 1950 the MPAA established an Advisory Unit to help foreign film producers adapt to the code so that their films would be acceptable for wide release; however, as *The New York Times* reported many Italian filmmakers questioned the gesture, wondering '... what changes will be necessary to make them "acceptable" and will those changes cripple the artistic quality of Italian films, which is the very thing that made them world famous?'[21]

Candid art

It is in the context of the debate over the legitimacy of film as a form of cultural expression that the understanding of art theatres developed into two opposing viewpoints. Increasingly films became seen as not only a serious art form but also as a means of dealing with mature themes. Film audiences demonstrated an interest in intelligent, serious films. The growing number of university film programs and 16 mm film societies legitimised the study of film.[22] The decision of some universities to include filmmaking and film appreciation in their curriculum both reflected and encouraged the growing interest in the serious consideration of film. As

Lauren Rabinovitz suggests, when the California School of Fine Arts included 16 mm filmmaking in its regular curriculum in 1947, 'the school's move ... helped to legitimate independent cinema's status as an artistic medium among the vanguard arts'.[23] The release of foreign and experimental films on 16 mm film allowed more people access to this work. Referring to experimental films, Arthur Knight wrote in the *Saturday Review of Literature*, '... these are pictures produced *con amore*, generally privately financed by young people who seek self-expression in the art that is closest to them, the art they grew up with'.[24] On a poster announcing the first Cinema 16 program in 1946, the film society declared its aim to show the 'scores of artistically satisfying, socially purposeful and thought-provoking 16 mm films [that] are gathering dust in film libraries'.[25] Both Knight's and Cinema 16's assessment of 16 mm films encouraged the serious consideration of film as an art form.

Whether or not they consciously defined their interests in endowing art houses with an image of prestige, certain groups did have a stake in increasing the cultural capital of these theatres and their films. Critics, art film exhibitors and art filmmakers could have all benefited from the increase in prestige afforded art films and art theatres. Critics increased the scope of their intellectual influence. The success of the art theatre as an alternative mode of exhibition, prompted the support of some critics who would benefit from the growth of an audience that embraced 'art' and considered films seriously (often seeking out intellectuals' views of films). Writing in *Variety*, Noel Meadow highlighted the role that film critics played in supporting foreign films:

> '[f]ilm critics, especially those interested in the film as art, helped the foreign pic boom along by lavish praise for most product ... This is an important factor, since a foreign film, because of the type of audience it attracts, lives or dies according to the critical consensus ...'[26]

Film critics seemed aware of their new importance for a segment of the film industry. *Theatre Arts'* Herman Weinberg noted that '[b]ad reviews will ruin a foreign film, since their audiences are generally more discerning. Bad reviews of an American film featuring a popular star hardly make an appreciable dent in the box office receipts ...'[27] Weinberg's move to depict the foreign film audience as being more 'discerning' and the Hollywood film audience as less thoughtful, not only encouraged art film attendance but also established the film critics as the cultural elite who could guide people through the unfamiliar realm of high culture.

By supporting the conception of art theatres as sites of cultural enlightenment, art film exhibitors attracted upper class and 'intellectual' audiences and avoided certain forms of censorship. These exhibitors fostered the cultural and intellectual image, providing not only more 'adult' films but also a cosmopolitan atmosphere expected to lure the adult 'lost audience' back to the urban theatres.[28] Modeling their theatres after places of highbrow, intellectual culture, exhibitors appealed to the public's attempt to differentiate themselves from mass audiences and supposedly passive viewers. Attempts to differentiate the experience of going to an art house support Gomery's observation that, 'The motto seemed to be: sell the art films to the rich and well educated and a sizeable group of the middle class might follow'.[29] Generally small theatres, art houses provided those in the audience a sense of exclusivity. Many art houses also used mailing lists to further the sense of attendees being 'in the know' and published newsletters that lent an intellectual feel to the art house culture. Most art houses further encouraged the serious image of their programs by refusing admission to children. Art houses also charged the highest admission price of movie theatres at the time, thus associating these film theatres with more high class, legitimate theatres.[30] The move away from selling popcorn, an inexpensive snack traditionally associated with lower class amusements,[30a] appealed to the middle and upper class pretensions of the US public at this time. Instead, many art houses offered coffee and even added cafés in their lobbies. An article in *Variety* summed up the attractions of art houses for their audiences, noting that these theatres 'tend to create a "loyal" clientele of their own which know the house, appreciates it and doesn't mind paying the extra charge for extra comforts, the service, the feeling of being with one's own'.[31]

In addition to the art house 'culture' fostered through the theatre environment, the advertising and promotion of art houses was often intended to support the high culture stature of the theatres. Many

of the foreign films did show more 'realistic' portrayals of love, sex and other themes that prevented a film from getting an MPAA seal of approval. However, in keeping with Bourdieu's idea that the marketing of 'culture' supported the 'disavowal of the economic',[32] many of the first wave of art theatres (at least in the early 1950s) publicly denied exploiting the sensational nature of their films, frequently professing a reserved approach to promotion in order to preserve the artistic integrity of art houses. In his article on art film production, Paddy Chayefsky expressed an idea that many people invested in the art film movement supported: 'Since your film is art, it is by definition not lewd and therefore you cannot promote an audience by provocative publicity and advertising, not that sensationalist advertising does really get people into the theatre ... whatever the case, the art producer does not want lascivious promotion'.[33] Furthermore, even if they wished to exploit the sensational nature of the films, most art cinemas could not afford large newspaper advertisements or promotions. Extended-runs and word-of-mouth, combined with a loyal clientele were the main forms of promotion used to attract audiences to art films.[34]

As pressure groups attacked the Hollywood studios for their willingness to produce teen exploitation films that lured young audiences (which accounted for the largest percentage of the film-going audience) into 'immoral' films in order to keep up revenues,[35] art houses avoided such attacks by creating a specialised, segmented audience. The frequent restriction of art houses to adults, allowed these theatres to claim that they took responsibility for the mature nature of their films. These business practices helped ascribe to art theatres the public image of sophisticated culture rather than exploitation for the sake of profit – a focus on art rather than economic gain.

Louis Sher owned a chain of 13 theatres in 1958 when *Business Week* described him as the head of the largest chain of art houses in the US in terms of the number of theatres.[36] The article on Sher's chain Art Theater Guild, Inc., written to coincide with the opening of Sher's Toledo Plaza (described as 'typical' of art theatres), demonstrates the way that art film exhibitors presented themselves to the public.[37] Sher described his interest in opening art theatres as stemming from his own feelings of alienation from more mainstream theatres. He said, 'I've gotten a very definite impression that commercial theatres have deteriorated to the point where they no longer served my purpose – which was to relax … Double features and kids thundering up and down the aisles, popcorn stands going full blast, all these things tend to discourage adults from attending the commercial theatres'. In an effort to promote adult attendance, Sher – who at the time operated theatres in ten cities in six states 'from Cleveland to Denver to Kansas City' – ran only single features, approximately 80 per cent of which were foreign films, in a 'relaxing' atmosphere with large, roomy seats (in revamping the Toledo Theatre Sher cut seating down from 700 to 480).[39] Encouraging his patrons to 'become our guests', Sher, nevertheless, did not offer popcorn or a concession stand claiming that they were not necessary: 'We run only well-planned, single features, so when you come in, it is not an expedition. You are in for only two hours and then on your way.'[40] *Business Week* echoed Sher's rhetoric about the comfortable and adult environment, describing the lobbies as resembling '… living rooms, with lots of comfortable seats, easy lighting, interesting pictures and decorations'.[41]

Business Week, also supported Sher's claim not to capitalise on the sensational nature of his films, writing that he '… makes no effort to exploit by life-size nudes or flamboyant billboards any sensational films. Pictures are advertised in a subdued and straight forward way.'[42] As a result of his avoidance of exploitation and the adults-only policy, Sher said '… we have had some battles with groups in cities we run in but when they find that we cater only to adults – and even exclude children – the pressure usually disappears'.[43] Sher's claim to an economically disinterested dedication to art houses and art films is questionable in the light of the fact that his chain (like many other art theatres) switched to become an adult ('nudie') theatre in the 1960s. However, for the purposes of this *Business Week* article, Sher clearly foregrounded his willingness to disregard economic considerations as much as possible in order to serve the adult audience. The cost of refurbishing the Toledo theatre to make it more comfortable, as well as the daily expense of serving free coffee, became unimportant in the light of Sher's personal devotion to motion pictures. Sher

recalled, 'My mother used to say that when I was a baby I'd let out a squawk every time she wheeled me past a movie house'.[44] Furthermore, commenting on his dealings with distributors, Sher suggested that they respect him and other art film exhibitors '… because they know that we go into this as a labor of love and not just to make a fast buck'.[45] Promoting the conception of film as an art form, art filmmakers gained status and increased demand for their productions. Paddy Chayefsky writing for the *Saturday Review* about the process of making 'good' films, defined 'good' films as art films.[46] Foreign filmmakers attempted to use the status of art as a way to get around the Production Code and therefore find wider distribution in the US. For example, representatives of the French film industry suggested (and were denied) a separate interpretation of the Production Code for French films.[47] US filmmakers often looked to foreign films, such as Italian neorealist films, for inspiration and for examples of the artistic freedom lacking within the studio system. Director Fred Zinnemann (*The Search, High Noon, Oklahoma!*, etc.) said that foreign filmmakers, '… are dealing with the world of today and the problems of today. Here in Hollywood we are going in circles'.[48]

Offensive entertainment

Remarks such as Zinnemann's illustrate that the film styles and themes connected to the increased cultural capital of cinema raised questions about the structure and output of the US film industry. Bourdieu wrote, 'To bring a new producer, a new product and a new system of tastes onto the market at a given moment, is to push the whole set of producers, products and systems of tastes into the past'.[49] The rise of 1950s art theatres provoked a counter reaction within the critical establishment, the film industry and local censoring groups. These groups attempted to weaken art films' connection with high culture by depicting them as films that exploit sex in order to make money, thereby exposing the economic side of the art film industry.

The rhetoric which associated art houses with sex films seems to have come from three camps: the 'anti-snob snob', the mainstream film industry and pro-censorship groups. The mainstream US film industry perhaps felt the most pressure from the suc-

Fig. 3. *Bitter Rice* (1950), starring Silvana Mangano, explores the lives of women working in the rice fields of the Po Valley. [Photo courtesy of Jerry Ohlinger.]

cess of these alternative theatres and their films. The refusal of the foreign film industry and the art houses to conform to the production code led the Hollywood film industry to label these films as 'immoral'. In 1950 the MPAA refused to give a seal of approval to Vittorio De Sica's *Bicycle Thief* because of two scenes: one in which a young boy goes to urinate and the other a brief scene in a bordello. As Bosley Crowther points out in *The New York Times*, other Hollywood films that made use of similar scenes received the seal.[50] The wide critical praise of *Bicycle Thief*, along with the general belief in the inoffensive nature of these two scenes, led to rumours that the US film industry wanted to discourage filmmaking outside Hollywood. Joseph Burstyn, the film's distributor, stated that 'Hollywood wants to discourage any pictures made outside the film capital'.[51] Crowther commented, '… one is impelled to wonder after a case such as this of *The Bicycle Thief*, whether the only considerations are those of 'purity'. One cannot help but wonder uneasily

whether the code has not here been used to support some parochial resentment toward alien and adult artistry'.[52]

Additionally, the success of these foreign films at a time when most of the film industry was losing its audience led these groups to suggest that sexual content helped make a film such as *Bitter Rice* the highest grossing foreign film at the time of its release in 1951. Critics ascribed the success of *Bitter Rice* to its 'volatile earthiness'[53] and its 'busomy Italian stars'.[54] An art film distributor in the postwar era, Arthur Mayer described *Bitter Rice* as a film with '… no cinematic merit, but it had a bountifully proportioned leading lady, Silvana Mangano …'[55]

According to Mayer, the charges that foreign films attempted to pass off sex films as 'art' were not completely unfounded. In his autobiography Mayer wrote, 'The only sensational successes scored by [partner] Burstyn and myself in the 15 years in which we were engaged in business were with pictures whose artistic and ideological merits were aided

Fig. 4. Ads for *Open City* playing at three Chicago film theatres – the LaSalle, the World Playhouse and the Alba. [All ads from the *Chicago Tribune* (April, July, August, 1946).]

and abetted at the box office by their frank sex content'.[56] Mayer charged exhibitors (not distributors or filmmakers) with promoting the sexual nature of films: '*The Bicycle Thief* was completely devoid of any erotic embellishments, but the exhibitors sought to atone for this deficiency with a highly imaginative sketch of a young lady riding a bicycle'.[57] An examination of the advertising of some film theatres in Chicago, however, illustrates that it was not necessarily art theatres that most blatantly used sex in their advertising of art films. Rather, successful films such as *Open City*, which were shown in mainstream theatres and exploitation theatres as well as art theatres were objects of more sensationalised advertising on the part of these non-

art film theatres (Fig. 4).[58] Additionally, that the 'sketch of a young lady riding a bicycle' which Arthur Mayer objected to in the advertisements for *The Bicycle Thief* was included in many different theatres' advertisements for the film (Fig. 5)[59] suggests that it was actually a pre-prepared advertisement (ad slick) which few (if any) art theatres could afford to have made and which probably came from the film's distributors (Joseph Burstyn and Mayer, himself). Clearly, the advertisements of art films and art theatres needs further examination in order to clarify the role of sex in the promotion of these films and the exhibitor's part in this sort of promotion.

The suspicions about the cultural validity of *Bitter Rice* bring up another group that questioned

Fig. 5. Ads for *The Bicycle Thief* playing at three Chicago theatres – the World Playhouse, the Alex and the Teatro. [All ads from the *Chicago Tribune* (March, April, May, 1950).]

the cultural status of art theatres: the 'anti-snob snobs', a term borrowed from a letter to the editor of the *Saturday Review of Literature* which objected to a critical article about art houses.[60] Art houses, previously the exclusive domain of the intelligentsia, grew into successful markets. As the middle classes pursued the emblems of high culture found in the art houses, some members of the 'intelligentsia' seemed to disapprove of the idea of being part of a profitable (and less exclusive) niche and rejected the art house culture. Cultural critics and intellectuals attributed the growing popularity of art films to their tendency to pander to the sexual desires of the viewers (in some later cases they probably responded to real changes in the Italian film industry).

Hollis Alpert, writing for the *Saturday Review of Literature* criticises:

> '... the taste snob ... [who] prefers all foreign movies to any home-manufactured product, although he is occasionally willing to lend his patronage to an American film of the documentary type. So prevalent has this sort of snobbism (or, more politely, preference) become that in recent years a sizeable number of movie houses have mushroomed throughout the land to cater to it.'[61]

Alpert also suggests that '... sex in frank, liberal doses helps a foreign film earn a profit' and scoffs at the art house that 'still assumes a tasteful audience'.[62] Richard Griffith wrote in the *Saturday Review of Literature* that, 'Examining the New York reviews and box-office returns it is not difficult ... for Italian [producers] to believe that the key to success is sex in the raw'.[63] Although Griffith questions the notion that it is only sex that attracts audiences to art films (because many films that offered filmgoers sex did not succeed), he notes that many American distributors '... believe and many European filmmakers have been convinced, that their [*Open City, Paisan* and *Bicycle Thief*] remarkable success is due not to their merit but to the frankly pornographic advertising used to exploit them here.'[64] Writing a bit later (in 1962), Pauline Kael expressed the anti-snob sentiment: '... the educated audience often uses "art" films in much the same self-indulgent way as the mass audience uses Hollywood "product", finding wish-fulfilment in the form of cheap and easy congratulation on their sensitivities and their liberalism'.[65] Kael then goes on to compare art films to 'nudie' magazines, associating art films with an overtly sexual product.

Fig. 6. The glorification of a thief: Lianella Carell and Lamberto Maggiorani (right) in *The Bicycle Thief* (1950). [Photo courtesy of Jerry Ohlinger.].

The pro-censorship movement took the lead in accusing art house culture and foreign films of perversity. For these guardians of US morality, foreign films provided a wonderful source of proof that films needed to be censored. Writing in *Catholic World*, John Sheerin referred to a film playing at the 'long-haired art theatres' as 'a thinly disguised art veneer covering a filthy sex picture'.[66] He went on to argue against '... pictures that have artistic value but with sordid themes making their way through the little art theatres. We [Catholics] want to see films made according to the best traditions of art and the eternal law of G-d.'[67]

Charges of Communism also became a common line of attack used against foreign films. In 1949 the Maryland censorship board refused a license to the documentary *On Polish Land* because the board did not '... believe that it presents a true picture of present day Poland'. Rather the board held that the documentary 'appears to be Communist propaganda'.[68] Italian neorealist films were considered to be examples of immorality on the screen simply because of the known fact that many of the filmmakers were leftists or even Communists.[69] In February 1951, seventy members of the Knights of Columbus went to a theatre in Queens, New York demanding that a showing of *Bicycle Thief* be cancelled because the film 'glorifies a thief'.[70] An exam-

Fig. 7. Ads for *Ways of Love* at the Paris
Theatre announcing the return of *The Miracle*.
[ads from *The New York Times*, January 1951.]

approved the film's exhibition in Italy, Spellman told his US followers, 'God forbid that the producers of racial and religious mockeries should divide and demoralise America so that the minions of Moscow might enslave this land of liberty'.[72] Spellman effectively associated the 'sacrilegious' film with Communism.

New York City's Paris Theatre received permission to continue exhibition of the film while the appeals board decided the fate of the film's license. Naturally, the volatile circumstances surrounding the film attracted crowds: people picketing the film, people picketing the picketers and many people waiting to see the scandalous film. Robert Wohlforth wrote that one Sunday afternoon over 200 picketers swarmed the theatre along with those people waiting to see the film.[73] Many of the picketers against *The Miracle* attacked it and its patrons as Communist and sexually perverse. According to Wohlforth, 'A few of them [picketers] ... announce, from time to time, that anyone walking along the south side of West Fifty-eighth Street is un-American, anti-Red Cross or a left-wing diversionist if he doesn't pass right by the theatre with his eyes straight ahead'.[74] One picketer illustrated the perception of the film as obscene when he asked a man waiting in line to buy a ticket, 'You wouldn't take your mother to see a picture like this?'[75] Another group picketed the theatre saying, 'Don't be a Communist. All the Communists are inside.'[76] Gilbert Seldes suggested that for different reasons '... the image of slobbering sexuality which does not appear in the picture' was added to the discussion of the film by people on both sides of the controversy.[77] Seldes wrote, 'The director, his enthusiastic critics and his enemies have all created a figure in our minds that does not exist on the screen'[78] in order to either outrage the public or attract audiences to the film. The advertisements placed by the Paris Theatre immediately following the rescinding of the film's license did not, however, attempt to sensationalise the controversy. Certainly the Paris Theatre indicated in its ads for *Ways of Love* when *The Miracle* had been restored to the trilogy (while the appeals board considered the case). These ads, though, focused on the restoration of the film to its original form, not on the risqué quality of what might be seen (Fig. 7).[79]

ination of the 1950 banning of Rossellini's *The Miracle* (a short film within the three-part feature *Ways of Love* which also included the French films *A Day in the Country* and *Jofroi*) illustrates the representation of art films and art houses at the time.

Initially given a license for public exhibition by the New York City Board of Regents, *The Miracle* later lost this license following an attack on the film by New York City Commissioner of Licenses, Edward McCaffrey and New York's Cardinal Spellman.[71] Despite the fact that the Vatican had

After effects

Clearly, the controversy had financial benefits for those involved with *The Miracle*. Throughout the protestation against the film, the Paris Theatre kept packing in standing room only audiences. Despite two bomb threats, the theatre, described in one article as showing 'exotic foreign films', continued to find audiences.[80] *Newsweek* reported that Burstyn was 'besieged by offers from a dozen theatres eager to show the still controversial film'.[81] There is no doubt that people saw this film because of the controversy, but it also exposed many people to foreign films and made many others consider the questions surrounding film censorship. The popular press and periodicals discussing this case of censorship appeared to side with those people who saw film as an art form deserving protection under the First Amendment. The pro-censorship movement came off as a group of reactionary, hard-line moralists. Cardinal Spellman threatened to call for a boycott of Radio City Music Hall if it went ahead with plans to host the New York Film Critics Circle's annual awards ceremony where *Ways of Love* was to receive the award for the year's best foreign film. While Spellman succeeded in getting the awards ceremony moved to the nearby Rainbow Room,[82] many articles questioned the Church's right to dictate what the general public could see in motion picture theatres. Some articles more blatantly attacked the censors. A *Time* magazine article scolded, 'Instead of simply staying away from *The Miracle* (like their Italian brethren), US Catholics tried to keep other people from seeing it and ... shouted "There ought to be a law!"'[83] An article in the *New Republic* sarcastically asserted, '... if the movies can be shown against the best judgment of Cardinal Spellman, we must plug the loophole that permits this shocking affront to clerical omnipotence'.[84]

The Supreme Court settled many questions of censorship when it made its first move to afford motion pictures the status of art protected under the First Amendment. The Court found it illegal to ban *The Miracle* for reasons of sacrilege. Cases continued to go to court in the 1950s that questioned the parameters of legal film censorship. In each case the courts determined that standards of morality could not be used to regulate filmmaking and film

exhibition. The Supreme Court ruled in 1955 that a Kansas ban on *The Moon is Blue* for reasons of obscenity violated the First Amendment.[85] And in 1959 the court determined that a ban against the exhibition of the French film *Lady Chatterley's Lover* (on the basis that it suggested that in some instances adultery was justifiable) suppressed ideas and violated the First Amendment.[86] The courts, however, continuously upheld the legality of prior censorship due to film's supposed potential to do harm.[87] What the court did was to limit the grounds on which a film could be refused a license for exhibition. With these changes the Production Code began to lose its power. The church, however, retained some of its control due to its ability to call boycotts. As the MPAA relaxed the Production Code standards, the Legion of Decency still had the power to persuade filmmakers to edit films that it deemed objectionable – even if the films had already received the MPAA seal of approval.[88] For many people, though, the events of the early 1950s prompted questions about the validity of censorship.

Much of the discourse surrounding art houses and their films suggested that censorship appeared most unnecessary. Following the refusal of the Production Code Administration to grant *Bicycle Thief* a seal of approval, most newspapers and periodicals joined together to denounce the censorship of art. *Life* magazine wrote that 'The Motion Picture Association of America ... has just made itself ridiculous'.[89] Throughout *The Miracle* controversy, as well, the popular press and periodicals tended to side with the artists, denouncing the church's attempt to control the films exhibited to 'adults only' in an environment that helped to expand the cultural horizons of the US public. The censorship of art films – even if more sexually explicit – was more difficult to justify than the censorship of mass entertainment. The *Newsweek* article that asked people 'How Do You See the Movies?' commented that 'Healthy-minded people appreciating them [motion pictures] as entertainment will naturally not wish to be plunged, or to have their children plunged, into violence and obscenity. On the other hand, people who care for them as art will insist that so long as they are art, dramatically strong, incisive representations of life, then violence and obscenity may be meaningful, bitter or tragic elements in the scheme of things.'[90] The cultural status of art films put them on the same level as theatre, painting and sculpture – media often afforded more leniency when pushing the boundaries of what is considered 'respectable'. However, the need to negotiate the cultural capital of art films and the economic capital necessary to maintain a commercial film industry – in other words the incomplete disavowal of the economic – within the shifting taste cultures of the postwar era resulted in contradictory and conflicting public rhetoric about the artistic legitimacy of films. The double-edged discourse surrounding art houses in the 1950s as being sites of high culture as well as places to see more sexually explicit films worked to open up a rupture within the then current perceptions of motion pictures. The contradictions that resulted from these discourses led to the questioning of the popular ideas about film and censorship, about art and entertainment. These ruptures certainly did not get resolved within the time period of neorealism but grew throughout the 1950s and the questions continued into discussions of the French New Wave and eventually mainstream Hollywood films.❖

Notes

1. Quoted in Richard S. Randal, *Censorship of the Movies: The Social and Political Control of a Mass Medium* (Madison: University of Wisconsin Press, 1968), 29.

2. The case of Mutual Film Corporation v. Ohio. Quoted in Randall, 19.

3. Pierre Bourdieu, 'The Production of Belief: Contribution to an Economy of Symbolic Goods', *Media, Culture and Society* 2 (1980): 262

4. Ronald J. Faber, Thomas C. O'Guinn and Andrew P. Hardy, 'Art Films in the Suburbs: A Comparison of Poplar and Art Film Audiences', *Current Research in Film* vol.4, edited by Bruce A. Austin (New Jersey: Ablex Publishing Corporation, 1988), 45.

5. ' Sureseaters', *Time* (17 October 1949), 102.

6. Bruce A. Austin, *Immediate Seating: A Look at Movie Audiences* (California: Wadsworth Publishing Company, 1989), 81.

7. Stanley Frank, 'Sureseaters Discover an Audience', *Nation's Business* (January 1952), 34.

8. Douglas Gomery, *Shared Pleasures: A History of Movie Presentation in the United States* (London: British Film Institute, 1992), 188.

9. Frank, 34.

10. Faber, O'Guinn and Hardy, 48; Dallas Smythe, Parker B. Lusk and Charles A. Lewis, 'Portrait of an Art-Theatre Audience', *Quarterly of Film, Radio and Television* 8 (Fall 1953): 30.

11. John E. Twomey, 'Some Considerations on the Rise of the Art-Film Theatre', *Quarterly of Film, Radio and Television* 10 (Summer 1956): 240; Gilbert Seldes, *The Great Audience* (New York: Viking Press, 1950), 22; Geoffrey Wagner, 'The Lost Audience', *Quarterly of Film, Radio and Television* 6 (Summer 1952): 340; Andrew Dowdy, *'Movies Are Better Than Ever:' Wide Screen Memories of the Fifties* (New York: William Morrow and Company, 1973), 2-3.

12. *Motion Picture Almanac* quoted in Ruth A. Inglis, 'Self Regulation in Operation' in *The American Film Industry*, edited by Tino Balio, 2nd ed. (Madison: University of Wisconsin Press, 1985), 385.

13. William K. Zinsser, 'The Bold and Risky World of "Adult" Movies', *Life* (29 February 1960), 82.

14. Twomey, 242.

15. Austin, 81.

16. Ellen Draper, '"Controversy Has Probably Destroyed Forever the Context": The Miracle and Movie Censorship in America in the Fifties', *The Velvet Light Trap* 25 (Spring 1990): 76.

17. 'Limit on Movie Censorship', *Business Week* (31 May 1952), 33.

18. 'How Do You See The Movies? As Entertainment and Offensive at Times or as Candid Art?', *Newsweek* (8 August 1955), 51.

19. Quoted in 'How Do You See The Movies?', 51.

20. 'Film Chain Finds Cure For Box Office Blues', *Business Week* (22 March 1958), 75.

21. Jane Cianfarra, 'Italian Film Industry is Wary of Americans', *The New York Times* (26 March 1950).

22. Austin, 82.

23. Lauren Rabinovitz, *Points of Resistance: Women, Power and Politics in the New Avant-Garde Cinema 1943-71* (Urbana: University of Illinois Press, 1991), 43.

24. Arthur Knight, 'Self Expression', *Saturday Review of Literature* (27 May 1950), 40.

25. Poster dated October 1946 in Cinema 16 files of Anthology Film Archives.

26. Noel Meadow, 'Getting Realistic About Those Foreign Films', *Variety* (4 January 1950), 175.

27. Herman G. Weinberg, 'The European Film in America', *Theatre Arts* (October 1948), 49.

28. Seldes, 42.

29. Gomery, 185.

30. Ibid., 79.

30a. Ibid., 186.

31. 'Four Kinds of Film Situations', *Variety* (28 January 1959), clippings files of the Museum of Modern Art.

32. Bourdieu, 283.

33. Paddy Chayefsky, 'Art Films - Dedicated Insanity', *Saturday Review* (21 December 1957), 16.

34. Frank, 36.

35. Zinsser, 86; 'The New Frankness in Films', *Saturday Review* editorial (19 December 1959), 18.

36. 'Film Chain Finds Cure', 75.

37. Ibid., 73.

38. Ibid., 75.

39. Ibid.

40. Ibid., 76.

41. Ibid.

42. Ibid., 75.

43. Ibid., 76.

44. Ibid., 75.

45. Ibid.

46. Chayesfsky, 16.

47. 'Film Censorship Stand', *The New York Times* (15 June 1955).

48. Quoted in Murray Schumach, 'Movie Creativity in Europe Hailed', *The New York Times* (13 May 1961).

49. Bourdieu, 290.

50. Bosley Crowther, 'Unkindest Cut', *The New York Times* (2 May 1950).

51. 'Banned Cicycle', *Newsweek* (13 March 1950), 78.

52. Crowther, 1950.

53. Hollis Alpert, 'Strictly for the Art Houses', *Saturday Review of Literature* (28 April 1951), 7.

54. 'Italian Movies - the Last Act?' *US News and World Report* (17 August 1956), 82.

55. Arthur Mayer, *Merely Colossal* (New York: Simon and Schuster, 1953), 230.

56. Ibid., 233.

57. Ibid. As filmmakers began to realise that money could be made with 'sexy' foreign films some undoubtedly chose to ignore even the pretension of art. Gunnar D. Kumlien, 'Sex in Italian Films', *Commonweal* (15 July 1955), 371; 'Italian Movies - the Last Act?', 84.

58. Advertisements for *Open City* from art theatre World Playhouse (*Chicago Tribune*, 20 April 1946, 15); small, independent theatre, LaSalle (*Chicago Tribune*, 24 July 1946, 25); Balaban and Katz's Alba (*Chicago Tribune*, 30 August 1946, 20).

59. Three advertisements featuring the same graphic for *Bicycle Thief* for the World Playhouse (*Chicago Tribune*, 11 March 1950, 15); the Alex (*Chicago Tribune*, 28 April 1950, part 2 page 14); the Teatro (*Chicago Tribune*, 7 May 1950, part 7 page 3).

60. Ernest Callenbach, Letter to the Editor, *Saturday Review of Literature* (26 May 1951), 24.

61. Alpert, 27.

62. Ibid.

63. Richard Griffith, 'European Films and American Audiences', *Saturday Review of Literature* (13 January 1951), 85.

64. Ibid.

65. Pauline Kael, 'Fantasies of the Art House Audience', *Sight and Sound* 31 (Winter 1961/1962), 5.

66. John B. Sheerin, C.S.P., 'Art, Movies and Censors', *Catholic World* (March 1954), 405.

67. Ibid.

68. Quoted in 'Moral Breach', *Time* (31 October 1949), 76.

69. Gunnar D. Kumlien, 'The Artless Art of Italian Films', *Commonweal* (22 December 1953), 177.

70. 'Miracle on 58th Street', *Harper's* (April 1951), 107.

71. Draper, 69.

72. Quoted in 'Miracle on 58th Street', 107.

73. Robert Wohlforth, 'People and Pickets', *New Republic* (5 February 1951), 13.

74. Ibid.

75.   Ibid.

76.   'Miracle on 58th Street', 108.

77.   Gilbert Seldes, 'Pressures and Pictures', *Nation* (3 February 1951), 105.

78.   Ibid.

79.   January advertisements for *Ways of Love* playing at the Paris Theatre: one announcing the return of *The Miracle* to the program (*The New York Times*, 1 January 1951, 14) and the other the advertisement that ran in *The New York Times* throughout most of the month of January.

80.   Draper, 73; Wohlforth, 13.

81.   'Freedom of Film', *Newsweek* (9 June 1952), 91.

82.   Seldes, 'Pressures and Pictures', 132.

83.   'The Miracle', *Time* (19 February 1951), 7.

84.   'Catholic Censorship', *New Republic* (29 January 1951), 7.

85.   'Film Censor Law in Kansas Killed', *The New York Times* (25 October 1955).

86.   'High Court's Ruling on Sex in Movies', *US News and World Report* (13 July 1959), 50.

87.   Randall, 38.

88.   'How Do You See The Movies?', 50.

89.   'The Evil-Minded Censor', *Life* (13 March 1950), 40.

90.   'How Do You See The Movies?', 50.

Film History, Volume 8, pp. 159–175, 1996. Copyright © John Libbey & Company
ISSN: 0892-2160. Printed in Australia

Evelyn Nesbit and the film(ed) histories of the Thaw-White Scandal

Stephanie Savage

'No, thank you', I laughed mirthlessly, 'if I want to be a freak I'll go and see Barnum'.

Evelyn Nesbit in her autobiography, *Prodigal Days: the Untold Story*.

12 September 1955

The cover of *Life* magazine features Joan Collins in a DeLuxe colour pink dress, aloft on a red velvet swing. The caption accompanying the photo reads: 'Joan Collins plays Gibson girl Evelyn Nesbit in movie of Thaw-White murder.' The five page cover story, however, pays little attention to the film. The article, subtitled 'The Thaw-White murder is recalled in new film,' uses the release of Fox's *The Girl on the Red Velvet Swing* as an opportunity to retell the story of the real life murder and the sensational trial that followed.[1] It is primarily a photo-essay composed of newspaper clippings and images of Nesbit, Thaw and White; it includes only three stills from the film and no production information. For *Life* magazine, then, the production of the film is an opportunity to retell the 'lurid story [of a] lovely girl,' an impetus for historical recollection and public titillation.[2] The *way* in which these two elements – history and sexuality – are dealt with in the production and reception of *The Girl on the Red Velvet Swing* provides a way of investigating the relation between the female body and Hollywood film culture. This essay relies on files from the Motion Picture

Producers Association and the Fox legal department and numerous newspaper, trade journals, magazine articles and clippings in order to trace the development of 'The Evelyn Nesbit Story' and examine its implications.[3]

25 June 1906

Harry K. Thaw and his wife of eleven months, Evelyn Nesbit, are watching the final number of the stage show *Mam'zelle Champagne* on the rooftop restaurant of Madison Square Garden. Renowned architect Stanford White is also in attendance. During the final chorus of 'I Could Love a Million Girls', Thaw approaches White's table and shoots three times, one bullet hitting White in the head. White falls dead, Thaw exits the restaurant and is peacefully escorted to the Tenderloin police station by an officer who is nearby.

5 February 1907

Thaw's murder trial begins. It ends 13 April, with a

Stephanie Savage is a PhD candidate in film studies at the University of Iowa currently working on her dissertation in Los Angeles. She writes on the body in American film, as well as scandal, pornography, and true crime narratives. Correspondence c/o Stephanie Savage 643 1/4 N. Spaulding Avenue Los Angeles, CA 90036 USA. as888@lafn.org

hung jury. His second trial begins the following January and lasts less than a month, at which point he is found not guilty by reason of insanity.

Nesbit was well known before her marriage to Thaw as an artist's model, a member of the 'Floradora' sextet, a Gibson cover girl and one of the most beautiful young women in New York. White was the architect who was changing the face of America with his Italian Renaissance inspired buildings: Penn Station, the Washington Arch, Madison Square Garden and the Boston Public Library to name a few. Harry K. Thaw was heir to a 40 million dollar mining fortune and known about town as 'the Pittsburgh Idler' and 'Mad Harry' for his trust-funded antics. Although each member of this trio had had their share of limelight before the murder, both the extent and the nature of the press coverage of the crime and the trial that followed were without precedent. The spectacle of the trial coverage itself became the object of public fascination, defining the paradigm of modern scandal that has served from this first 'Trial of the Century' to our most recent one in Los Angeles in 1995.

Sometime in the fall of 1901

Stanford White and Evelyn Nesbit are in a room on the second floor of his E. 22nd Street studio. He is pushing her in a red velvet swing that hangs from the ceiling. She goes so high that her toes break the paper of a Japanese parasol that is suspended from the roof.

8 February 1907

New York Times headlines proclaim that Evelyn Nesbit begins to tell her story. Thaw's defence lawyer has somewhat facetiously proposed that Thaw suffers from 'Dementia Americana', which compels a man to right the wrongs done to his wife. To this end, White's character is attacked by Thaw's defence. Nesbit's, correspondingly, is speculated upon by the prosecution and the media. The outcome of the case hinges upon whether or not Thaw was 'driven' to kill White because he believed White had drugged and raped Evelyn in her youth, years before his marriage to her. Nesbit is alleged to have told Thaw of a night in 1901 when she

passed out after drinking champagne. She woke up in bed with White, naked, next to her and blood on the sheets.

Much later, in her 1934 autobiography, *Prodigal Days: The Untold Story*, Nesbit claims to have perjured herself in order to save Thaw's life, explaining that White, whom she loved, did have sex with her while she was passed out, but that White did not drug her. Of course, no one will ever know what really happened, but at trial, whether White actually *did* drug and rape Evelyn was in any case irrelevant – and in fact, inadmissible. What was at stake was what Thaw believed. And since the 'facts' of the murder – that Thaw shot White in the head – were uncontested, the centre of both courtroom and media debate around the trial was the alleged crime against Nesbit.

For the public, more at issue than the extent of White's licentiousness was Nesbit's willingness to submit to it: how was it that fifteen-year-old Evelyn came to be unchaperoned with White in his bachelor's studio, drinking champagne late at night in a mirrored boudoir? This question opened up the murder, made it more than a debate over one man's morals or another's sanity. It raised the curtain on an entire world of champagne and sex parties, thick steaks at Louis Sherry's and late nights at the Casino Theatre or the rooftop restaurant at Madison Square Garden. It was a story played out across the exotic backdrop of Stanford White's self-styled fantasy made real, a night-world richly appointed with imported antique furniture, bear skin rugs, expensive Japanese kimonos and a red velvet swing that hung from the roof of his Gramercy apartment. And what else could emerge from this explosive combination of elements but a story of sex, brutality, betrayal and death?

Nesbit's *Variety* obituary focuses not on her career, but on the murder and trial. It asserts that 'The incidents [of the events leading up to the murder] brought out by the newspapers' leering prose and the trial examination was to serve Sunday supplements for half a century of … scandal and [t]he original circulation impact of the Harry K. Thaw case … can hardly be credited.'[4] A scandal may be defined as 'a grave loss or injury to reputation resulting from … [a] breach or violation of morality, ethics, propriety or law' coupled with 'something untoward, shocking, or reprehensible to the public'.[5] The narratives that circulate *as* scandals constitute key sites for negotiating the relation of the public and private spheres, particularly with respect to issues of sexuality and gender.

Thaw's trial is considered the crystallisation of sob sister journalism, a mode initiated by the Hearst-hired women writers who penned melodramatic accounts of popular news stories.[6] These reports relied upon a rhetoric of disclosure that created a confessional mode, foregrounding the drama – and trauma – of telling and revelation itself. Even *New York Times* reports of the trial focus on the 'performance' of testimony and the reaction of the courtroom audience in a way that shifts the actual object of the story away from the reporting of information meant to reconstruct a past event (June 1906) to a sensational description of present-day spectacle (February 1907).

When Evelyn testifies, for example, the women in the courtroom 'bow their heads and hide their faces'; Thaw had seemed to have his

Fig. 1. Joan Collins as Evelyn Nesbit and Ray Milland as Stanford White in *The Girl on the Red Velvet Swing* (20th Century-Fox, 1955): historical recollection and public titillation.

> ... heart stealed against the pain of an old wound being reopened. But when his wife, with her soft, black hair dressed so that the coiffure rested between her shoulders, with a linen collar, simple black tie and blue jacket that a child might have worn accentuating the girlishness of her form, began to tell of her meeting with White, Thaw shuddered, drew his brown overcoat closer about his shoulders and began to sink in his chair.[7]

The stony-faced jury, however, was not so moved on that day: 'Not a man of the twelve showed a crinkling of the eyelids, a deepening of the lines from the nose to the chin, a bit of moisture at the lashes'.

A few weeks later, March 1907

Nickelodeons are being condemned as a menace to society, theatres are being closed down and exhibitors, arrested. In the middle of reform-era concern about the cinema and public morals are the films of the Thaw-White murder. When the censorship of films begins in earnest with the formation of the Chicago Municipal Censor Board in November 1907, it is in the midst of a proliferation of controversial film dramatisations of the case.

In *Behind the Mask of Innocence*, Kevin Brownlow describes how 'the Chicago *Tribune* launched an attack on nickelodeons, describing their influence as "wholly vicious",' citing Sig Lubin's ambitious, eleven minute long re-enactment of events from the lives of Nesbit, Thaw and White (including Evelyn's ride on the infamous swing, White's boudoir and Thaw's murdering), *The Unwritten Law: A Thrilling Drama Based on the Thaw-White Case* (1907).[8] Two days after the shooting, police shut down a showing of *The Thaw-White Tragedy* (American Mutoscope and Biograph, 1906, shot by Billy Bitzer and featuring screenwriter/actress/stuntwoman Gene Gauntier as Evelyn, and in New York, in May 1907, the Children's Society had a nickelodeon proprietor arrested for showing *The Great Thaw Trial* (1907) to an audience largely composed of school children.[9]

In addition to this connection with the onset of film censorship, Brownlow suggests that 'the [Thaw-White] story has so many ramifications into the world of cinema that an entire book could be devoted to them'.[10] One of White's studios became the headquarters of Reliance Film Co.; Peter Cooper-Hewitt (the inventor of mercury-vapour lights) worked in the studio above White's; White sent Nesbit to the DeMille school in Pompton, New York, run by the mother of William and C.B. (William was living at the school while Evelyn attended); Nesbit was courted by John Barrymore; prosecutor Jerome raised funds for the Technicolour Corporation; and in the 1920s, Thaw became the movie producer who brought Anita Page to Hollywood.[11]

Clearly, the Thaw-White case problematises many of the arguments made today regarding that symptom of our postmodern era, the so-called 'crisis in representation'. Many of the assertions about reality-based television programs, 'tabloid' TV and journalism, or feature and made-for-TV movies that blur distinctions between 'news' and fiction could be made equally well about the 1907–19 period which saw Nesbit and Thaw in newsreels, as characters in fact-based fiction films and similar themed fictional melodramas, newspaper headlines and book-length biographies and autobiographies *all at about the same time*. And then there are the film-acting careers of Harry K. Thaw and Evelyn Nesbit themselves. Thaw's moments on screen are rather brief, spurred as they are by his escape to

Canada from Matteawan, the asylum for the criminally insane where he was incarcerated after the second trial. *Harry K. Thaw's Fight for Freedom* (Hal Reid, 1913), later elaborated as *Escape from the Asylum*, consisted of 500 feet of the real Harry eating, talking and looking out his cell window while a fugitive in Sherbrooke, Quebec.[12] Evelyn's career, however, had more breadth and longevity.

25 October 1910

Evelyn gives birth to a son, whom she names Russell Thaw. Although Harry has been incarcerated since 1907, Evelyn gives Russell his name and sues Harry for support (unsuccessfully), claiming that her child was conceived one night at Matteawan when Harry bribed his guards in order for them to be alone together.

1914–1922

All told, Nesbit appears in ten films: *The Threads of Destiny* (directed by Joseph Smiley for Lubin, 1914); *Redemption* (1917) and *Her Mistake* (1918), both by Julius Steger for Triumph; *The Woman Who Gave* (1918), *I Want to Forget* (1918), *Thou Shalt Not* (1919), *A Fallen Idol* (1919), *My Little Sister* (1919) and *Woman, Woman* (1919), all for Fox; and *The Hidden Woman* (Allan Dwan for Joseph Schenck, 1922). In the first several of these films, Evelyn appears with her son, Russell, billed by both Steger and Fox as 'Evelyn Nesbit and Her Son Russell Thaw'.

Nesbit's films are all hearty melodramas, featuring plots such as white slavery (*My Little Sister*) or the Russian massacre of the Jews (*Threads of Destiny*). Some feature characters very much like her own public persona: women who are fallen, but with a good heart, plenty of regrets and a willingness to reform. The heroine of *Redemption* is an actress who gains notoriety in her youth, comes clean with her marriage and is then haunted by her past – one of her ghosts being a former lover who is a wealthy architect. *The Woman Who Gave* is promoted as 'The gripping story of an artist's model who came to fear her own beauty as she feared her titled husband', and the artist she models for is suggested to be Charles Dana Gibson.[13] But more

Fig. 2. Evelyn Nesbit 'and her son Russell Thaw', both billed above the title in a trade ad for *Redemption* (Triumph, 1917). *Exhibitors Trade Review*, 26 May 1917.

than anything else, all of Nesbit's films sell Evelyn Nesbit, the woman herself.

Like the stage variety acts she performed both before and after her film period, her films are exploited with respect to her real-life experiences. Their promotion suggests that the audience will find pleasure in simply observing her past-laden form on the stage or screen. Discourses of truth, disclosure, illicit sexuality and 'real life' figure in the promotion of all her films. *My Little Sister*, for example, deals with a 'vital topic of today', bearing 'the horrible mystery that lies behind the disappearance of those thousand of girls who are sacrificed every year on the altar of lust and brutality'.[14] *Redemption* is tagged as 'A photo-drama of life depicted with relentless truth'.[15]

Although her acting is often praised in reviews, the main draw, according to most trade journals, is 'the value of the name'.[16] In *The Woman Who Gave* promises, 'Curiosity seekers will be satisfied with the mere screen showing of an unfortunate woman'.[17] Exhibitors of *I Want to Forget* should '[p]lay up the star ... [a]nnounce her as Evelyn Nesbit, "the woman who wanted to forget"'.[18] *Woman, Woman* attempts to 'solve the eternal riddle – woman', and features Nesbit's character sculpting, a talent she developed after divorcing Thaw.[19] But even in 1918, only twelve years after the actual murder, another discourse is already being introduced into the reception of Evelyn Nesbit: forgetting.

The Nesbit-Thaw-White affair is in the headlines more or less continuously for 15 years as one scandal gives way to the next. There are a series of post-trial legal battles, the birth of Nesbit's son, Thaw's escape from Matteawan to Quebec and return to New York, his release and divorce from Evelyn, his re-institutionalisation after being found guilty of whipping a young boy, his re-release from the asylum and another series of lawsuits. Yet the *Variety* review of *The Woman Who Gave* suggests that it will find its best returns outside of cosmopolitan New York City, 'where the name Evelyn Nesbit Thaw has not been forgotten'.[20] At some point along the way, the Thaw-White scandal begins to pass from current event to historical memory and its designation as the 'trial of the century' changes its meaning as the century wears on.

4 August 1952

In a memorandum to Charles Brackett, Darryl F. Zanuck's comments at an earlier meeting are restated. Spoke Zanuck:

> The name Evelyn Nesbit means nothing to modern audiences, although to the older people it still has a certain flavour of scandal. This might turn out to be a very good story, but it does not have any pre-sold value.[21]

According to Zanuck, the Evelyn Nesbit story has not been preserved culturally. Rather, it is only

maintained in the memories of individual historical bodies.

30 July 1954

Evelyn Nesbit is showing some of her sculptures at a Long Beach ceramics show. The *Los Angeles Times* runs a human interest story on Nesbit and her art work. Author Bill Dredge begins, 'The cloak of obscurity fell aside briefly yesterday from a woman whose name in the year 1906 was known throughout the country'. While to most visitors to the show, the name that hangs above her booth means nothing:

> ... white-haired grandmothers, who devoured every glowing word of her Thaw trial testimony back in 1906, stop to visit in a day-long stream. They want to talk – to touch – the woman whose name meant glamour in their youth. They come away savouring memories.

The concept that, for those over sixty, Nesbit is a site for personal reflection and reverie is also reflected in many reviews of *The Girl on the Red Velvet Swing*.

Motion Picture Daily singles out 'women and those film goers who were around at the time of the celebrated case' as the segment of the audience most likely to respond favourably to the film.[22] *The New Yorker* is less enthusiastic, suggesting '[u]ndoubtedly, this provided superior newspaper fare back in 1906 – I know several members of the older generation who are only too anxious to relive it all at cocktail parties or the Yale Club bar'.[23] That the Thaw-White case is nothing if not an excuse to gather together and talk with others who recall it is also evidenced in *The Hollywood Reporter*, where a writer refers to his own memory of the case, now 49 years past:

> One of the happiest memories of childhood is my recollection of being smacked on the behind and told to run and play somewhere as my mother and the other virtuous matrons of the neighbourhood discussed the Harry K. Thaw case. It was the type of thing that little boys were supposed to learn of behind the barn and I was overjoyed when we finally got rich

enough to own a horse and build a stable behind which I was filled in on the more exciting elements of the moral storm that involved Thaw, Evelyn Nesbit and Stanford White.[24]

Embedded in this exposition, as a part of the preservation of the Thaw-White scandal, are the reviewer's own experiences of the very elements central to the case itself – homosocial interaction, sexual awakening, even violence and new-found wealth.

Every article that features Nesbit comments in some fashion on the distance between 'Evelyn Nesbit – Then and Now'. Many feature a postcard image circa 1906 next to a recent snapshot.[25] The difference between 'then' and 'now', however, is not characterised as natural and an inevitable result of the passage of time, but as dissonant – even unlikely – and always, the result of an unfortunate 'decline'. Indeed, the harsh realities of Nesbit's life in the 1950s – that she is poor, that she is alone and that her health is infirm – are displaced on to her body so that the aging process itself is infused with pathos. The 1954 article about her ceramics show describes the 71 year old woman: 'She is five feet four and a half inches tall, but she's no longer slim. Her weight is 135 pounds'.[26] When meeting Nesbit for the first time, Adela Rogers St. Johns can hardly contain her disbelief that Nesbit 'was wearing, of all things, dark brown linen slacks that did not conceal her "middle-aged spread"'.[27]

Her contemporary tragedy, it would seem, is to have outlived not only all the other players in the original scandal, but also her youth and beauty. She is represented as a woman who, simply by surviving, has found herself out of step with the march of time. Adela Rogers St. Johns sees the Nesbit she interviews as emerging out of nowhere, like a ghost from another time. 'When I told some of my acquaintances that I was going to sit down and talk with Evelyn Nesbit Thaw, they looked at me as though I had announced that I was on my way to call on Madame Pompadour or Mary Queen of Scots'. Although presented as if from the past, however, her form is not ethereal or ghostly, but only too corporeal, with wide hips, coarse grey hair and feet that are heavy in clunky shoes.

But if the press is preoccupied with Nesbit's perceived physical 'decline', it is her very real econ-

omic one that makes her an appealing target for Fox.

29 July 1952

Brackett writes to Zanuck that he believes 'Evelyn Nesbit is still alive, but she's broke and only too anxious to sell her story'. Once Nesbit has been contacted, her hard-luck and loose-lips are again referred to: in an inter office correspondence addressed to Zanuck, David Brown writes that '[s]he works in a ceramics factory in a ramshackle district of downtown Los Angeles. She talks quite freely of her champagne and mirrored-room days in New York'.[30] The project seems to be viable.

Only weeks before the note from Brown, Brackett is pleased when he comes across the Charles Samuels Pocket Book based on Thaw's first trial transcripts, *The Girl on the Red Velvet Swing*. Brackett writes that '[e]ven a cursory glance will indicate what rich material it is for a great, big, sex-laden, dynamite-loaded production'.[31] Although recognising that this pulp publication might not strike Zanuck as sufficiently 'classy', Brackett sees possibilities for big box-office: 'I do not think we should let the fact that it is a 25 cent yellow-back deter us. Those cheap books are the only real best sellers these days'.[32]

By 1953, the pulp publishing industry was well into its post-war boom. The end of wartime paper rationing in 1950 and a growing awareness of 'adult' audiences created a swell of recreational reading material that was not marketed, like film and television, to families. Serials and paperback books took on the look of true crime and romance magazines, with racy illustrated covers and captions. For example, even the cover of Signet's pocket-size *The Catcher in the Rye*, published in 1953, warns that '[t]his unusual book may shock you' and features an illustration of young Holden Caulfield on a tough-looking dark street plastered with posters for a girlie-show and populated by a blonde and a man in a dark overcoat. As represented in *The Seven Year Itch* (1955), not only fiction, but books of a social scientific nature – especially sociology and psychoanalysis – get repackaged to maximise their potentially 'cheap' appeal. This is the case with a series of books by

Fig. 3. Off screen, Nesbit was an amateur sculptor and ceramicist. This still from *Woman, Woman* (Fox, 1919) shows her 'making her artistic skill useful', according to the original caption.

Mentor in the early 1950s, which manage to put naked people on the cover of books on economics, mythology and genetics. Transcripts of famous trials – especially those with a racy content, like Leopold and Loeb or Thaw – are also marketed to produce titillation.

Confidential, the scandal magazine with the largest circulation, promises to 'tell the facts and name the names'. Stories containing sex and violence were told in a confessional I-was-there/it-happened-to-me mode and accompanied by suggestive photographs. Publisher Robert Harrison relied on a network of small-time Hollywood players, prostitutes and private detectives to supply stories disclosing the infidelities, drunken antics and interracial romances of stars, socialites and politicians.

'Men's' magazines also flourished, from pulp publications like *Photo*, which mixed stories of war, crime and modern medical breakthroughs with pin-ups and photo-essays of curiosities (like sumo wrestling, the birth of a lamb and a man crushed by a giant anaconda, all featured in the April 1953 volume) to glossier, more upscale varieties like *Playboy*. In December 1953, the first issue of *Playboy*, with its Marilyn Monroe centrefold, hits the stands. It is into this context that Evelyn Nesbit and her story resurface into public view.

18 June 1953

Fox story department employee Jim Fischer takes Evelyn Nesbit out to lunch. He pitches their story idea and suggests a fee. Evelyn leaves happy, saying she will think about it.[33]

The deal goes forward in essentially the form it was offered to Nesbit, with $5,000 for an option and an additional $40,000 if Fox decides to produce the picture ($5,000 for extending the option and three equal payments over a three-year period for the remaining $35,000). They aren't going to use the Samuels book without a satisfactory 'release and covenant' from Nesbit, so the entire project rests on securing her consent to grant Fox the 'exclusive right ... to the story, events and incidents of [her] life and career'.[34] Originally, Russell Thaw, who was acting with power of attorney on his mother's behalf, is expected to sign a waiver as well, but when he withholds his signature Fox decides they don't need him after all and note that Russell won't feature as a character in the film. They also decide they don't need the rights to Evelyn's autobiography, *Prodigal Days: The Untold Story*, which she mistakenly believes she owns outright. In the end, Fox goes forward with Nesbit and the Samuels book, bought for $2,500, which they are primarily interested in for the title.

From the beginning, there is no mistaking that it is Nesbit's story which is to be told. Until the script is written for *The Girl on the Red Velvet Swing*, all correspondence features her name as their subject and nowhere is there evidence of discussion indicating that either Thaw or White might provide a central focus. With 'Mad Harry Thaw' being found not guilty by reason of insanity and no question as to who murdered Stanford White or why, it is also not a story well-suited to a courtroom drama or detective film featuring a gallant private eye, prosecutor, or defence attorney. But in any event, in the Thaw-White scandal Zanuck is looking for 'a sort of New York turn of the century *Moulin Rouge*', not a tense thriller or social issue film.[35] (Zanuck does, however, send the script to Elia Kazan. He's 'not interested').[36] Although arguably, given the choices, Nesbit remains the most appealing and sympathetic of the three main characters – and the most exploitable – bringing her story to the screen presents some fundamental problems related to Hol-

lywood narrative convention and the Production Code. Writes Zanuck, 'what is more important – who do we root for'?[37]

In earlier, written full-length narratives of the case, this question has been answered by providing either the point of view of the author, or leaving events and interpretations suggestively ambiguous. *Prodigal Days* has us 'rooting' for Evelyn. *The Traitor*, Harry K. Thaw's rambling 1926 opus, is certainly his own version of events despite its insistently objective subtitle, 'Being the Untampered With, Unrevised Account of the Trial and All that Led to It'. Frederick L. Collins' 1932 book *Glamorous Sinners* and *The Girl on the Red Velvet Swing* take a wider view, less concerned about who is to blame for what and more focused on presenting the colourful world of the case. Source material is also an issue. For narratives that do not rely on the personal experience of the author, trial transcripts do not provide a definitive version of the Thaw-Nesbit-White triangle. As Fox reader Desmond Knott observes, Evelyn's 'testimony was based on at least one big lie which even the prosecutor, Jerome, was reluctant to expose'.[38]

Nesbit has sex underage, out of wedlock, with a married man; then she perjures herself at her husband's murder trial. Even if a moralistic ending portrays her learning from her mistakes and being punished for her sins, in this case, the events of the story simply cannot be reconstructed without either presenting White as a rapist or Evelyn as a perjurer. If Stanford White did not drug Evelyn and she never told Harry Thaw that he did, then she has perjured herself and a guilty man has got away with murder. If he did, then the movie is the story of a young woman raped by her mentor, beaten and betrayed by her husband and left penniless.[39] It is at its base a complicated and depressing story that for all its glamour and 'meaty' sexual intrigue, hardly inspires an emotion more lofty than cynicism.

It is the opinion of a Fox reader that the script attempts to deal with this difficulty by presenting Evelyn as 'such a nice little girl who got the worst of a bad bargain that we can only admire and feel sorry for her in the end ... a much nicer and more genuine girl than she really was, even in her own book'.[40] Presenting her in a 'much better light' means correcting the perceived faults of the Evelyn in *Prodigal Days*, 'too self-indulgent to remain the "nice" girl she always claimed she was and not smart enough to capitalise on it in a big way'.[41] Surprisingly, however, the new and improved 'nice' Evelyn is 'an ardent young girl who becomes infatuated with a charming older man, White and practically throws herself at him'.[42] Here, improving Evelyn's moral character takes the form of making her sexually aggressive. Ascribing desire and agency to her character eradicates the possibility of rape and sets up a tragedy based on impossible love lost, an unhappy marriage of convenience and the legacy of a life alone. Perhaps incidental to the concerns of the Fox production team but not to the argument presented here, it also takes away any possibility of social critique, of investigating why a resourceful young girl was willing to resign herself to a life of ersatz prostitution. But the main issue for Fox is that this revisionist story is going to run into some trouble with the Motion Picture Producers Association.

According to an MPPA checklist sent 10 August 1955, the final film's ending is 'unhappy' (as opposed to 'happy' or 'moral'). The film contains violence and adultery but, in the opinion of its raters, no illicit sex, seduction or rape is indicated. 1954–55 is a year when films such as *The Moon is Blue* (1953), *Blackboard Jungle* (1955) and *The Man with the Golden Arm* (1955) are running into real trouble with state censors and *The Man with the Golden Arm* is actually denied an MPPA seal.[43] Foreign films from France and Sweden excite public censorship battles. Home grown exploitation films like *Mom and Dad* (1947, produced by Kroger Babb and road-shown for over twenty years), and *Teaserama* (1955), with Tempest Storm and Betty Page, are also causing controversies. Fox certainly had the option of pushing a more explicit version of *The Girl on the Red Velvet Swing*, but this never appears to have been an intention. The film passes through the MPPA relatively effortlessly and runs into little objection by censors or reviewers. There are, however, a few hurdles that need to be cleared.

Early versions of the script use the swing to stand metonymically for the sexual encounter between White and Nesbit, charging the space with implications of sexuality and using verbal innuendo to make it clear what climbing into the swing will ultimately involve. As in many melodramas, here the *mise-en-scène* carries the burden of signifying a narrative action that cannot be shown directly. This coding of prohibited interaction, however, does nothing to obscure the essentially immoral nature of the characters. The MPPA's main objections to the original script submitted are that 'there seems to be an over-all condoning of the adulterous affair between White and Evelyn and there is no moral recognition of Evelyn's perjury'.[44]

In addition to these general objections, Geoffrey Shurlock's office finds Fox's wily use of imagery none too subtle. 'Of course, the phallic symbolism … of Evelyn's foot piercing the paper of the parasol, so clearly refers to the breaking of the hymen that it is totally unacceptable' and '[t]he central gimmick of the story, "the room with the red velvet swing", is so symbolic of erotopathy as to be offensive to our family audiences'.[45] Fox's Frank McCarthy suggests that the swing problem may be resolved by altering the set design so that it does not 'contain prominently featured divans or that sort of thing', which might 'delineate this room and its appurtenances as a setting for erotic orgies'.[46] One strategy in particular stands out:

> It was agreed that the set would be so constructed as to remove any erotic symbolism surrounding these appurtenances. Along the line someone suggested that the 'room with the red velvet swing' would be decorated to represent a 'picnic' theme. In this way the audience would get the impression that the room was designed for a lover of the great outdoors, who, by force of circumstances, lived in a penthouse.[47]

Clearly, Fox needs the swing in order to build up promotion around the title (and, even, for the title to make sense); a reader of the MPPA file senses their resolve to keep it at any cost. But in solving their immediate censorship problem, they create another one. In de-eroticising the swing, the film loses its sexual centre. Its strongest symbol neutralised, some other element will have to carry 'sex'.

The fall of 1955

Marilyn Monroe was constantly in the headlines from 1953 to 1955. And it is her sexuality that is, again and again, in one way or another, their topic. As mentioned previously, her nude calendar shot appears in *Playboy* in 1953. The dress she wears to receive a 1953 *Photoplay* award is publicly criticised by Joan Crawford: 'Sex plays a tremendously important part in every person's life. People are interested in it, intrigued with it. But they don't want to see it flaunted in their faces'.[48] She is greeted at the premiere of *How to Marry a Millionaire* (1953) by thousands of fans shouting her name. There are her contract disputes with Fox, her marriage to Joe DiMaggio and their subsequent separation and divorce, throughout which time there are rumours of pregnancy.

In January 1954, Marilyn Monroe is put on suspension by Twentieth Century-Fox for failing to show up on the set for the first day of shooting on *Pink Tights* (never produced), a musical to be directed by Henry Koster, starring Monroe and Frank Sinatra. Money would seem to be a factor in the dispute, (Monroe was Fox's top grossing

Fig. 4. Joan Collins tries out Fox's 1955 version of the notorious swing. A bit of ivy suggests the picnic theme, 'designed for a lover of the great outdoors'.

star and still paid a weekly salary of $1250 per week), but script approval is the main issue, part of her overall desire to become a serious actress that results in the formation of Marilyn Monroe Productions with Milton Greene in the summer of 1955. She 'is "tired of sex roles" and definitely wants no more of them'.[49] In January 1955, Monroe is again suspended, this time for refusing *How to be Very, Very Popular* (1955, with Sheree North).

The Girl on the Red Velvet Swing plays a role in Monroe's war with Fox 'over frothy roles'.[50] Days after Monroe's first suspension is announced, an item appears in the LA *Daily News* announcing that

The Girl on the Red Velvet Swing has received 'clearance' from 'Evelyn Nesbitt (sic) and all the still-living dramatis personae involved' and that 'it looks certain for Marilyn Monroe to play Evelyn'.[51] It is difficult to imagine that at this point anything is certain regarding Monroe's future at Fox. Regardless, days before her second suspension Monroe is again linked with *The Girl on the Red Velvet Swing*. An item in the *Mirror News* reports, '[s]tudio officials said they are also planning her next film, *Girl on the Red Velvet Swing*, the life story of Evelyn Nesbit Thaw'.[52]

The film, in fact, was conceived with Monroe

in mind. This hardly makes sense in terms of casting. Monroe's plump and platinum image could not be more different from Nesbit's dark haired, black eyed waif and even at a youthful 27, Monroe would be considerably older than Evelyn, who was still only 20 at the time of the trial (Joan Collins, who ends up in the role, is 22). But the similarity that Fox sees between Marilyn and Evelyn is not physical.

One of the earliest correspondences in the Fox legal files is a note from Charles Brackett to Darryl Zanuck, dated 29 July 1952: '[writer] Walter Reisch has suggested that an enormously effective role for Marilyn Monroe would be that of the girl who symbolised illicit sex for the nineteen hundreds: EVELYN NESBIT'. Brackett glosses the story and then comments, 'every element of the case has the kind of headline quality with which Monroe should be surrounded'. Indeed, one can almost imagine that Fox intends to promote this Monroe film much in the same way they promoted Nesbit's films almost forty years earlier. For Fox, Monroe is the 1950s version of Nesbit, each in their era 'the girl who symbolised illicit sex'.

Of course, a symbol for illicit sex is precisely what this movie needs. Fox knows from the beginning that there can be no actual illicit sex in the film and as we have seen, the MPPA will significantly curtail the use of other symbols within the setting and dialogue of the film. But the right female body inserted into the film – and exploited outside of it – could achieve this result. It is without irony, then, that it is Monroe's own struggle for autonomy from the studio and control over her image that prevents her from being this body.

In the end, Fox casts Joan Collins in the role, but her inexperienced and relatively unknown body can hardly symbolise sex in the way that Monroe's might. In order to promote the film, Fox turns to their elderly former starlet, 'who was once as widely photographed as Marilyn Monroe' and whose Gibson portrait 'for all its modesty and simplicity became as famous a "pin-up" as a full-colour calendar of another beauty fifty years later'.[53] *Hollywood Citizen* columnist Hal Boyle comments that Nesbit looks like a 'greying retired schoolmarm', but also notes that no schoolmarm 'quite has her memories'.[54] And so it will be Nesbit's body, with beauty faded and health ailing, that provides an authentic link to a well-publicised, scandalous, sex-

uality. Her body, as the living repository of these memories, is the ligature that binds the promotion of the film and acts to insert, through extra-filmic discourse, sexual content into the film's narrative. Although Darryl Zanuck and a score of reviewers are quite sure few people have any knowledge of the original scandal, revisiting the past becomes the only way to tell the story.

9 June 1955

Evelyn Nesbit is hospitalised after a stroke. The *Los Angeles Times* reports that 'the attack was apparently brought on by overexertion and excitement during the filming of a movie based on her life'.[55]

October 1955

Twentieth Century-Fox's CinemaScope version of the Nesbit-Thaw-White story begins with the following written preface:

> In 1906, the Thaw-White murder case rocked America. Because it involved a man of great consequence, another of great wealth and a girl of extraordinary beauty, it remains unique in the annals of crime ...

> What follows is taken from the actual reports of the trial and from personal interviews with Evelyn Nesbit.[56]

Nesbit's name appears everywhere the film does; and of course, she *is* the 'girl in the red velvet swing'. The national ad campaign for the film proclaims 'The rise ... the fall of Evelyn Nesbit Thaw!' and shows Collins in the red velvet swing, toes pointed upward.[57] The red velvet swing is the central iconographic image of Evelyn's past with Stanford White at the first trial. And in all subsequent representations, it comes to be associated with that which is unknowable and un-representable: the first sexual encounter between White and Nesbit. In effect, the swing foregrounds the history to which Evelyn's body was in fact subject.

As discussed earlier, the 1955 film uses the swing to stand in for Evelyn and Stanford's first encounter. Because of the requirements of the MPPA, the scenes that deal with this are handled rather awkwardly and would be downright confus-

Fig. 5. The celebrity of sexual scandal: Joan Collins wards off autograph seekers in *The Girl on the Red Velvet Swing.*

ing without any previous knowledge of the case. This confusion might be cleared up later in the film. The swing features prominently when Evelyn experiences a delirious fit after being left at a girls' school by White. A shot of the empty swing initiates an elaborate series of dissolves between shots superimposing images such as 'Evelyn's tortured face tossing' with the 'swing swaying over it', 'Evelyn's body lying prone on the beach, waves washing over it' and White with two dancing girls.[58] The final scene of the film shows Evelyn as a showgirl – even a stageshow – now seemingly older and alone, in a red velvet swing in front of an audience of leering men. The film thus aligns the swing with both Evelyn's subjectivity and her objectification – her personal memory and our cultural one.

In some instances the disparity between earlier versions of the story and the 1955 film are attributed to Fox's use of Nesbit. The reviews in both *Variety* and the *New York Times* note the fact that Nesbit is still alive and state that this has had an obvious

influence on the film. The *Times* asserts that the story has been 'penned with an evident eye on the law of libel (since Miss Nesbit is still alive)'.[59] Both reviews also inscribe a sense of oral history and even gossip into the film's narrative, suggesting that the film is not 'true' by using phrases like 'the way we have always heard it', 'according to this story' and 'the side of the story never told'.[60] In these examples, the existence of other stories is pointed out in order to criticise the film for 'siding' with Evelyn and not being 'objective', rather than drawing attention to the various institutions of Hollywood filmmaking that shaped it. This is not the case everywhere, however.

The idea of getting to the 'true' story is also the main focus of an article in *Inside Story*, the 1950s scandal magazine with the next highest circulation after *Confidential*.[61] The banner, 'Yesterday's Inside Story' runs across the top of the first page of the article, linking the project of the magazine (giving the 'scoop' on current scandals) an historical bent.[62] Its claim that '[the] movie version is strictly a whitewash job on a sex-and-murder triangle that decent people wouldn't discuss – even in whispers'! further inscribes the Nesbit-Thaw-White story into the discourse of gossip and oral history.[63] In this example, it is a story that can *only* be transmitted truthfully outside of 'decent' channels. Thus it is with a wilful and self-realised hypocrisy that the article goes on to spend over seven pages telling the 'true' story, complete with pictures of the real trio, Nesbit's popular 'Polar Bear Rug' photo and a postcard image of the rooftop garden where White was shot.

The story also shows Nesbit together with Collins on the set of the film with the caption: 'Evelyn Nesbit, now 71, discusses script with lovely Joan Collins, who portrays ex-Floradora Girl in watered-down film of famous scandal'.[64] We can see how in this example, Nesbit is inscribed as 'real' precisely because the document which the two hold together, as the entire story seeks to prove, is *not*. In Nesbit we are given the bearer of truth, a body that embodies a historicised, lived, experience; in Collins, a body that embodies the fiction of the script, Hollywood 'whitewash'. A comparison with a very similar photograph that appears in a November 1955 *Photoplay* feature story on Joan Collins reveals the vested interests of the two magazines.

This article describes Nesbit as 'that beautiful and tragic central figure in one of the nation's most sensational murder trials'.[65] On its first page, it displays a photo of Collins with Nesbit on the set of the film. As in the *Inside Story* photograph, we see past and present conjoined, a living legend copresent with a representation of herself. But rather than holding a script – a narrative that in *Inside Story* is constructed as false – they hold Gibson's famed drawing of Nesbit, 'The Eternal Question'. The drawing is necessarily tied to the time of its historical production because both its style and its subject are archaic (a pen-and-ink drawing, Evelyn's 'old fashioned' hair style) as well as iconic (it is recognisable as a Gibson, even as 'the Eternal Question'). But the (re)presentation of the drawing indicates that it can exist outside of its time – indeed, without time – in a way that Nesbit cannot. The young Nesbit 'em'bodied by Collins meets the 'authentic' one, but the 'trueness' of the real Nesbit is ultimately contested by the Gibson drawing. For the drawing serves only to authenticate *Collins* – as likeness of

young Nesbit. Thus the filmic representation is validated as accurate, with the real Evelyn Nesbit acting not as the guarantor of truth, but of *history*. Here, her body bears witness to the time that has elapsed between past and present and creates a 'then' and 'now'.

A striking photograph of Nesbit in the *Life* article mentioned at the beginning of this essay also plays out the theme of past and present via Evelyn's body. While the series of small photographs arranged chronologically that compose the bulk of the piece necessarily chronicle Nesbit's aging (from a circa 1905 photo with her Gibson hairstyle to middle-age in 1931, having 'earned a precarious living entertaining at resorts'), one photo in particular presents this sense of time passing with particular pathos.[66] In the foreground of the image, 'Evelyn Nesbit today, a 71-year-old grandmother' holds up a glass covered 'The Eternal Question', while in the background her now aged profile is reflected beneath her youthful one.[67] As in the picture with Collins, we can see how Nesbit's body – her very *un*-recognisability – is the concrete link from present to past. The difference between the old Nesbit and the young one is what allows us to speak of a history that is precisely not the present, but one that may still be with us as both living and popular memory. Thus we can see how in each of these cases, although the aims and means are different, history is inscribed into the text through Evelyn Nesbit's body, as though the wrinkles around her eyes can somehow be read like the rings that form a tree trunk.[68]

One night in September 1901

Evelyn Nesbit enters Stanford White's mirror room and finishes a glass of champagne. Everything goes black. When she wakes up she is naked, with White next to her in bed. When Evelyn begins to cry, White holds her and says, 'It's all over now'. He holds her and tells her everything is okay.

As a 17-year-old, Evelyn wrote in her diary that she had stopped reading a novel because she did not like the heroine, whom she described as 'a nice, natural character ... as good as an angel ... too good for this world'.[69] Nesbit went to her grave proclaiming that Stanford White was the only man she ever loved.

The final image of *The Girl on the Red Velvet*

Fig. 6. In 1955 Nesbit posed nostalgically with Charles Dana Gibson's portrait of her as 'The Eternal Question'.

Swing, Evelyn leered at in a prop swing, may be seen as a *mise-en-abyme*. This swing stand in for all the others, all the moments throughout her life that Evelyn Nesbit's body has been trotted out and displayed as a spectacle. In her youth, Nesbit's own memory of the red velvet swing and the events that transpired during her first night with White were denied to her, an amnesia brought on by White's drugging, or her own imbibition of too much cham- pagne, or perhaps, a society that does not allow women to speak of their desire. A proliferation of narratives and images were generated to fill up this absence of personal memory and a collective mem- ory was born. It is this memory – not her own – that Nesbit is used to bear witness to in *The Girl on the Red Velvet Swing* and its reception. Yet it is the concept of Evelyn Nesbit's lived experience and 'em'bodiment of the past that imbues the film with its sexual content and sense of history. Despite Nesbit's active participation in the production and promotion of *The Girl on the Red Velvet Swing*, in 1955 her 71-year-old body represses an eternal question of another kind: how is it possible that, in Hollywood cinema, a woman's body can represent sexuality and history, while a woman's sexual history cannot be represented?✣

An earlier version of this paper was presented in 1994 at the Film Studies Association of Canada conference under the title, 'How to Bury Some Millionaires: Evelyn Nesbit and the Thaw-White Murder Case'.

Notes

1. *Life* 12 September 1955, 70+.

2. *Life*, 70.

3. Thanks to the Margaret Herrick Library at the Academy of Motion Pictures Arts and Sciences, arts special collections at UCLA and special collections at the University of Iowa.

4. *Variety*, 25 January 1967.

5. George Kohn, *Encyclopedia of American Scandal* (New York: Facts on File, 1989) ix.

6. see Phyllis Leslie Abramson, *Sob Sister Journalism* (New York: Greenwood, 1990).

7. *New York Times* 8 February 1907.

8. Kevin Brownlow, *Behind the Mask of Innocence* (New York: Knopf, 1990) 4.

9. Brownlow, 4. Yet another Thaw-White film is *In the Tombs* (American Mutoscope and Biograph, 1906), a one shot film featuring Evelyn and Mother Thaw visiting Harry Thaw while he was incarcerated.

10. Brownlow, 143.

11. Brownlow, 143–4.

12. Brownlow, 146. Brownlow recounts how when a film featuring a fake Harry, *Harry Thaw's Escape from Matteawan*, appears on the market, Harry sends Reid a telegram giving him permission to sue all imitators. Reid declines the legal advice, but uses Thaw's telegram in the advertising of his film.

13. *Moving Picture World* 5 October 1918, np.

14. *Motion Picture News* 28 June 1919, 233.

15. *Exhibitors Trade Review* 26 May 1917, 1750.

16. *Variety* 4 May 1917, 28.

17. *Moving Picture World* 2 November 1918, 2796.

18. *Moving Picture World* 14 December 1918, 1252–3.

19. *Moving Picture World* 8 February 1919, 809.

20. *Variety* 1 November 1918, 38.

21. J. Johnson, correspondence with Charles Brackett, 4 August 1952.

22. *Motion Picture Daily* nd, np.

23. *The New Yorker* 29 October 1955, np.

24. *The Hollywood Reporter* 12 October 1955, np.

25. *Los Angeles Times* 19 June 1955.

26. *Los Angeles Times* 30 July 1954.

27. Adela Rogers St. Johns, *American Weekly* 14 August 1955, 6.

28. St. Johns, 6.

29. Charles Brackett, correspondence with Darryl Zanuck, 29 July 1952.

30. David Brown, correspondence with Darryl Zanuck, 19 June 1953.

31. Charles Brackett, correspondence with Darryl Zanuck, 27 May 1953.

32. Brackett, 27 May 1953.

33. David Brown, 19 June 1953.

34. Release and Covenant, 15 September 1953.

35. Darryl Zanuck, correspondence with Charles Brackett, 5 June 1953.

36. Frank Ferguson, correspondence with Lew Schreiber, 9 March 1955.

37. Darryl Zanuck, 5 June 1953.

38. Desmond Knott, *Comparison*, 4 April 1955.

39. It does not seem to occur to anyone, including Nesbit herself, that even if White didn't deliberately drug her champagne, if she was unconscious, the sex they had on that night was not consensual. Knott says he thinks Nesbit totally made up the champagne story in *Prodigal Days* so as not to have to take any responsibility for her actions and thus appear in a more favourable light.

40. Desmond Knott.

41. Desmond Knott.

42. Desmond Knott.

43. *Film Daily Yearbook of Motion Pictures* 1956, np.

44. Geoffrey Shurlock, correspondence with Frank McCarthy, 17 March 1955.

45. Geoffrey Shurlock, correspondence with Frank McCarthy, 17 March 1955.

46. Frank McCarthy, correspondence with Geoffrey Shurlock, 1 April 1955. 'Memo for the files' 29 March 1955.

47. 'Memo for the files'.

48. As reported by columnist Bob Thomas, taken from Norman Mailer, *Marilyn* (New York: Warner, 1973) 144.

49. *New York Daily News* 8 January 1955.

50. *Mirror News* 10 January 1955.

51. *Los Angeles Daily News* 9 January 1954.

52. *Mirror News* 10 January 1955.

53. *Los Angeles Times* 28 June 1955. Harry Brand, Vital Statistics, nd.

54. *Hollywood Citizen* 19 September 1955.

55. *Los Angeles Times* 22 July 1955.

56. Continuity Script, reel 1, page 1. Because the film is not available on video or available for viewing in the Los Angeles area, all references to the content of the finished film are taken from the continuity script found in the Fox collection at the University of Iowa.

57. See *Variety* 14 September 1955, *New York Times* 18 October 1955, *Los Angeles Times* 12 Octover 1955.

58. Continuity Script, reel 7, page 9.

59. *New York Times* 20 October 1955.

60. *New York Times* 20 October 1955 *Variety*, 12 October 1955.

61. Alan Betrock, *Unseen America: The Greatest Cult Exploitation Magazines 1950–1966* (Brooklyn: Shake Books, 1990) 52.

62. Barnaby Murray The Shocking Truth about that Girl on the Red Velvet Swing, *Inside Story* March 1956, 40.

63. *Inside Story* 40.

64. *Inside Story* 43.

65. Hyatt Downing, Cool, Crazy and Jolly Exciting, *Photoplay* November 1955, 102.

66. *Life*, 76.

67. *Life*, 71.

68. Arguably, this entire nexus of issues related to history and authenticity are tied to a sense of historical consciousness that is *nationally* specific. For example, a British fan magazine, *Picturegoer*, presents a serialised account of *The Girl on the Red Velvet Swing* (7 January 1956). The story re-told, however, is the story of the *film* and although it is clear that it is 'based on' a true story, it is not accompanied by a single photo of the real players. There is no sense of a 'truth' that is inarticulable, or a past that is irrecoverable: the temporal distance inscribed is only the time from the production of the film to its release and the story is 'complete' as is.

69. *New York Times* 27 February 1907.

Film History, Volume 8, pp. 176–185, 1996. Copyright © John Libbey & Company
ISSN: 0892-2160. Printed in Australia

Warner Bros.' Yellowstone Kelly

A case study of the interaction of film and television in the 1950s

Jerome Delamater

'**H**is calling card had claws on it' was the headline of a full-page advertisement for United States Savings Bonds that appeared in *Variety* early in 1956. The featured reference was to a nineteenth-century mountain man, adventurer and sometime army scout named Luther Sage Kelly, popularly known in his time as 'Yellowstone' Kelly. Noticing that ad, someone in the Warner Bros. organisation decided to pursue the subject as a possible source for a film and from the filing of a title registration with the MPAA on 1 February 1956,' to the premiere of the film in Denver on 18 August, 1959, *Yellowstone Kelly* wended its way through a maze of circumstances that reveal information about the possible relationships among the production system, the formal images produced and the evolution of the genre; about the indecisiveness of a studio in a period of transition and financial upheaval; and perhaps most important, about the interaction of television and film in the late 1950s. From original conception as a major film with full-scale commitment, *Yellowstone Kelly* seemed to descend the scale during production to a minor film only half-heartedly given studio support. Not sure how to deal with the subject, Warner Bros. eventually treated the film like an expanded episode of a television series.

In September 1955, several months before the appearance of the *Variety* ad, a new television Western, *Cheyenne*, starring Clint Walker, an unknown actor recently under contract to Warner Bros., had premiered as part of a trilogy series entitled *Warner Bros. Presents*. The other two components, *Kings Row* and *Casablanca*, based, of course, as was *Cheyenne*, on Warners' films from the 1940s, did not last the season, but *Cheyenne*, sometimes credited with ushering in the adult television Western that dominated American television for the next decade,[2] survived for eight years. According to Erik Barnouw, until 1954 'Jack Warner [had] frowned on any appearance of a television set in a home scene in a Warner feature',[3] but Warners' shift to television production, characterised fully in Christopher Anderson's *Hollywood TV*,[4] seems in some respects an attempt to hold on to a semblance of its former way of operating. For example, although not unique at the time, the fact that Clint Walker was under contract was in itself a holdover from that former system.

Particularly striking is the symbiosis between its new mode of production for television and its loyalty to the former system as seen in *Yellowstone Kelly* and *Fort Dobbs*, a low-budget Western released in 1958, written and directed by Burt Kennedy and Gordon Douglas, the same team who eventually did *Yellowstone Kelly*. *Fort Dobbs* was the first feature film Clint Walker made after achieving stardom as the eponymous hero of *Cheyenne*. Furthermore, the evidence of the archival materials

Jerome Delamater, Author of *Dance in the Hollywood Musical,* is Professor of Communication at Hofstra University. The following is for correspondence: School of Communication, Dept of Audio/Video/Film, 111 Hofstra University, Hempstead, NY 11550-1090, USA. e-mail: avfjhd@Hofstra.edu

Fig. 1. Clint Walker stars as television's Cheyenne Bodie.
[Photo courtesy of Warner Bros.]

Preproduction

Walter MacEwen, who had been Hal Wallis's assistant at Warners and who had subsequently become responsible for supervising a considerable amount of production at the studio, sent a memo to Carl Milliken, Jr., Head of Research, on 27 February 1956: 'I think you should proceed to dig up all the research material you can on Yellowstone Kelly. The producer is Richard Whorf and the writer will probably be Irving Wallace'. Warners' interest in the project was clearly based on the myth and image of the generic Western hero as represented by Kelly. The image of the mountain man had been popularised in two best-selling novels by A. B. Guthrie, *The Big Sky* (1947) and *The Way West* (1949), and the former had been filmed in 1952 by Howard Hawks (the latter was subsequently made into a film in 1967). Moreover, the success of *The Kentuckian* (1955), for which Guthrie had written the screenplay, *The Indian Fighter* and Walt Disney's *Davy Crockett* television series (1954–55) made Yellowstone Kelly an ideal story project. Kelly's own life, however, contained little enough action of the kind they deemed acceptable in a movie, for MacEwen wrote to Jack Warner and Steve Trilling, Warner's executive assistant, in late February that any film would be 'highly fictionalised'.[6] To exploit that image further – and of course, presumably to create a market for any possible film – Warners negotiated a deal with Western novelist Clay Fisher (pseudonym of Henry W. Allen) to write a novel about Kelly.[7] In May 1956 Fisher wrote to story editor Finlay McDermid about his approach to using the Kelly material:

for each film reveals aspects of the 'package-unit system', noted by Janet Staiger,[5] combined with an earlier, more traditionally autocratic studio control. At a later time both films would likely have been made-for-TV movies, appealing as they did primarily to the television audience by casting Walker in versions of his Cheyenne Bodie persona. Indeed, the exploitation of his television persona (and his financial battles with Warner Bros. over his role in *Cheyenne* at precisely this time) also reflected the way television was subsuming the genre during the late 1950s and early 1960s.

The main problem has been to keep away from any biographical feeling – to keep the thing strictly an adventure story based on fact and a love story based on invented fiction ...[8]

Fisher's work on his novel seems to have constituted Warners' action throughout 1956. However, after the novel's publication in 1957 – promoted, of course, by the studio for its movie tie-in[9] – the records indicate renewed studio consideration – this time, quite logically, in the form of commissioning a screenplay.

Since Warner Bros. had eliminated 'the entire story department' as part of its extreme cost-cutting measures in April 1951,[10] script writers were hired on an *ad hoc* basis. Although of necessity this practice was maintained for *Yellowstone Kelly*, nevertheless, the writing itself followed traditional patterns of the old studio 'writing stables'. Several writers (but never Irving Wallace) worked on the project, contributing to and revising other writers' work. D. D. 'Bud' Beauchamp (who had also worked uncredited on *Fort Dobbs*) and Elliot Asinof contributed script material during the first several months of 1957.[11] The records are not clear about the nature or the length of their contribution to the script at this stage, but Burt Kennedy, the credited writer, who had been working at the studio since April preparing the script for *Fort Dobbs*, was assigned to the project in August[12] (he also continued making post-production contributions to *Fort Dobbs* through October) and initially spent eight months writing *Yellowstone Kelly*.

Throughout the entire process – including production on location more than a year later – the studio officials (the producer, Jules Schermer[13] and even Warner and Trilling) kept close watch on the project. An interchange of memos dated 7 January 1958, for example, demonstrates everyone's concern for – and involvement with – the film's dramatic possibilities. (See note for a brief plot synopsis.[14]) Apparently there had been objections – very possibly from 'JL' (Jack Warner) himself – to the death of Anse Harper, Kelly's young-gun sidekick, halfway through the film and the originally scripted death of the Indian girl Wahleeah at the end. Kennedy wrote Schermer a mild protest ('If Kelly finds young Anse alive ... and he stays alive through the remainder of our story I feel that we would lose a

powerful third act'), but he did offer a summary of changes ('... if we have no choice in the matter ...') and included two pages of script amendments that included Anse's survival; at the bottom of the second page, though, Kennedy wrote: 'The girl living presents a bigger problem but I'm working on it.' He concluded his letter, 'This is weak compared to the other but it would work'. At the bottom of one copy of the memo, 'Steve [Trilling]' had a handwritten note to 'J.L.: 1/10/58 Boys now on rewrite for approx 3 days to accomplish this – and still make it *strong* [underlined four times]!'

Clint Walker's continued success in *Cheyenne*'s first two seasons obviously made him an attractive consideration for the starring role in *Fort Dobbs*. Since this film was being handled at a considerably lesser level than *Yellowstone Kelly* was initially, it was easier to complete at a faster rate and principal photography was accomplished during the summer of 1957. Although shot on location in Utah, *Fort Dobbs* had a relatively short, four-week shooting schedule and only a half-million dollar budget.[15] The film was released around the country early in 1958, opening in Los Angeles on a double bill with *Escape from San Quentin* on 5 March. Sometime during the 1957–58 television season, Walker began to express dissatisfaction with playing *Cheyenne*, particularly at his contract salary. The salary sheets for *Fort Dobbs* make his complaints understandable; although the star of the film, since he was 'contract talent', Walker made only a total of $8750 (seven weeks at $1250 per week). The other leading player, his co-star Virginia Mayo, was also under contract but at 'picture rate' and earned $66,250. Brian Keith, as the film's antagonist, was paid $15,000 'free lance' for only a few days' work. Shortly after the release of *Fort Dobbs*, prior to production for *Cheyenne*'s fourth season, Walker was refusing to continue to play that role. And, indeed, *Cheyenne* ran the entire 1958–59 season without Clint Walker. Having been promoted as Walker's first film, *Fort Dobbs* ironically provides the reason for his protest against the studio. Significantly, *Yellowstone Kelly* would become the vehicle for his restoration to the studio's good graces and to his small-screen role.

Clearly the studio did not know what to do with the *Kelly* property during 1958. In January Clay

Fisher wrote Finlay McDermid about his concern for the studio's commitment to the project:

> I read recently where Clint Walker was grow-ing weary of his Cheyenne role and wanted to do an entertainment film. Why not let him do the Yellowstone Kelly thing, with an idea to starting a new TV series after the motion picture has given the project a boost?

> Nowhere among the published lists of Warner Bros. films for 1958 do I see mention of Yellow-stone Kelly. A grievous error in company pol-icy, old boy.[16]

By this time and perhaps indicative of the change in the film's status, Clint Walker had appar-ently become their primary consideration for the role (he was 'handed [a script] personally' on 1 April, 1958)[17], although discussion of other figures did arise. James Garner, for example, known then for his part in the TV series *Maverick*, was mentioned for the lead at one point[18]. Most interesting, though, Jules Schermer wrote to Jack Warner on 15 April that John Wayne was interested in the film 'with John Ford directing' if the studio would approach him to do it. 'I am conveying this message to you because I believe the script is a great one and with Ford and Wayne this package can get whatever money is around. The combination of Wayne, Ford and an outdoor Western with this scope has always clicked big and I would be negligent in my duty to Warner Bros. if I did not pass this information on to you.' Perhaps Schermer was just indulging in wish-ful thinking, for there was never any follow up on his memo. An earlier reference to Wayne in the role had occurred in a trade-press release of 8 August 1956: 'D. D. Beauchamp has been engaged to write the film script of *Yellowstone Kelly*, a historic western drama to star John Wayne. One of the biggest productions on the studio's winter schedule, the picture will be produced by Richard Whorf'. In the two-year interim, however, the film had become a small, frequently postponed production.[19]

The television connection of *Yellowstone Kelly* becomes particularly evident when the studio – early in 1959 – finally began to consider actually putting the film into production. The tentative cast list of 16 February 1959, proposes several names for consideration in various roles (although only Walker's for the title character), many of whom were television personalities. The first-listed for the two other major male roles – both of whom are in the final film – were primary players in other War-ners' TV shows: Edward Byrnes, who played Kookie on *77 Sunset Strip*, was the choice for the sidekick (for some reason called Ben on this list but returned to the scripted name Anse Harper for the film itself) with John Russell, star of *Lawman*, featured as Gall, the Indian chief.

Televison stars in movie roles

Warner Bros. further exploited the actors' identifi-cation as television performers throughout the film's production. Burt Kennedy's original decision to have Anse Harper die was retained in the shooting script, but press releases during April 1959, when the production was on location in Flagstaff, Ari-zona, reveal a fascinating confusion of actor, TV character and film role by playing up the 'outrage' of teenage fans that 'Kookie' was slated to die in the film. One group is alleged to have petitioned the studio to keep 'Kookie' alive and the production stills include photographs of teenage girls picketing the location, carrying signs protesting 'Kookie's' demise. Not being teen-age idols, neither Clint Wal-ker nor John Russell was burdened with that same putative hysteria, but all publicity for the film did emphasise them as television figures. Every studio announcement about *Yellowstone Kelly* presented 'John "Lawman" Russell' in a straightforward ac-knowledgment of his popular, television persona. More ambiguous, however, were the references to 'Clint "He's Back" Walker'. In contrast to the preceding year's references to 'Clint "Cheyenne" Walker' in *Fort Dobbs*, nowhere in the publicity materials during production of *Yellowstone Kelly* nor the promotional materials during the film's re-lease is there a specific reference to his TV role. Nevertheless, the Clint Walker persona, presented primarily through the character of Cheyenne Bodie, is strong in *Yellowstone Kelly*, as it was in Gar Davis, his role in *Fort Dobbs*. He was a wanderer and loner whose commitment to justice prevailed when con-fronted with evil and wrongdoing. In terms of Wal-ker's television image, though (and perhaps the semantic imperative of *Cheyenne*, explicitly de-picted in both films), was the excuse for Walker

Fig. 2. Television stars: Edward 'Kookie' Burns as Anse Harper with Clint 'He's Back' Walker as Kelly in a scene from *Yellowstone Kelly*. [Photo courtesy of Warner Bros.]

always to display his bare-chested physique at some crucial moment. Having settled his contract dispute with Warner Bros., 'Clint "He's Back" Walker' had indeed returned in *Yellowstone Kelly*, his persona and his chest in tact.

There is no evidence that the pressure to keep 'Kookie' alive in the film was ever given serious consideration. Apparently the attempts to modify the script in that regard a year earlier had not succeeded. The ending of the film is a different matter altogether, however, and reflects a persistent concern about the dramatic qualities of the death of Wahleeah, the Indian woman, when she rides into the middle of the battle at the end of the film. Moreover, it is clear that through the preview system some audience influence on particular films still prevailed. Wahleeah's death was Burt Kennedy's preference, to be sure, and remained the ending of choice into production. In March 1959, Kennedy, by this time under contract to Batjac, John Wayne's production company, was loaned to Warner Bros. for 'some additional non-exclusive service-

s ... on the screenplay of *Yellowstone Kelly*'[20] and participated in location scouting with director Gordon Douglas and was present on location throughout production. The blue script-revision sheets dated during location shooting clearly indicate Kennedy's involvement in the decisions about the film's ending. Indeed, the final script includes an 'Alternative Tag', dated 6 April, one day before principal photography began, which eventually became essentially the film's actual conclusion.

Alternate endings

In the tag – and the film, of course – Wahleeah, though wounded, stays with Kelly rather than returning to her people. Earlier endings had her sacrifice herself in order to achieve peace between the warring Indians and soldiers (whom Kelly was reluctantly assisting). Alternative endings must have been shot in Arizona, but not until late in July, about three weeks before the film's premiere, probably after preview screenings, did the studio finally de-

Fig. 3. Wahleeah (Andra Martin) with Kelly (Walker) in *Yellowstone Kelly*.
[Photo courtesy of Warner Bros.]

cide to keep the character alive. Production notes indicate attempts to cope with the ending in three different ways. (1) After Wahleeah's death Kelly and Gall, the Indian chief, meet in truce on the battlefield, where Kelly 'tells Gall to take his people out of this country and ride north, where they can live in freedom and not have to die for it'.[21] This is essentially the ending of the original script. (2) As the battle between the Indians and the soldiers rages, Wahleeah 'gallops toward Gall offering herself as a sacrifice to bring peace'. There is no meeting between the antagonists.[22] (3) 'Caught in the crossfire, she is wounded and both Kelly and Gall go out to her. Gall, realising that her action was prompted by her love for Kelly, tells him to take her and go, then leads his braves away as Kelly lifts her in his arms.'[23] In the actual film, after Wahleeah runs between the opposing forces, Kelly meets with Gall but refuses to allow him to take Wahleeah and says to him, 'Take your warriors and go away from this place. The land no longer smiles on your people.' A final scene recapitulates the opening as Kelly – now with Wahleeah by his side, however – waits to intercept a river boat coming upstream after

the spring thaw. Audience previews with the different endings must have convinced Warner Bros. that keeping Wahleeah alive had the strongest impact; most interestingly it provides the film with a closure that is different from certain generic norms for that time, particularly in its acceptance of a relationship between an Indian woman and a white man.

Representing native Americans

As an example of a late, classical Western, one that has few elements associated with the revisionist Westerns of the 1960s and 1970s, *Yellowstone Kelly* raises a number of interesting questions about the genre at this time. The roles of the Indians, for instance, suggest a genre in transition. Typically, the leading Indian characters – Gall, Sayapi and Wahleeah – are played by white performers who were then promoted for their Indian characteristics. Production stills – staged photographs completely unrelated in this instance to any activity in the film – of Andra Martin as Wahleeah show her as a stereotyped squaw holding Indian corn and making bread. Ironically, other studio publicity materials emphasise the Navajos employed as extras to lend 'authenticity' to the production: 'The Navajos proved to be fearless riders and their coyote-like yelps as they charged the cavalry made the sequence spine-chillingly real even to those working on the sidelines'.[24] Various, usually undated, press releases during principal photography in April 1959 reveal the studio's inconsistency about the Indians – an inconsistency reflected to some degree within the film itself. Some releases, for example, point up the Navajos' non-Anglo characteristics, whereas others note the influence of Anglo culture: 'Times have changed for the Indian and also have changed him. Tall, lean, warrior-type Indians are almost impossible to find.'[25] Similarly, publicity made an issue of the emergency need to procure wigs from Hollywood when the extras all showed up wearing crew cuts. (The same story was part of studio publicity for *Fort Dobbs*. Was this just another publicity gimmick or did nobody – including Gordon Douglas, who directed both films – remember such details from one picture to the next?) Later publicity, associated with the film's actual release, emphasised the Indians' innate skills, whereas earlier press releases noted the need to camouflage the overweight and out-of-condition extras. And within the film, an early conversation between Kelly and Anse Harper, in which Kelly admonishes Anse not to get involved with Wahleeah because of the impossibility of 'taming' an Indian, contrasts with Kelly's own Indian-like existence and his acceptance of Wahleeah as his mate at the end.

Warner Bros.' perceptions about the Indians also carry through to its attitudes about the potential audiences for such films. There are numerous discrepancies between *Yellowstone Kelly* as a formal entity and the materials associated with it as determined and defined by its system of production. Attempts at period authenticity during pre-production gave way to the expected compromises necessitated by the exigencies of location production, on the one hand, and by studio perceptions of audience desires, on the other. Research records reveal a careful concern for historical accuracy during the preliminary development of the project with requests for period maps and detailed information about settlements, trapping and ways of living. The film itself, however, suggests a considerably more cavalier approach to costuming and historicity,

both giving way apparently to dramatic and budgetary concerns. Moreover, in spite of the fact that both *Fort Dobbs* and *Yellowstone Kelly* are serious/adult Westerns akin to others of the late 1950s, they were advertised primarily for children. *Kelly* had a comic-book tie-in, for example, while *Fort Dobbs* was promoted in connection with colouring contests and cowboy and Indian costume screenings, gimmicks obviously directed at a juvenile audience. In general Warner Bros. must have considered that its television Westerns appealed to children – at least to a degree. During the fall of 1959 (and clearly *Yellowstone Kelly* was released in August to exploit the tie-in to Clint Walker's return as the star of *Cheyenne*), Warner Bros. had several Westerns on television in addition to *Cheyenne*: *Sugarfoot*, *Bronco*, *Colt .45* and *Maverick*. All of them were in the earliest prime-time broadcasting slots, not one ending later than 8:30 p.m., contrasting sharply with the blatantly adult *Gunsmoke* and its long reign at 10:00 p.m. on Saturdays. The television influence on *Yellowstone Kelly* may have extended beyond its use of the small screen's stars and encouraged the discrepancy between the film and its surrounding promotion and publicity and the discrepancy between the film and its fellow Westerns of the period.

Hollywood and history

An analysis of the archival information about *Yellowstone Kelly* reveals the complexity of Hollywood's relation to the history of the West and Hollywood's relation to television in the 1950s. Indeed, inquiry into a non-canonical film like *Yellowstone Kelly* may be analogous to the microhistory that has become so important in repositioning previously subordinated populations of the past.

Natalie Zemon Davis, for example, in *Society and Culture in Early Modern France* (and, of course, in her better-known *The Return of Martin Guerre*), has made 'local history [of Lyon, France] ... an occasion to ask general questions'.[26] Similarly, Carlo Ginzburg's *The Cheese and the Worms* has explored the nature of larger social and ecclesiastical practices by concentrating on the effects that the Inquisition had not on the rich and famous but on one individual who was a newly literate member of the populace.[27] In both of these cases significant

Fig. 4. White actors play Native American parts: John 'Lawman' Russell (right), another television star, plays Gall; Martin (lying down) stars as Wahleeah. [Photo courtesy of Warner Bros.]

archival research was necessary to understand the historical contexts in which such people lived during the sixteenth and seventeenth centuries. Moreover, their studies suggest that different sets of questions often need to be asked when investigating the non-canonical, the less important, the historically ignored.

Two concepts of microhistory that raise questions of class interaction in respect to popular culture seem of particular interest here. First is what Carlo Ginzburg in his introduction to *The Cheese and the Worms*, calls *circularity*: '... between the culture of the dominant classes and that of the subordinate classes there existed, in preindustrial Europe, a circular relationship composed of reciprocal influences, which travelled from low to high as well as from high to low'. Second are the *discrepancies* between the artifacts of a culture and their reception, '... the existence of a gap between the [popular literature of the period] and the way ... it was in all

probability read by the popular classes'.[28] The pre-industrial model is by no means perfect, but the cultural interaction provided by Hollywood's system of previewing films and the studio's inferences about what a television audience wants in movies both seem possible contemporary avenues of circularity. More significant is the studio's apparent inability or unwillingness to confront the underlying cultural problems demonstrated most specifically in *Yellowstone Kelly*'s treatment of Indians. These discrepancies seem particularly manifest in the images of publicity and promotion of the films under consideration.

One can infer certain principles and raise particular questions from an archival exploration of Hollywood production in the late 1950s. First, it is clear that certain studio practices of the earlier contract period are, *mutatis mutandis*, generally still operative for these late-studio examples but with a confusion about priorities and decision making that reflected the problems of the industry as a whole.[29] At Warner Bros. the new package-unit system prevailed for high-budget independent productions, whereas something akin to the old system operated for television programs and low-budget films. Second, the comparison of production materials with the formal qualities of the actual films suggests the complexity of the artistic and economic enterprise, particularly in terms of the circular and reciprocal interaction with television. Had *Yellowstone Kelly* not been so closely tied to its television roots, it very likely would have been able to be more daring in its confrontation with cultural values of the period. To a certain degree, it does seem evident that when television became the primary site for the Western, in movies the genre began increasingly to re-evaluate the norms by which it had operated for the previous decades, a re-evaluation that this film attempts only modestly. Third, the publicity and other exploitations of the films during production and exhibition (often the major means by which people initially receive films) were sometimes only tangentially related to the films themselves. Such discrepancies surely had some influence on the evolution of the Western, which changed so definitively during the next several years. Models of microhistory suggest that exploring certain overlooked details of popular culture (e.g. printing workers in the sixteenth century or non-canonical films in the twentieth century) becomes a primary means of attempting to understand the shifting contexts of historical development. The various questions raised require continued investigation.❖

Notes

1. The copy of *Variety* in the Warner Bros. archives at the University of Southern California is dated 9 February 1956, eight days later than the title-filing date. It is clear from other references, however, that the *Variety* ad was the original source of their interest. My assumption is that the ad, though first noticed before 1 February was clipped from the 9 February *Variety* 'for the record', fortunately a compulsive practice at that studio. Hereafter all references to the material from the Warner Bros. collection at USC will be designated WB/USC.

2. For example, in *The BFI Companion to the Western*, ed. Edward Buscombe (London: André Deutsch/BFI Publishing, 1988), 401: *Cheyenne* was 'Perhaps

the Western series most responsible for the small-screen stampede of the late 1950s ...' It is important to remember, however, that both *The Life and Legend of Wyatt Earp* and *Gunsmoke* also began in September 1955.

3. *Tube of Plenty: The Evolution of American Television* (New York: Oxford UP, 1975), 193.

4. Christopher Anderson, *Hollywood TV: The Studio System in the Fifties* (Austin: university of Texas Press, 1994), Chapters VII–IX.

5. 'The Package-Unit System: Unit Management after 1955' in David Bordwell *et al.*, *The Classical Hollywood Cinema: Film Style and Mode of Production to 1960* (New York: Columbia University Press, 1985), 330–337.

6. Memorandum of 27 February 1956. The Research Records for 16 February 1956, from '[Richard] Whorf' request 'Maps of period and locale/additional material on/which to hang a story – /there is nothing in Kelly's life which gives [a] necessary story line'. Interesting in this regard, too, is the comment in studio attorney Albert Howson's letter to the MPAA, Aug. [Apr?] 23, 1956, ' ... we have acquired the rights to the *novel* [emphasis added] by Luther S. Kelly'. (WB/USC) Kelly's autobiography, *Yellowstone Kelly: The Memoirs of Luther S. Kelly*, was edited by M. M. Quaife and published by Yale University Press in 1926, two years before Kelly died.

7. Allen (who maintained the Clay Fisher pseudonym – even in his signature – in all correspondence with Warner Bros.) wrote to Robert L. Gale, *Will Henry/Clay Fisher (Henry W. Allen)* (Boston: Twayne, 1984), 126, n. 12,: 'I did the book in conjunction with Warner Brothers film company, a once-only effort of this nature'.

8. Letter of 8 May 1956. He continues: 'and I am satisfied this is being done. Kelly's actual life was so rich in useless detail and so damned utterly devoid of useful drama that I have had, as indeed we all anticipated, to pull out all the stops in setting up this novel.' (WB/USC)

9. The studio released an announcement to the trade press on 27 August that *Yellowstone Kelly*, 'which Warner Bros. is to make into a motion picture, goes on sale in book form this week'. It listed Jules Schermer as producer and Burt Kennedy as script writer. (WB/USC)

10. Thomas Schatz, *The Genius of the System: Hollywood Filmmaking in the Studio Era* (New York: Pantheon, 1988), 437–438.

11. Their Research Records requests begin 7 January

1957 and end 21 May 1957. (One can only wonder about their notions of the film's themes and structure when considering the Research Records: obvious requests for Kelly's autobiography, information about Indian names and stories of Indian lore are supplemented by requests for copies of *Lady of the Lake* [Sir Walter Scott's?], *Hamlet* and Turgenev's *A Month in the Country*.)

12. Warner Bros. released an announcement to the trades on 9 August, which appeared in *Hollywood Reporter* and *Variety* on 12 August 1957, that Burt Kennedy was assigned to *Yellowstone Kelly*. His Research requests begin on 16 August 1957 and continue through 18 February 1958. (His services were completed as of 31 March 1958, per memo from MacEwen to Obringer.) There are subsequent requests in 1959 immediately prior to and during production when Kennedy had been hired again for the film. In May 1959 when the film was finally being prepared for release, neither Beauchamp nor Asinoff voiced objections to Kennedy alone receiving script credit. (WB/USC)

13. The first time Schermer's name is mentioned as producer is in a *Variety* announcement of 9 April 1957 (8), that Asinof has been 'set ... to screenplay' the film. The last appearance of Whorf's name as producer is in a trade-press release of 8 August 1956. (WB/USC)

14. In the film, Yellowstone Kelly and Anse Harper, his sidekick, occupied primarily as fur trappers, become involved in two conflicts: One is an intra-tribal battle between Gall, an Indian chief, and Sayapi, a young rebel, over an Indian girl, Wahleeah; the other is a battle between the Indians and the cavalry, a fight Kelly tries to mediate. In the course of the action, Anse Harper is killed by the Indians and Kelly kills Sayapi in a climactic battle between the cavalry, whom Kelly reluctantly supports, and the Indians. Wahleeah, who loves Kelly, rides into the midst of the gunfire and causes the opposing forces to cease fighting. Kelly and Wahleeah are united at the end.

15. The estimate was $578,000; actual cost was $678,751.38. (WB/USC)

16. Letter of 14 January 1958 to Finlay [McDermid] signed Clay. (WB/USC)

17. Per Steve Trilling memo. (WB/USC)

18. He was also – and more seriously – considered for the young-gun role; a rewrite of pages 4 to 22 was undertaken specifically considering 'ANSE for Garner'. Note from 'Johnny' to MacEwen, n.d. (WB/USC)

19. One other indication of the film's diminished status

may be that, although *Yellowstone Kelly* is in colour, it was not shot in a wide-screen format. In addition, the archival materials suggest a confused decision-making process at Warner Bros., reflective perhaps of the studio's conflicted attitudes about the package-unit system in contrast to the producer-unit system that had worked so effectively for them in the years when Hal Wallis was 'associate executive in charge of production'. See especially Staiger, 326–327, and Aljean Harmetz, *Round Up the Usual Suspects: The Making of Casablanca – Bogart, Bergman and World War II* (New York: Hyperion, 1992).

20. Memo from Walter MacEwen to Roy Obringer, 11 March 1959, authorising payment of $3750 per week to Batjac. (WB/USC) Kennedy told me in an interview that whenever he was on loanout from Batjac he and John Wayne split the difference between his regular Batjac salary and the additional money charged to the other party for his services.

21. Synopsis dated 6 May 1959, 3. (WB/USC)

22. Synopsis of 2 June 1959, 3. (WB/USC)

23. Synopsis of 17 July 1959, 3. (WB/USC)

24. Production Notes dated 31 July 1959, 4. (WB/USC)

25. Press release, n.d., from Flagstaff, AZ. (WB/USC)

26. Interview with Natalie Zemon Davis in *MARHO: The Radical Historians Organisation, Visions of History* (New York: Pantheon, 1983), 99.

27. Natalie Zemon Davis, *Society and Culture in Early Modern France* (Stanford: Stanford UP, 1975); Carlo Ginzburg, *The Cheese and the Worms: The Cosmos of a Sixteenth-century Miller,* trans. John and Anne Tedeschi (1976, Harmondsworth: Penguin, 1982). Among others, Emmanuel Le Roy Ladurie and Edward P. Thompson are also especially noted as pursuing the practice of microhistory.

28. Pp. xii and xvi. Ginzburg does not claim originality for these ideas; the first he attributes to Mikhail Bakhtin and the second to Geneviève Bollème. The concept of circularity also seems akin to the ideas about the audience-filmmaker relationship that is so fundamental to most understandings of the development of genre. See, among others, Jane Feuer's comments about the ritual approach to genre in 'Genre Study and Television', in Robert C. Allen, ed. *Channels of Discourse, Revisited: Television and Contemporary Criticism,* 2nd ed. (Chapel Hill: University of North Carolina Press, 1992), 138–159.

29. Anderson, Chapter IX.

Film History, Volume 8, pp. 186–208, 1996. Copyright © John Libbey & Company
ISSN: 0892-2160. Printed in Australia

The Circus: a Chaplin masterpiece

Jeffrey Vance

The Circus: finding its rightful place

There has been an unfortunate tendency amongst modern film commentators to underrate Charlie Chaplin's 1928 film, *The Circus*. Sandwiched between Chaplin's great silent masterworks, *The Gold Rush* (1925) and *City Lights* (1931), *The Circus* has been passed over or even forgotten. The failure to canonise the film cannot fall squarely upon critical appreciation, depreciation, or passing tastes. Chaplin himself (never one to remain silent in the face of his own genius) failed to devote one word to the film in his principle volume of autobiography.[1] Chaplin also refused to revive *The Circus* until 1970, some 42 years after its original release. The film's more privileged counterparts, *The Gold Rush* and *City Lights*, enjoyed their cinematic revivals decades earlier.

Chaplin's dismissive view of *The Circus* is incongruous in the light of the quality of the film. *The Circus* explores complex themes, striking resounding chords both autobiographical to the filmmaker and universal to his audience. Employing a tightly organised plot, Chaplin tells the story of the Tramp and the beautiful equestrienne with seamless fluidity. The film is at once funny, poetic and ultimately 'Chaplinesque' as the great clown raises the slapstick banality of circus life to the sublime. Chaplin had displayed the same genius in telling the story of the Lone Prospector and would do so again in convincing the world that a blind flower-girl could mistake the Tramp for a millionaire. By any critical standard, *The Circus* demands comparable acclamation.

Audiences across the boundaries of time agree with this assessment. The film opened in 1928 to a balance of enthusiastic reviews and enjoyed magnificent runs in the cinemas. Modern film-goers at triumphant revivals in Washington DC, Los Angeles and New York City have turned out in the thousands to revel in this rarely-revived film.

Chaplin certainly could recognise his own artistic gifts, yet he relegated *The Circus* to critical obscurity by shelving it for nearly a half century. The key to this ostensibly enigmatic behaviour lies in the production history of *The Circus* itself. The circumstances surrounding the filming of *The Circus* were so disastrous that Chaplin in turn suffered threats to his film, his studio, his career and ultimately his life. It would be these grim recollections and not the comedic poetry or critical reception of *The Circus*, that would colour his memory of the film. The solution to *The Circus'* enigma – the delay in reviving the film while other Chaplin masterworks flourished and the consequential dearth of any detailed critical analysis of the film – lies in this enervating production history, not the calibre of the film.

Today, *The Circus* has cast off its once constraining inaccessibility. A CBS/Fox laser disc of *The Circus* (containing never before published studio records, out-takes and press-book) and revivals of the film in major cities (boasting live orchestral accompaniment and prints carefully prepared from the best-surviving negative) have engendered a renaissance. At no other time in the film's nearly seventy year history has it enjoyed such accessi-

Jeffrey Vance received his MA degree in English Literature from Boston University in 1995. Currently, he is completing a lecture tour with Chaplin's *The Kid* and preparing the final edit of the late Lita Grey Chaplin's second memoir, *Wife of The Life of the Party*. Address correspondence to: 10900 Bluffside Drive, Studio City, California 91604, USA.

bility. The time has finally come, therefore, to give *The Circus* its rightful place in the Chaplin canon.

Chaplin in 1925: genesis of *The Circus*

After the critical and commercial success of *The Gold Rush*, Chaplin was at a loss. He considered *The Gold Rush* to be the summit of his art and believed that surpassing (or even equalling) the success of the film was a near impossible task. He first thought of producing an adaptation of Robert Louis Stevenson's novella, *The Suicide Club*, for his next film project.[2] This idea was quickly aborted in favour of a comedy production tentatively titled *The Dandy*. The *New York Times* on 29 November 1925 reported that Chaplin was to produce the comedy picture *The Dandy* and then commence production on a 'great picture' to be called *The Clown*:

> It is called *The Clown* and in it Chaplin is to be clad as a circus clown except for his big shoes, his little cane and his tiny bowler hat. This story was described as another dramatic comedy and in its method something after the style of *The Gold Rush*, except that it was to have a tragic ending – the fun-maker impersonated by Chaplin is supposed to die on the tanbark while the spectators are applauding his comic pantomime.[3]

There are enough similarities to suggest that ideas from *The Clown* were incorporated into Chaplin's *Limelight* (1952). Indeed, *The Clown* prefigures *Limelight's* final sequence of the ageing clown Calvero (played by Chaplin) dying after performing a magnificent music-hall pantomime.

It should be noted that *The Circus* also has many similarities to *Limelight*. Both films explore similar themes: age giving way to youth (in each film an older man gallantly relinquishes his love for a younger woman to a younger man), clowns who lose their ability to make people laugh and what Ira S. Jaffe has termed 'the anxious labour of performance'.[4] *The Circus* and *Limelight* are both set in a theatrical milieu, as well as being more noticeably autobiographical than any of Chaplin's other works.

The Charles Chaplin Film Corporation daily production reports indicate that when production commenced on 2 November 1925, the third Chaplin United Artists picture had the working title *The Traveller* and was projected to be a five reel comedy film, a less ambitious project than the nine reel *The Gold Rush*.[5] By 3 December 1925, Chaplin had a circus tent under construction and was rehearsing on a tightrope, which was to be used in the film's climatic sequence. Henry Bergman (1868–1946), a Chaplin associate since appearing in Chaplin's Mutual Film Corporation two-reeler *The Pawnshop* (1916), remembered the genesis of *The Circus* in an interview:

> Before he had made *The Circus* he said to me one night, 'Henry, I have an idea I would like to do a gag placing me in a position I can't get away from for some reason. I'm on a high place troubled by something else, monkeys or things that come to me and I can't get away from them.' He was mulling around in his head a vaudeville story. I said to him, 'Charlie, you can't do anything like that on a stage. The audience would be uncomfortable craning their necks to watch a vaudeville actor. It would be unnatural. Why not develop your idea in a circus tent on a tightrope. I'll teach you to walk a rope'.[6]

The Suicide Club, *The Dandy* and a film about Napoleon Bonaparte had been discarded.

Chaplin assembles his team

Prior to the commencement of a remarkable production history Chaplin began to assemble a creative team and principal players who would bring his vision to life on the screen. Along with Bergman, Chaplin engaged Harry Crocker as his assistant (Crocker would later join the cast as Rex, the tightrope walker) and Allan Garcia (1887–1938) as the circus proprietor. Allan Garcia had first worked for Chaplin at First National in such shorts as *The Idle Class* (1921) and *Pay Day* (1922). *The Circus* was Garcia's first major role in a Chaplin film. Chaplin originally wanted Henry Bergman for the role of circus proprietor, but Bergman insisted he was not suited for the part. Bergman told Chaplin: 'No, Charlie, I'm a roly-poly kind-faced man, not the dirty heavy who would beat a girl'.[7] Instead,

Fig. 1. Publicity portrait: Charlie Chaplin in *The Circus*.
[Copyright Roy Export Company Establishment.]

Bergman would play an old clown. The other principal cast member, Merna Kennedy, was engaged to play the young equestrienne.

Chaplin's long-time cameraman Roland Totheroh (1890–1967), who had been with Chaplin since Mutual, would once again be director of photography, with Jack Wilson and Mark Marlatt

as cameramen. Charles D. Hall (1899–1959), who had designed *The Gold Rush*, was engaged as art director. Of the major members of *The Circus* production, only Crocker and Kennedy had not worked with Chaplin before.

Harry Crocker (1893–1958) came from a prominent banking family in San Francisco and had attended Yale University. Chaplin met Crocker through Marion Davies, the actress who has been linked romantically to Chaplin as well as newspaper tycoon William Randolph Hearst. Crocker was a frequent guest at Hearst's legendary estate, San Simeon, where Chaplin spent an occasional week-end. Crocker came to Hollywood in the autumn of 1924 to pursue a career in films. He acted in productions of the Los Angeles Playhouse Company and did extra work in such films as King Vidor's *The Big Parade* (1925). Although he had little motion picture experience, Crocker had an enthusiasm which was attractive to Chaplin and so vital a quality in assisting the master filmmaker. Chaplin hired Crocker originally as his production assistant for *The Circus* and the two men went to the Pebble Beach Lodge, Del Monte, California from 9–18 November 1925 to further develop the film's scenario. As Chaplin's assistant, Crocker acted as a sounding board for story ideas and recorded them as the day's gag 'suggestions'. The suggestions from the trip survive in the Chaplin archives and several were reprinted in David Robinson's *Chaplin: His Life and Art*.[8]

As indicated by the use of her name in the daily production reports and extant *The Circus* story notes, Chaplin had originally intended the role of the equestrienne to go to Georgia Hale, who had appeared with Chaplin as the dancehall girl in *The Gold Rush*. Hale's contract expired on 31 December 1925, however and was not renewed.[9] No primary source adequately explains the reason for this occurrence, but it is believed that Hale was anxious to expedite her career. The production of *The Circus* would move along too slowly for Hale, so she had decided to move on herself.[10] In Georgia Hale's place, Chaplin signed Merna Kennedy as his leading lady.

Merna Kennedy (1908–44) had been the childhood friend of Lita Grey, Chaplin's second wife. Lita Grey (1908–95) was the screen name Chaplin had created for Lillita MacMurray, who appeared as the flirting angel in *The Kid* (1921) and as a maid, along with her mother, in the Chaplin two-reeler *The Idle Class* (1921). Originally cast as the dancehall girl in *The Gold Rush*, Chaplin married Lita Grey on 25 November 1924 after she became pregnant with their first child. According to Lita Grey Chaplin:

Merna Kennedy and I had been friends ever since dancing school together when we were small children. When Mr. Chaplin made it known that he was planning a film on the Circus, it occurred to me that my friend Merna would be ideal for the leading lady and I asked him if he would consider testing her. He did not like me, or for that matter his crew even, to make suggestions about these matters, but he finally, after my pestering him, agreed to make a test of her. Mr. Chaplin was very pleased with the test and paid me a compliment for suggesting that he consider her.[11]

Kennedy, along with her brother Merle, had toured in vaudeville in a dancing act. She had not only a pretty face but also the developed legs and figure which would be convincing in her role as trapeze artist/equestrienne. Her contract commenced on 2 January 1926.

With the principal players in place, Chaplin began shooting *The Circus* on Monday, 11 January 1926.

Production history

Film historian David Robinson writes that *The Circus* 'was to be a production dogged by persistent misfortune. The most surprising aspect of the film is not that it is as good as it is, but that it was ever completed at all'.[12] Indeed, *The Circus* faced many potentially life-threatening pitfalls, four major disasters in all, suggesting a Chaplinesque version of 'The Four Horseman of the Apocalypse'.

When Chaplin began filming, his first order of business was to shoot the tightrope sequence – the seminal idea that had led him to create a film about a circus. To shoot the climatic sequence first was not in keeping with Chaplin's method of filmmaking. Chaplin generally shot his films in chronological order. However, since Chaplin had been training to walk the tightrope and this sequence was fully worked out in his head, he decided to commence the production with the difficult tightrope sequences.

On 6 December 1925, an incident occurred which was to foreshadow the four major disasters which were to plague the production. On the afternoon of the sixth, a violent storm tore apart the

Fig. 2. The Tramp breaks bread with the equestrienne. Merna Kennedy and Chaplin in *The Circus*. [Copyright Roy Export Company Establishment.]

nearly-completed circus tent on the studio back lot, destroying the film's largest set. Although the tent was reconstructed, a more tempestuous storm was brewing in the Chaplin Studio laboratory. The first of the film's four major disasters struck as the studio's film processing laboratory discovered that the rushes of the tightrope scenes, shot during the first month of production, were marred with scratches. There is no record of what exactly occurred, but an incensed Chaplin fired his entire laboratory staff. The memo in the Charles Chaplin Film Corporation daily production report of 12 February 1926 notes: 'Did not shoot. Rain. Making change in Laboratory force. New employees started last night'. [13] On 16 February 1926 the daily studio report records: 'Starting today to do all previous scenes over again on account of developing and printing'. [14] In the wake of this disaster, Chaplin placed his studio laboratory under the supervision of William E. Hinckley. Chaplin must have been pleased with

Hinckley's work, for he granted him a rare screen credit in the completed film. Nevertheless, Chaplin was forced to retake the difficult tightrope sequences all over again after weeks of arduous tight-rope training and shooting. For Chaplin, however, the ordeal of filming *The Circus* was only beginning.

Several months later, on 28 September 1926, the second major disaster, a fire, swept through the studio. Before the fire was brought under control, the interior stage, props, electrical equipment and thousands of glass panes in the side walls and roof were destroyed by fire and water. The daily production report chronicles the event with the following:

> Were shooting scenes in entrance to dressing rooms on enclosed stage. Fire broke out and whole interior of stage was burned – burning sets, props, etc. [15]

While the damaged sets and props were being rebuilt, an undaunted Chaplin began filming a new sequence with himself, Kennedy, Crocker and Doc Stone (in a dual role as prizefighter Twin Spud and his twin brother) on 3 October 1926. The sequence was finished on 14 October. Chaplin, however, did not see fit to include it in the finished film. The unedited footage exists in the Chaplin archives as the only sequence of Chaplin's United Artists films that survives in unedited form. The sequence was assembled by Kevin Brownlow and David Gill and played in its entirety in the third programme of their documentary, *Unknown Chaplin* (1983), where it can be seen as a delightful, perfectly constructed comedy sequence.

The sequence begins with the Tramp waiting outside of the equestrienne's wagon practising high wire walking along the handle of a nearby rake. The girl appears at the unfortunate moment when the Tramp manages to hit himself in the face with the rake's handle. The two walk arm in arm to the cafe, coming across Rex the tightrope walker along the way. A one-sided rivalry develops as the Tramp attempts to top Rex's acts of gallantry (toward a woman who has dropped her handbag for example). This 'rivalry' ends in disaster for the Tramp as his attempt to aid a woman with her unruly parcels devolves into a slippery stream of fish spilling upon the pavement. Finally at the cafe, the Tramp endures the taunts of Twin Spud, a famous prizefighter. Spud subjects the Tramp to a constant barrage of flying sugar cubes until the Tramp can no longer contain himself and leaves. Spud pays his bill and follows closely behind. Spying a golden opportunity, the little fellow cuts a deal with Spud. Spud is to 'throw' an impromptu fight against the Tramp in order for him to finally wrestle the girl's affections away from Rex. The two re-enter the cafe and perfectly execute the plan. All seems well until Spud's twin brother appears. Thinking he is Spud, the Tramp decides to go another round. Not knowing why this little fellow has attacked him, Spud's brother quickly knocks the Tramp to the ground. In the end, Rex comes to the Tramp's rescue and effortlessly executes the single knockout punch that sends Spud's brother to the canvas. Rex summons the adoring equestrienne to his side and the couple leaves. The Tramp quickly settles his debt with 'Spud' (by removing a five dollar bill from his pocket) and follows the couple out of the cafe.

Eighteen minutes of this out-take footage are included in the supplemental section of the CBS/Fox laser disc version of *The Circus*, with commentary by film historian David Shepard.

The cut cafe sequence was not the only film shot during the production of *The Circus* destined never to be shown in the cinema. While working on *The Circus*, Chaplin commenced for the first (and last) time upon producing a film by another director. Josef von Sternberg, who had caught Chaplin's eye directing Georgia Hale in *The Salvation Hunters* (1925), was to be the writer and director of *A Woman of the Sea*, an Edna Purviance vehicle. Chaplin's first film for United Artists, *A Woman of Paris* (1923), had failed to meet Chaplin's expectations in establishing Purviance as a dramatic actress. Chaplin hoped von Sternberg could utilise his early directorial promise by making *A Woman of the Sea* (and Purviance) a success.

With the working title *Sea Gulls*, production of *A Woman of the Sea* commenced on 16 January 1926, almost simultaneously with *The Circus*. Although Chaplin had no hand in the film, members of the *The Circus* crew did: Mark Marlatt (cameraman for *The Circus*) was cameraman for *A Woman of the Sea* and Charles D. Hall (*The Circus'* art director) was the film's art director. *A Woman of the Sea* told the story of two daughters of a fisherman on the California coast. Purviance portrayed the good sister, Joan and Eve Southern was cast to play Magdalen, Joan's manipulative sibling. The story was nothing more than a simple melodrama. The bad sister, Magdalen, leaves her fisherman fiance, Peter (Raymond Bloomer), to seek the hedonism of the big city with a playboy novelist (Gayne Whiteman). Following Magdalen's departure, Joan marries Peter and begins a modest, yet happy, life with him. Soon Magdalen returns and attempts, with some initial success, to tear Peter away from her sister. Magdalen's efforts are ultimately dashed, however, as Joan and Peter reconcile to resume their life together at the film's close.

The shooting of *A Woman of the Sea* began on 8 March and was completed on 3 June 1926, but the film was never released. Upon seeing the finished version, Chaplin deemed it a failure. *A Woman of the Sea* was the property of the Charles Chaplin Film Corporation. This gave Chaplin the authority to shelve the film indefinitely, which he promptly did. Ultimately, the negative of *A Woman*

Fig. 3. Chaplin gazes at the damage caused by the studio fire, 28 September 1926. [Copyright Roy Export Company Establishment.]

The Circus. Chaplin had married Lita on 25 November 1924 upon his discovery that she was pregnant with their first child, Charles Chaplin, Jr. The marriage was never more than a perfunctory one. Lita Grey, 16 years old at the time of the marriage, was wholly rejected by Chaplin from the moment the marriage vows were uttered. By the summer of 1926, the marriage had completely deteriorated. Chaplin had been totally absorbed in the filming of *The Circus*, making any of Lita's attempts at marital bliss impossible. For Chaplin, balancing domestic tranquillity and the filming of *The Circus* was becoming impossible. In Lita Grey's divorce complaint, the following exchange is alleged to have occurred between Chaplin and his increasingly estranged wife:

'Why, Charlie, I don't understand how I interfere with your work. I never see you or annoy you.' And he replied in a tone of exasperation: 'That isn't it. It is just the fact that you are here; and I am supposed to give the usual attention to a home and family. It annoys me and irritates me; and I cannot work'.[16]

of the Sea was destroyed by fire for tax purposes in 1933 and the film remains unseen to this day. Although scholars may never definitely know what qualities of *A Woman of the Sea* compelled him to shelve the film, Chaplin's second attempt at making Purviance a star in her own right had failed. The anxiety of creating a film, as well as making the executive decisions regarding another, had placed a tremendous strain upon an increasingly harried Charlie Chaplin, during an increasingly difficult period of his professional career.

    The divorce from Lita Grey was the third and most devastating disaster to strike the production of

Occasionally, however, Chaplin would engage Lita in sexual relations (albeit devoid of any real affection) and one such union produced a second child, Sydney Earl Chaplin, who was born on 30 March 1926 (the day Chaplin and Crocker were in Venice Beach looking for locations for *The Circus*). Although Chaplin was pleased at the arrival of another healthy child, according to Lita Grey Chaplin, the birth of Sydney was but a momentary respite of a doomed marriage.[17]

    The events leading to the inevitable separation came early in the month of November 1926 when Lita invited Merna Kennedy to spend a weekend at the Chaplin estate. Kennedy was sporting a diamond bracelet which she revealed to Lita to be a gift from Chaplin. According to Lita Grey Chaplin:

> Merna came to spend a weekend and she showed me a beautiful diamond bracelet. I thought that maybe she had a rich boyfriend. But this particular night, we were in the bedroom and she said 'Charlie gave me this bracelet, but I didn't want to tell you because I thought maybe you'd think something was going on between us'. I just listened. I knew what a tightwad Charlie was and how I had to beg him to get me a diamond ring. I knew then the two were having an affair. I finally got out of my bed and walked through the bathroom to Charlie's room. Charlie had just come in. I said 'Charlie, I've had it with you and I think I'm going to leave you. I've known for a long time that you've been playing around with different women but, having an affair with Merna, this is the last straw'.[18]

Chaplin asked Lita to reconsider and suggested she take a holiday to think things over. Lita sailed for Honolulu, Hawaii with her mother and Charles Chaplin, Jr. (Sydney was too young to travel) for a three week trip. Upon her return, she decided to separate immediately, taking the children with her. Lita Grey left with their two sons on 30 November 1926 and filed for divorce on 10 January 1927.

The divorce complaint, by any lawyer's standards, was extraordinary. While a normal pleading ran four or five pages, Lita Grey's complaint totalled 42 pages.[19] It traced the unseemly events that had led to the Chaplin separation in lurid detail. So vivid was the description of Chaplin's married life to Lita, that profiteers pandered the document on the black market. Though the text of the complaint was a personal embarrassment to Chaplin, what concerned him deeply was the structure of the litigation. Chaplin had been joined as a defendant with the Chaplin Studio, the Charles Chaplin Film Corporation, his valet, his manager and various banks and corporations. All of Chaplin's marital and separate property (allegedly totalling $16 million) were placed into receivership pending the outcome of the divorce litigation. In short, through the magic of the

legal rules of civil joinder and attachment, Lita and her attorneys had embroiled every penny of Chaplin's financial life into the divorce litigation. Desperate to save his studio and his film, on 3 December 1926 Chaplin had nine reels of cut positive and thirteen reels of uncut scenes of The Circus packed for removal to safety in New York. Remembering his previous difficult divorce (from Mildred Harris during the filming of The Kid), Chaplin had the foresight to protect his work early before plaintiff lawyers and court orders could seize it.

As devastating as the divorce from Lita Grey had become, it was but one of Chaplin's legal problems in January 1927. Just three days before Lita filed for divorce, Chaplin filed a complaint in federal court against Pictorial Review, a magazine which had just published the first instalment of a four-part biography purporting to be the 'Real Life Story' of Charlie Chaplin. The articles had been written by Jim Tully, a Chaplin employee during the production of The Gold Rush who was known professionally as the 'hobo writer'. Fearful that the Tully biography would generate negative publicity that might affect the impending divorce, Chaplin sued Pictorial Review on the grounds that the biography was unauthorised. Chaplin's attorney, Nathan Burkan, sought $500,000 in damages for the first published article and an injunction to prevent the release of the remaining instalments. On both counts, Chaplin was unsuccessful. Judge Thatcher denied Chaplin's request for monetary damages and an injunction, allowing the remaining instalments of the biography to be published on schedule. Even with a wealth of legal resources (and in no position to endure further public humiliation), the 'Tramp' had been bested by the 'hobo writer'.[20]

Adding to Chaplin's already woeful legal problems (and amounting to the fourth major disaster to beset The Circus), the Internal Revenue Service declared that Chaplin and the Charles Chaplin Film Corporation owed over $1,670,000 in back taxes.[21] The IRS promptly put a lien on Chaplin's financial assets (the second lien to be placed on his property in January). The Chaplin Studio, however, had suspended operations on 5 December 1926. The Charles Chaplin Film Corporation daily production report of 6 December 1926 states:

> Studio operations suspended temporarily.

Staff of employees cut down throughout studio, including actors, with exception of those remaining on list.[22]

The chosen few on that list were the film's principal players: Chaplin, Henry Bergman, Harry Crocker, Merna Kennedy and Allan Garcia.

On 16 January 1927, the *New York Times* reported that the strain of these crushing legal and financial blows had finally taken its toll on Chaplin. While visiting his attorney Nathan Burkan in New York, Chaplin reportedly suffered a nervous breakdown.[23] He would not work on *The Circus* again for eight months. A divorce settlement agreeable to Lita Grey and Chaplin's attorneys was finally entered on 19 August 1927, which was approved in Los Angeles Superior Court by Judge Guerin on 22 August 1927. Lita Grey withdrew her elaborate charges and asked for an interlocutory decree of divorce on the charge of extreme cruelty. A cross-complaint Chaplin had filed was also withdrawn. The settlement agreement provided Lita Grey with $825,000 ($625,000 for herself and $100,000 in trust for each son) and custody of the children.[24]

Financial, legal and personal trials of the magnitude suffered by Chaplin during this period would have destroyed a lesser man. It is a testament to Chaplin as a man and as an artist that he was able to overcome these difficulties. Chaplin's sheer determination to continue making *The Circus*, and the public's affection for him and his art would prevail. Throughout the eight month hiatus, Chaplin sought refuge in New York City. The influential press of that city supported him, its society embraced and entertained him and its citizenry delighted him with mountains of fan mail. Chaplin would never forget how the city of New York rejuvenated him during this difficult period. In appreciation, Chaplin rewarded his loyal New York admirers by holding the world premiere of *The Circus* in Manhattan on 6 January 1928 at the Mark Strand Theatre.

After eight months of inactivity, Chaplin finally returned to his studio on 23 August 1927 and resumed production of *The Circus* on 6 September 1927. The film was virtually complete at the time of the suspension; the material shot in the remaining weeks after work resumed was to fill out and refine what had already been photographed. Chaplin, upon his return, spent time cutting and titling the picture. Ever the perfectionist, Chaplin would shoot 211,104 feet of film (on one camera) which were reduced to 6,500 feet, the length of the finished film.[25] In these final weeks there was to be, however, one last trial to beset the production of *The Circus*. On 11 October, the production unit discovered that the circus wagons, which were to be used in the final scene of the picture, were missing. The police discovered that they had been taken by some students to be used for a bonfire. An entire freshman class was arrested, but Chaplin declined to prosecute. The wagons were subsequently returned. Although minor in comparison with the other catastrophes, the wagon incident was but a final salvo to barrage the most difficult production of Chaplin's professional life.

These nightmarish incidents that besieged Chaplin during the production of *The Circus* inevitably sullied his recollections of this period of his life. Perhaps this enervating production history explains why Chaplin failed to devote one word to *The Circus* in his principle volume of autobiography and why he neglected to revive the film for so many years after its initial release. Jerry Epstein, Chaplin's long-time friend and assistant, explained Chaplin's dismissive view of the film in this way:

> The affair [the divorce to Lita Grey] coloured all Charlie's memories of *The Circus* – which, despite the pressures and interruptions, emerged as a charming film with a light, improvised feel. But Charlie could only remember the heartaches behind the scenes. When the film was re-released in 1970, Charlie was thrilled at how modern audiences responded and all bitter associations faded.[26]

The Circus as autobiography

Inevitably any critical study of *The Circus* leads to the inescapable conclusion that the nature of the film is intensely autobiographical. *The Circus* stands as the filmmaker's attempt to explore, confront and perhaps even release issues deeply personal to him at a given time in his life. The central theme of *The Circus*, the clown's struggle with the comic muse, mirrors Chaplin's trepidation that his dissatisfying personal life was quashing his ability to create comedy. Another vehicle for Chaplin's catharsis, comic devices evoking terror, reflects the struggles Chaplin faced during the difficult production of the film.

The Circus has the most self-referential narrative premise of Chaplin's silent films. The film is an exploration of the nature of Chaplin's own art – the art of making people laugh. Only in Limelight would Chaplin revisit this highly personal theme. In The Circus, Chaplin portrays the Tramp as a circus performer who is funny when he does not mean to be and who is unfunny when he tries to get laughs. This dichotomy inevitably reflects Chaplin's own deepest fears – that as a director and as a performer he would be unable to equal the comedic artistry he had realised in The Gold Rush.

Further exacerbating Chaplin's artistic self-consciousness was his strained relationship with Lita Grey. No doubt when the equestrienne becomes the cause of the Tramp losing his ability to be funny, Chaplin in real life believed that Lita Grey was inducing a similar effect. Lita Grey, in her divorce complaint, alleges that Chaplin once exclaimed: 'Go away some place for awhile; I can't work or create when you are here. You are ruining my career'.[27]

The seminal idea which inspired The Circus, the Tramp on the tightrope beset by three escaped monkeys, is suggestive of the nightmarish setbacks that besieged Chaplin throughout The Circus' production history. In The Circus, terror and agony are transformed into sequences which amuse Chaplin's ever demanding audience, a reflection on the painful process of creating comedy.

As the monkeys attack the Tramp, teetering perilously on the rope, the little fellow attempts to realise his dream of winning the girl's love and usurping Rex, the king of the air. His attempt is a failure and before an entire audience he must suffer this failure. The Tramp's safety-belt comes loose, he loses his trousers and is attacked by monkeys. It is one of the most interesting passages in all of Chaplin's work. For some, it is Chaplin at his comic best. Others, like Alexander Bakshy, found the scene unsettling:

> This latter scene, however, includes a struggle with monkeys which strikes a somewhat alien, discordant note. Its scarcely premeditated effect may be ascribed to the change in the dra-

matic style of the scene which from a situation artificial and farcical passes into realism and borders upon tragedy.[28]

Near tragedy, terror and agony are transformed into comedy throughout the film. When the Tramp is chased into the big top by the police, his terror and agony are recast into an act to amuse the public. Although the Tramp is actually a terrified fugitive, the circus audiences see him as nothing more than a funny man. Another terrifying experience, the little fellow's flight from the donkey, is the source of another public success.

Chaplin himself was fearful of performing before live audiences after he left Karno [29] for a career in films.[30] Chaplin's dramatisation of the Tramp's failure with the circus spectators (in a much greater and nightmarish degree than any scene in Limelight) illustrates that even over a decade after his meteoric rise from stage to film, Chaplin still harboured such terror toward live performances. It is telling that this secret fear would surface in a work where Chaplin was plagued with a heightened awareness of the potential price of failure.

Chaplin's filming of sequences in which the Tramp must face terrifying animals further evinces the notion that the production period of The Circus was the most terrifying of Chaplin's career. The little fellow's flights from an irate donkey, for example, become a circus routine to amuse the demanding audience. It is the donkey who chases the Tramp into the lion's cage where the bulldog barks at him (threatening to wake the slumbering lion) despite the little fellow's pleas to go away. The dog persists and bites the Tramp's trouser leg, refusing to let go. The tightrope sequence finds the little fellow attacked by three escaped monkeys. Even when biting an apple, the Tramp encounters a worm.

It is worth noting that the Tramp does leave the lion's cage and the tightrope unharmed. This is perhaps symbolic of Chaplin's own troubles; like the Tramp, Chaplin entered the struggle and endured danger yet left the predicament relatively unscathed.

Therefore, despite the ostensibly negative aspects of autobiographical comedy steeped in terror, the Tramp's narrow escapes throughout the film were perhaps subconsciously placed to assure the audience (and perhaps Chaplin himself) of the resilience of both Chaplin and the Tramp in the face of danger and almost insurmountable odds.

Chaplin's romantic triangle

The Circus, as with the other silent Chaplin feature-length comedies, is essentially a refinement of the Chaplin short films. Influences upon *The Circus* can be found from many of his early films, the most important being *The Tramp* (1915), *The Vagabond* (1916) and *Sunnyside* (1919). These three earlier films, like *The Circus*, explore the romanticism of the Tramp. The same romantic triangle exists in all of these films.

In the Essanay two-reeler, *The Tramp*, the Tramp saves a farmer's daughter (Edna Purviance) from some thieving toughs and subsequently aborts their attempt to rob the farm. The little fellow falls in love with the girl, but upon the appearance of the girl's handsome young fiance, the Tramp realises the true situation. He quietly leaves the farm, leaving a note to the girl:

> i thout your kindness was love but it ain't cause i seen him.

The Tramp then makes his classic fade-out for the first time, shuffling down a country road with his back to the camera. Chaplin was to develop and perfect this ending in *The Circus*. The closing moments of the *The Circus* find the little fellow standing within what was the centre ring of the circus. The Tramp settles on an abandoned crate and wistfully reflects on his fate. As he sits quietly, his gaze turns forlornly toward a paper star – not unlike the one the equestrienne had joyfully burst through in the opening scene of the film. Chaplin takes the paper star and for one moment the great clown directs his eyes toward the camera – thereby involving the audience in a way that he had not in *The Tramp*. This act of inclusion affords the sequence a heightened sense of poignancy as the Tramp shuffles off toward new horizons.

In the Mutual two-reeler, *The Vagabond*, the little fellow is a street musician who saves a Gypsy drudge (Edna Purviance) from the cruel Gypsies (who anticipate the cruel step-father of *The Circus*). The Tramp loves the little drudge, but a handsome young artist encounters the girl and they fall in love. Before the film's happy conclusion, there is a scene

in which the artist and the girl's long-lost mother take the girl away from the Tramp, leaving the little fellow disconsolate. Again, Chaplin has employed the triangle of the Tramp, the young girl and the handsome young man who takes the girl away from the little fellow.

Finally, in the three-reel First National film *Sunnyside*, the Tramp is a farm-hand who finds he has a rival in the city chap for the affections of the girl (Edna Purviance). The subtitle 'His last hope' introduces the little fellow in a feeble attempt to imitate the city chap, supplementing his best clothes with stockings over his boots to suggest the city chap's spats and his bamboo walking-stick which, through home-made modification, attempts to suggest the city chap's cane with its built-in lighter for his cigarettes. The little fellow's attempts to mirror the city chap prefigures the Tramp's fruitless attempts to dress in Rex's clothes and assume the mantle of the tightrope walker.

The romantic triangle is the most obvious example of earlier ideas which were to be reworked and fully developed in *The Circus*. The constant employment of the romantic triangle mantra also suggests something of the character of Chaplin the man. Indeed, Chaplin once mused: 'I am physically not equipped for romantic roles. I am no Valentino'.[31] Yet in *The Circus*, romanticism is arguably at its most intense – more so than in *City Lights*, a 'Comedy Romance in Pantomime' which tells the story of the little fellow's love for a blind flower-girl. It is the Tramp in *The Circus* who is blind: blind to success, to the hopelessness of his quest, to everything but the beautiful little equestrienne. Indeed, Chaplin's idolatry of women reaches its apogee in *The Circus*. The Tramp worshiping the equestrienne from afar manifests the purest example of Chaplin placing his leading lady on a pedestal.

The Circus as a reflection of the 1920s

The Circus is a reflection of its time, a creation of the late 1920s. Three aspects of the decade weave their way into the film, providing a window through which film historians can understand this remarkable era of American life and filmmaking. Unabashed indulgence, the cinema inspired by E.A. Dupont's *Variété* (Variety, 1925) and the birth of the 'talkies', all provide the canvas upon which

Chaplin paints his *The Circus*. Hints of Chaplin's preoccupation with each of these developments can be found throughout the film.

Like the decade of indulgence that spawned it, *The Circus* lavishly eschews any notions of economy in film production. Indeed, one of the film's outstanding qualities is its high production values, most noticeably prevalent in the authenticity of the circus atmosphere. The one-ring circus created by Charles 'Danny' Hall, the film's designer, is superb. The exemplary designs were further highlighted by the circus animals and the numerous extras engaged to create an authentic circus atmosphere. Chaplin's attention to the authenticity of his cinematic worlds would lessen in his subsequent films, opting in later years for inexpensive process screens rather than constructing authentic environs. Chaplin was certainly not the only filmmaker engaging in elaborate film production with *The Circus*. One need only look at the films of Chaplin's friend and United Artists partner, Douglas Fairbanks, whose *Douglas Fairbanks in Robin Hood* (1922) and *The Thief of Bagdad* (1924) were the apex of costly, larger-than-life cinema. In a time when Americans indulged themselves on bathtub gin, Babe Ruth and the Charleston, filmmakers had to compete for popular attention by providing comparable spectacle in the cinema.

The Circus is one of many films that exploited a genre which thrived in the 1920s as a result of E.A. Dupont's influential film *Variety*, which explored the world of the variety stage, inspiring many filmmakers of the 1920s to create pictures concerning music-hall, theatre or circus life. The menagerie of a circus gave Chaplin the opportunity to use a wide selection of props to engender comedic circumstances. Indeed, Chaplin had originally decided to make a film about the circus expressly for that purpose. Not unlike the commedia dell'arte, Chaplin chose a setting first, knowing that comic situations would develop from the location. Some film critics and historians have posited that Chaplin's influences during the filming of *The Circus* stretched beyond *Variety* to early classic examples of clowning. According to a *New York Times* article, Chaplin had studied the early traditions of clowning as traced in M. Willson Disher's book *Clowns and Pantomimes* in preparation for filming *The Circus*.[32] Chaplin's link to clowns of the past

was not a novel conception. As a result of the tremendous success of *The Gold Rush*, the intellectual critics had begun to crown Chaplin a counterpart to such great clowns as Grimaldi and Grock. M. Willson Disher suggests *The Circus* when he writes that: 'Charlie Chaplin begins as a half-wit, grows into an artful dodger and threatens to develop the theme of a clown's unrequited love in a serious cinema tragedy'.[33] Created at the height of Chaplin's fame and popularity, *The Circus* embodies the traditions of both popular cinema and classic clowning influential to Chaplin as an artist in the 1920s.

Perhaps the greatest influence on Chaplin's psyche, however, as he began to piece together the comic routines, situations and circumstances that would become *The Circus* was the arrival of talking pictures. It is a well known fact of cinema history that Chaplin was the final hold-out against dialogue films. Refusing to let go of the art he had pioneered and perfected, Chaplin continued to make silent pictures right up until the little fellow reluctantly shared his gibberish swan song with the world in *Modern Times* (1936). In 1927, talkies were still a novelty, but the spectre of sound film was not lost on Chaplin. Nowhere is this conflict more evident than in the final sequence of *The Circus*. As the Tramp sits alone in what once was the centre ring of the circus, Chaplin's metaphor is apparent. Not unlike Chaplin, the Tramp arrived at the circus and revolutionised the slapstick comedy that no longer pleased the audience. The Tramp had been wildly successful for a time under the big top, but now that time has passed. The show is now moving on, leaving the Tramp alone in the very spot where he had enjoyed his great success. Chaplin must have felt the same profound isolation, as his fears that talking pictures may soon leave him and his subtle artistry behind. Chaplin began shooting the film's final sequence on 10 October 1927, four days after the premiere of *The Jazz Singer* (1927). Indeed, the musical score for this scene makes a direct reference to *The Jazz Singer*. When Chaplin and Arthur Kay compiled a score for the premiere of *The Circus* (see below), Chaplin completes his metaphor by underscoring the film's final sequence with one of the songs that had made *The Jazz Singer* a popular success – Irving Berlin's 'Blue Skies'. Chaplin rejected Al Jolson's exuberant rendition of the Berlin standard, opting instead to have it played slowly and sorrowfully. It is the final ironic comment in *The Circus*, one of the finest films of the 1920s and the last Chaplin film made in the silent film era.

The lion's cage

The Tramp trapped in the lion's cage is one of the most memorable sequences in *The Circus*. Indeed, it is as perfectly conceived, choreographed and executed as any sequence in all of Chaplin's work. A possible influence for this sequence is Max Linder, who in his feature *Seven Years Bad Luck* (1921) enters a lion cage to elude the police.[34] Prior to filming the lion sequence, Chaplin had rehearsed a sequence which involved snakes and would later, when the lion scene was virtually finished, film a sequence which included several tigers.[35] Unlike the Tramp's encounter with the lion, the snake and tiger scenes were later discarded. According to the daily production reports, shooting began on the lion sequence on 4 August 1926. Chaplin would continue to refine the scene over the next two weeks of shooting, as indicated by the bit of business with the bulldog, which was to be incorporated into the sequence on 7 August 1926. Chaplin tentatively finished the scene on 13 August, after nine days work, edited the scene and shot retakes on 17 August 1926. The daily production report of 20 August indicates that Chaplin was finished with the lion segment and was now 'Cutting and working on balance of story'.[36] Ever the perfectionist, 25 August found Chaplin again shooting the lion sequence. This would be the final day he would devote to this important sequence of the film. After three weeks of work, Chaplin had made more than 200 takes in the lion's cage.

The finished lion sequence lasts only three minutes (at 24 frames per second), indicating the care and precision Chaplin spent on this scene.[37] In the completed film, a tiger only briefly appears when Charlie opens a small hatch in the lion cage revealing a snarling tiger in an adjacent wagon.

L'Estrange Fawcett, the British film critic for the *London Morning Post,* recorded his impressions of watching Chaplin film the lion's cage sequence in both the *New York Times* and in his book *Film: Facts and Forecasts*.[38] Fawcett corroborates that the lion cage sequence was a special one for Chaplin, who considered it the only true 'gag' in the picture. Fawcett quotes Chaplin as saying:

> In this film we have a continuous working story and this scene with the cage is the only bit that can really be called a gag. In other words, we are interrupting the story momentarily to put this scene in. Hence, it must be exactly right, otherwise we shall spoil the general sense and upset the audience. You are only entitled to switch from the main theme if the switching is worth while.[39]

Chaplin evidently thought this endeavour to be worthwhile, demanding countless rehearsals and retakes. In recounting Chaplin's arduous work schedule with this scene, Fawcett observed Chaplin lament: 'I'm tired out and my clothes are wringing wet with the heat'[40] after a day's work. Despite his fatigue and the constant heat, Chaplin worked diligently on the sequence. He would rehearse his part without the lion in the cage, showing the cameramen exactly what he wanted to be photographed. Chaplin would then indicate to the lion trainer what was expected from the lion. Fawcett recalls Chaplin explaining this method:

> 'Look, I'll show you just what we want', says Mr. Chaplin and he lies on the ground in the corner imitating the lion. He moves, grunts and bares his teeth. He hunches round the cage on all fours, rolls over in the dust, feet and arms in the air and rubs his back artfully against the bars.[41]

Chaplin acting out every part – even the roles of the animals – was part of his directorial method. It was a difficult sequence for Chaplin, as the animals in the sequence, a lion, a tiger and a bulldog, did not take the exact direction to which the master filmmaker was accustomed. Captain Charles Gay, the lion trainer, had to induce the lion with various odours (meat, garlic, perfume) in order for the lion to adopt the proper attitude Chaplin wanted (twitch, bare its teeth, etc.). In fact, two lions were used in the scene. According to David Robinson:

> Two animals were hired (at a cost of $150 a day, including the trainer). One was docile, but the other was a spirited creature. In at least one scene that appears in the finished film, as

Chaplin would unashamedly point out in later years, the fear on his face was not pretence.[42]

The bulldog (named Buddy), the other key four-legged player in the scene, had to bite Chaplin's leg at a certain moment. The dog had its own trainer, Henry East. Chaplin had to wear a special leather legging to prevent the bulldog's sharp teeth from tearing into his flesh.

When Chaplin was behind the camera in rehearsals, Harry Crocker would 'play' Chaplin's role. Fawcett recalls Crocker having to play the Tramp in the lion's cage the particular Saturday Fawcett happened to be watching. Harry Crocker, in his memoirs, writes:

> One of the more curious facets of my job was playing Charlie Chaplin in rehearsals. When a scene had been set to Chaplin's satisfaction, he would retire to the camera and cry, 'All right, let's see it!' With Chaplin's famous battered derby upon the top of my head – I stand an even six feet – and with the limber cane in my hand, I would run through the actions of the scene with the other members of the cast.

It was no surprise when Chaplin would explode at me, 'No, no, no, he wouldn't do that!' and leap into the fray to play the scene himself.[43]

Given the endless rehearsals, the heat and the dangers with the animals, the labour involved in filming the scene was extraordinary. After watching a day's shooting, Fawcett observed simply: 'I don't believe Mr. Chaplin enjoyed the experience very much'.[44]

The tightrope

The seminal idea which inspired The Circus was the climatic scene of the Tramp on the tightrope. Cha-

Fig. 4. The Tramp in the lion's cage. Chaplin considered this sequence the only true 'gag' in the film. [Copyright Roy Export Company Establishment.]

plin's only comments on the scene are found in his last volume of autobiography, My Life in Pictures:

> The big scene of The Circus is when I have to take the place of the tight-rope walker at the last moment and a safety-belt enables me to make a spectacular start; but then I discover it has come loose just as some monkeys who have escaped from their cage begin to crawl all over my face.[45]

The sequence was influenced by the aerial scenes in Dupont's Variety, as well as the moment in Harold Lloyd's Safety Last (1923) where Lloyd, attempting to climb a skyscraper, is besieged by several pigeons. However, Chaplin's construction of an encounter with mischievous creatures while in danger would be uniquely his own. Chaplin had used thrill comedy as early as the Keystone one-reeler *The New Janitor* (1914). Arguably his most memorable use of this comedic genre was in the climax of *The Gold Rush*, where the Tramp and his prospector partner Big Jim McKay try to escape their storm-ravaged cabin that is dangerously teetering on the edge of a precipice. The tightrope scene, however, demanded great labour on the tightrope itself, not merely the reliance upon models (as with *The Gold Rush*) to convince the audience of the danger. To make the tightrope sequence believable, Chaplin would have to summon skills from his earliest comedic training with Karno. It was Chaplin's employment of difficult physical comedy sequences throughout his films that had convinced audiences he was a man who could seemingly do anything.

In an unidentified interview, Henry Bergman explains that it was he who taught Chaplin to walk the tightrope:

> I taught Charlie to walk a rope in one week … We stretched the rope this high from the floor [he indicated a foot high to the interviewer] then raised it as high as the ceiling with a net under it, but Charlie never fell. He walked it all day long. You didn't see anything in the picture of what he did on that rope.[46]

Along with Chaplin, Harry Crocker learned to walk the tightrope. It was Crocker's natural athletic ability that won him the role of Rex, the tightrope walker. According to Harry Crocker:

> It was characteristic of Chaplin that he determined to shoot the tightrope scenes on an actual tightrope stretched thirty-seven feet above the sawdust between two giant tent poles. This necessitated the building of a series of platforms beneath the rope in case of a spill. Giant parallels were constructed for the cameras. In any other studio, the rope would have been located above the stage floor with a tent top in correct perspective above it, thus enabling the camera staff to work in comfort on the stage floor level. As part of the preparation of the film, Chaplin learned to walk the tightrope. Again, in any other studio, technical experts and actual circus tightrope walkers would have

been engaged to instruct the star. With his fetish for doing everything himself, Charlie had a rope stretched about a foot above the stage floor. With a pole he set out to master the art himself. While he was resting from the arduous exercise, I essayed the task. In a short time we were walking a rope eighteen feet above the stage … As a result of my proficiency, and the fact it would save salary, Charlie cast me in the role of the circus tightrope star, 'Rex, King of the Air'.[47]

The tightrope scene, executed perfectly in the film, involved an enormous amount of effort. The tightrope sequence was the first to be filmed on 13 January 1926 and also the last, a series of retakes on 7 November 1927. In all, Chaplin shot more than 700 takes on the tightrope. Technically, the camera placements for the tightrope scene are excellent (indeed this is true of the entire film, most notably the 'Mirror Maze' sequence) and Chaplin's method of infinite practice to make his actions appear seamless and natural had paid off. Once again, however, he was to deal with animals that were not inclined to take Chaplin's exact direction. Three monkeys were to attack the Tramp on the tightrope. In the finished film the scene flows easily, but at the expense of many calculated risks as well as physical pain. One monkey bites Chaplin's nose twice and his nose becomes discoloured despite the greasepaint make-up he is wearing. Also noticeable upon careful inspection is that the monkeys have fine string leashes around their necks. Judging by the tension given to the strings, a production member off-camera must have been tugging at the strings and directing the monkeys to the desired movements. No doubt this was also a precaution to protect Chaplin himself as the aggressive monkeys were dangerously close to his face. Only Chaplin's unyielding dedication as a filmmaker could sustain him to continually retake a sequence which involved monkeys biting his nose, scratching his face and placing their tails in his mouth. The finished sequence, however, is a triumphant dance of physical comedy. The scene contains escalating comedy alongside the thrill of the little fellow's peril and embarrassment, giving the scene a balance and rhythm absent in the thrill sequences of Harold Lloyd.

Fig. 5. The climax of *The Circus*: the Tramp on the tightrope beset by three escaped monkeys. [Copyright Roy Export Company Establishment.]

The use of monkeys was common currency in film comedy, but Chaplin's film seems to have triggered ideas in Harold Lloyd and Buster Keaton. Although Lloyd used a monkey briefly in *Dr. Jack* (1922), Lloyd and Keaton both enlisted monkeys to a greater degree following Chaplin's filming of a monkey sequence for *The Circus*. A monkey is the scene-stealer in Harold Lloyd's *The Kid Brother* (1927) and Buster Keaton used a playful primate throughout *The Cameraman* (1928). That the three great silent clowns should all incorporate a monkey or a monkey sequence into a film of around the same period is unlikely coincidental. Since Chaplin began shooting *The Circus*' tightrope sequences as early as January 1926, it is not unlikely that contemporary comedians were influenced by Chaplin's use of monkeys. It is possible that information regarding the monkey sequence was leaked out and Lloyd and Keaton set about to incorporate a monkey in their own films.

The finale

Chaplin's only documented recollection regarding the memorable ending of *The Circus* is found in *My Life In Pictures*. Chaplin writes: 'The film has a poetic and touching ending, with the circus slowly packing up and moving off, leaving me quite alone on the deserted ground'.[48] Although Chaplin had used the Tramp taking to the road to great effect in the Essanay two-reeler *The Tramp*, the image of the Tramp alone at the conclusion of a film is uncommon for Chaplin's mature silent features. The final moments of *The Gold Rush*, *City Lights* and *Modern Times* all find the Tramp paired with (albeit, however, intermittently) the girl. Perhaps the reason for this anomaly (the Tramp alone at the end of *The Circus*) lies in the personal torment Chaplin had undergone during the production of the film. Following his difficult marriage, separation and divorce from Lita Grey, Chaplin must have felt truly alone. This mood is reflected in *The Circus'* haunting finale, which has the distinction of being the saddest ending of all Chaplin's silent films. Theodore Huff has noted:

> Toward the close of the film, he had the daring to turn his personal troubles to advantage before the camera. The last scene was deliberately photographed in the harsh, early morning light to bring out the careworn lines of his face. This adds great poignancy to his representation of the tragic emotions of the eternal frustrated misfit.[49]

Chaplin gave special consideration to the filming of the final sequence of the film, as indicated by the following contemporary description of Chaplin at work on 10 and 11 October 1927, reprinted in David Robinson's *Chaplin: His Life and Art*. Although the moving conclusion of *The Circus* truly speaks for itself, the unidentified reporter's description is reproduced here to provide a sense of how Chaplin accomplished the filming of this memorable scene.

> Perspiring men rush about the Chaplin studio. Carpenters, painters, electricians, technical minds, labourers. Charlie must not be held up. A caravan of circus wagons are hitched on behind four huge motor trucks. They start for Cahuenga Pass. A long and hard pull to Glendale. The location is flooded with light. It comes from all directions. The dynamo wagon hums. So the men work through the night.
>
> Daylight breaks. The morning is cold. Cracklings echo from a dozen fires. It is an unusual Californian crispness. Cars begin to arrive. The roar of exhausts signals their coming. There is an extra-loud rumbling. The big blue limousine comes to a stop. *The Circus* must be finished. Everyone is on time. Cameras are set up. Now the sun is holding things up. Why doesn't it hurry and come up over the mountains? It is long shadows the Tramp wants.
>
> Six o'clock and half the morning wasted. The edge of the circus ring is too dark. It doesn't look natural. The Tramp refuses to work artificially. Men start to perspire again. Thirty minutes later the soft voice speaks, 'Fine! That's fine! Let's shoot!'

> Cameras grind. Circus wagons move across the vast stretch of open space. There is a beautiful haze in the background. The horses and the wagon wheels cause clouds of dust. The picture is gorgeous. No artist would be believed should he paint it. Twenty times the scene is taken.
>
> The cameras move in close to the ring. Carefully the operators measure the distance. From the lens to the tramp. He is alone in the centre of the ring.
>
> He rehearses. Then action for camera. Eighty feet. The business is done again. And again! And again! Fifty persons are looking on. All members of the company. There are few eyes that are not moist. Most of them know the story. They knew the meaning of this final 'shot'.
>
> 'How was that?' came inquiring from the Tramp. Fifty heads nodded in affirmation. 'Then we'll take it again; just once more', spoke the man in the baggy pants and derby hat and misfit coat and dreadnought shoes. The sun was getting high. The long shadows became shorter and shorter. 'Call it a day', said the Tramp, 'we'll be here again tomorrow at four'.

Chaplin is then described watching the day's rushes at three o'clock the following morning:

> The little fellow in the big black leather chair was no longer the Tramp. But he was watching him on the screen. Charlie Chaplin was passing judgment. 'He should do that much better'. 'He doesn't ring true'. 'He has his derby down too far over his eyes'. 'They have burned his face up with those reflectors'. A severe critic, this Chaplin. The Tramp doesn't please him. The stuff must be retaken. A leap from the leather chair. Speed, dust, location.[50]

Chaplin was satisfied that he had captured the feeling of isolation and melancholy on film after some additional retakes on 14 October. As the above commentary suggests, *The Circus'* ending sequence contains the essence of Chaplin: his humanity, his humour and his genius. The emotional element of the final scene cannot be adequately expressed in words. Suffice it to state that the finale of *The Circus*, like the ending of *City Lights*, tran-

Fig. 6. The haunting finale of *The Circus*. [Copyright Roy Export Company Establishment.]

scends the mere implication of heart to the sublime suggestion of soul.

The premiere film score of 1928

Musical accompaniment was always a major concern to Chaplin. L'Estrange Fawcett, a British journalist who visited the set of *The Circus* to interview Chaplin, recounts Chaplin's interest in the musical accompaniment provided to his films:

> 'Music is extremely important', he [Chaplin] said; 'that is why I welcome the efforts being made to provide music by mechanical systems, such as the De Forest and the Vitaphone. Mechanical music which has the quality of a symphony orchestra is much better as an accompaniment than feeble vamping on a piano or the excruciating efforts of an incompetent and ill-led orchestra'.[51]

Chaplin was a self-taught musician with a gift for melody. Through the Charlie Chaplin Music Publishing Company, Chaplin published three songs he composed: 'There's Always One You Can't Forget' (1916), 'Oh That Cello!' (1916) and 'The

Peace Patrol' (1916). In the 1920s, Chaplin composed themes for *The Kid* and *The Idle Class*, published two more songs: 'Sing a Song' (1925) and 'With You Dear in Bombay' (1925) and helped prepare the cue sheets and compile accompaniments for the premiere performances of *A Woman of Paris* and *The Gold Rush*. For *The Circus*, Chaplin demonstrated a similar interest in musical accompaniment and engaged Arthur Kay to help compile appropriate music for the film. Kay was a conductor who previously had been with the Boston Symphony Orchestra. In a distinguished career, Kay would hold such positions as general music director of Fox Movietone and music director of the LA Civic Light Opera.

The Charles Chaplin Film Corporation daily production reports indicate that Chaplin began preparing the musical score with Kay after the first preview of *The Circus*, which was held at the Alex Theatre, Glendale, California on 28 October 1927. The task for Chaplin and Kay was to compile fitting pre-existing music to accompany the finished film. Operatic, dance band, popular and incidental music were incorporated into the score. To complement the opening moments of the film, Chaplin and

Kay chose music from Leoncavallo's *I Pagliacci* to emphasise that the film was Chaplin's version of the Pagliacci story. For the Tramp's bravado in the lion's cage, the pair chose the Toreador song from Bizet's *Carmen* as a musical joke to emphasise the little fellow's false bravery (for he is hardly a toreador). For the Tramp on the high wire, unaware that his safety belt has become detached, a dance band arrangement of James P. Johnston's 'Charleston' was employed to underscore the little fellow's frantic dance on the tightrope. Similar fast-paced music, Minot's 'Hurry No. 26', accompanies the Tramp being beset by the mischievous monkeys on the wire. Finally, for the dramatic ending for the film, Chaplin chose an arrangement of Irving Berlin's 'Blue Skies' which was to be played in a slow legato.

The completed score was first utilised at the film's premiere at the Mark Strand Theatre on 6 January 1928 and was used continually at the Strand for the original run of the film. After 1928, the score remained unperformed until Gillian Anderson, music specialist in the Library of Congress Music Division, was invited in April 1992 to do an inventory of music material from the silent era at the Chaplin archives in Vevey, Switzerland. In the basement archives of the Chaplin estate, Anderson discovered that Chaplin had preserved the original scores and orchestral parts to the premiere performances of *A Woman of Paris*, *The Gold Rush* and *The Circus*. The Chaplin family was particularly interested in a performance of *The Circus* with its original score. Roy Export Company Establishment (the company which distributes the Chaplin-owned film properties) consented to Anderson conducting live orchestral presentations of the film with its original musical accompaniment. Roy Export also prepared new 35 mm prints for these performances. The premiere was held at the Library of Congress, Washington, DC in October 1992 and enjoyed performances in Los Angeles (March 1993) and New York City (February 1994).[52]

The 1928 score illustrates that popular music choices lend an extra dimension to an audience's understanding of the action of the film. Chaplin deliberately chose music for *The Circus* that would be familiar to audiences in the 1920s. The popular music, underscoring a certain segment of the action, could assist the audience in knowing what a character was thinking or feeling. When the bareback

rider first meets Rex, for example, the music Chaplin chose was 'For I'm Falling in Love with Someone'. A close-up of the equestrienne's face accompanied by this song provided the audience with all the information they needed to understand how the girl felt upon seeing Rex for the first time. Similarly, for the ending of the film Chaplin employed the Berlin ballad 'Blue Skies'. Audiences in 1928 were familiar with Berlin's lyrics and therefore knew what the little fellow was feeling as the circus wagons pulled away without him. The music Chaplin chose for the premiere score, therefore, fit the film expertly not only in terms of action, but also in adding an extra emotional element to the thoughts and feelings of the characters. This technique undoubtedly enriches an audiences viewing of the film through heightening their awareness of the characters thoughts and emotions.

The reissue film score of 1970

In 1968, Chaplin began work on his own original musical score for the theatrical reissue of *The Circus*. William Lambert Williamson, who had worked with Chaplin previously with the music of *A Countess From Hong Kong* (1967), is credited in the reissue version for the score's arrangement. As he had done with *A Countess From Hong Kong*, Williamson extended and arranged Chaplin's musical ideas. Eric James, who had also worked with Chaplin on the music for *The Chaplin Revue* (1959) and *A Countess From Hong Kong* (and would assist Chaplin throughout the 1970s on other reissues), is credited as musical associate. Chaplin cut the film slightly (removing unnecessary intertitles), but left the action of the film itself intact for the reissue.

The music Chaplin composed for the reissue is quite different from the premiere score of 1928. Instead of the operatic, dance band, popular and incidental music which were standard in the 1920s, the reissue score utilises techniques of 19th century theatre music, which had permeated Chaplin's boyhood. Gillian Anderson compares the two scores thus:

> In a sense, the music for the 1928 score emphasises the slapstick aspects of the film and the reissue version shows his evolution as a composer and heightens the pathetic aspect of

Fig. 7. Filming the tightrope sequence of *The Circus*. [Copyright Roy Export Company Establishment.]

the film. It's a question of taste. Both scores are great. One happens to be of a younger man and the other reflects forty years of experience – musical and otherwise – and also a different phase and age of the man.[53]

For the opening of the reissue version of *The Circus*, Chaplin replaced *I Pagliacci* with a ballad entitled 'Swing, Little Girl'. Chaplin sang the expressive lyrical ballad himself over remade opening credits. In place of Bizet's Toreador song from *Carmen*, Chaplin underscored the lion sequence with a simple vamp complemented by an ominous lion theme (to mimic the lion's yawn) interspersed with a dainty string phrase (to emphasise the Tramp's caution). For the sequence where the high-wire walking Tramp encounters the bites and paws of the monkeys, Chaplin had initially employed Minot's 'Hurry No. 26' to mirror the action. For the reissue, Chaplin chose a slow, pleasant waltz as an effective counterpoint to the chaotic action. Finally, for the

ending of the film, instead of Berlin's 'Blue Skies', Chaplin began the closing sequence with a dramatic fanfare (in a minor key) as the circus wagons pull away leaving the Tramp alone in the centre ring. Following the fanfare, Chaplin employs a ballad (still in the minor key) which builds its sad melody to a crescendo as the Tramp walks down his lonely road.

On the whole, Chaplin's 1970 reissue score conveys a more effective marriage of image and sound.[54] Like so much of his music, the best word to describe Chaplin's 1970 reissue score of *The Circus* is quite simply that it is Chaplinesque and indeed some of the finest music Chaplin ever composed.

Conclusion

In 1929, the first year the Academy of Motion Picture Arts and Sciences presented awards for excellence in filmmaking, Charles Chaplin received a Special Award for *The Circus*. The citation on the statuette captures his total commitment as an artist to the production of a film. It reads: 'Charles Chaplin for versatility and genius in writing, acting, directing and producing *The Circus*'. Despite this tribute and the commercial and critical success of the film, Chaplin chose to bury *The Circus*. Following the most catastrophic production history of his career, Chaplin could not bear the pain that images of *The Circus* evoked. Indeed, it was during the production of *The Circus* that Chaplin's greying hair turned white virtually overnight and he reportedly suffered a nervous breakdown.

It remains a testament to Chaplin's genius as a filmmaker and commitment to his art that *The Circus* ever reached the screen. Despite the many trials that beset the production, Chaplin ultimately summoned the strength to construct a beautiful film, complex in its emotions and sublime in its execution. It is unfortunate that Chaplin was unable to look toward these qualities of the film and not the agonising personal and professional troubles that accompanied its creation.

Now, nearly seventy years after *The Circus'* initial release, modern commentators and audiences are in an unique position to savour this remarkable film. Once relegated to infrequent revivals and a dearth of critical analysis, *The Circus* now enjoys a renaissance. The CBS/Fox laser disc version of the film, as well as the current theatrical revivals, ensure its reassessment. Charlie Chaplin's *The Circus* deserves to be elevated to the critical status of his other silent masterworks. The time has come to recognise *The Circus* as a true Chaplin masterpiece.❖

Acknowledgements: I would like to record a special thanks to three friends: to Jon Bouker, Jr. for his excellent suggestions which helped shape this monograph, to David Shepard for invaluable advice and encouragement and to Pamela Paumier of Roy Export Company Establishment for her support and for making available material from the Chaplin archives.

Notes

1.   Charles Chaplin, *My Autobiography* (London: The Bodley Head, 1964). Chaplin mentions the film in passing within the context of his mother's death. He records that while filming *The Circus*, his mother had died (page 288). Actually, Hannah Chaplin died 28 August 1928, during the production of *City Lights*. Of Chaplin's other autobiographical volumes, only *My Life in Pictures* (London: The Bodley Head, 1974) discusses the film.

2.   *New York Times*, 29 November 1925 section 8 page 5. Theodore Huff in *Charlie Chaplin* (New York: Henry Schuman, 1951), 208 and David Robinson in *Chaplin: His Life and Art* (London: Collins, 1985), 360, write that Chaplin was considering a film version of Stevenson's *The Suicide Club*. However, L'Estrange Fawcett, in his book *Films: Facts and Forecasts* (London: Geoffrey Bles, 1930), 156, writes that Chaplin's *The Suicide Club* would be based on an original story and not on the Robert Louis Stevenson novella.

3.   *New York Times*, 29 November 1925 section 8, 5.

4.   Ira S. Jaffe, 'Chaplin's Labor of Performance: *The Circus* and *Limelight*', *Literature/Film Quarterly* 3 (1984): 202–210.

5.   Charles Chaplin Film Corporation daily production report (2 November 1925).

6.   David Robinson, *Chaplin: His Life and Art* (London: Collins, 1985), 360–361. Robinson identifies this source in his notes as 'Interview with Henry Bergman, in cutting from unidentified source'.

7.   Ibid, 367.

8.   Ibid, 363–365.

9.   Ibid, 366.

10. See Theodore Huff, *Charlie Chaplin* (New York: Henry Schuman, 1951), 208 and David Robinson, *Chaplin: His Life and Art* (London: Collins, 1985), 366. Georgia Hale's memoir, posthumously published as *Charlie Chaplin: Intimate Close-Ups*. Edited with introduction and notes by Heather Kiernan (Metuchen, NJ: Scarecrow Press, 1995), reveals no new information about Hale's leaving the Charles Chaplin Film Corporation for Paramount Pictures.

11. Lita Grey Chaplin in letter to the author, 29 November 1993.

12. David Robinson, *Chaplin: His Life and Art* (London: Collins, 1985), 360.

13. Charles Chaplin Film Corporation daily production report (12 February 1926).

14. Charles Chaplin Film Corporation daily production report (16 February 1926).

15. Charles Chaplin Film Corporation daily production report (28 September 1926). Roland Totheroh had the presence of mind to photograph 250 feet of the

studio fire and a frantic Chaplin. The footage was shown for publicity purposes in several metropolitan theatres which had booked *The Circus*. The footage of the studio fire survives in the Chaplin film vaults in England.

16. Ed Sullivan, *Chaplin vs. Chaplin*. Foreword by Walter E. Hurst and Frank Bacon (Los Angeles: Marvin Miller Enterprises, 1965), 13.

17. Interview with Lita Grey Chaplin in West Hollywood, California, 21 August 1993.

18. Interview with Lita Grey Chaplin in West Hollywood, California, 21 August 1993. This account is at variance with other accounts of the separation (see *New York Times*, 2 December 1926 section 1 page 1, the Lita Grey divorce complaint, reprinted in Ed Sullivan, *Chaplin vs. Chaplin* (Los Angeles: Marvin Miller Enterprises, 1965), as well as Lita Grey Chaplin's own memoir, *My Life with Chaplin* (New York: B. Geis, 1966)). In her explanation of the varying accounts, Lita Grey Chaplin told the author that she had very little to do with her divorce complaint, 'I was so young, I just left it to the lawyers'. As to errors in her memoir, she revealed that 'Morton Cooper rewrote my 600 page manuscript. As a result, there are errors in dates and how things actually happened'.

19. The complete divorce complaint and Chaplin's answer are reprinted in Ed Sullivan, *Chaplin vs. Chaplin*. Foreword by Walter E. Hurst and Frank Bacon (Los Angeles: Marvin Miller Enterprises, 1965).

20. See *New York Times*, 8 January 1927 section 1 page 19; 9 January 1927 section 1 page 8; 14 January 1927 section 1 page 15 and 15 January 1927 section 1 page 11 for an account of the *Pictorial Review* dispute. The Tully articles were published in *Pictorial Review* in four instalments (January–April 1927 issues) under the title 'Charlie Chaplin: His *Real* Life Story'.

21. See *New York Times*, 18 January 1927 section 1 page 1; 26 January 1927 section 1 page 9; 28 January 1927 section 1 page 7 regarding Chaplin's difficulties with the Internal Revenue Service. Chaplin finally settled with the IRS on 12 January 1928. See *New York Times* 10 February 1928 section 1 page 26.

22. Charles Chaplin Film Corporation daily production report (6 December 1926).

23. *New York Times*, 16 January 1927 section 1 page 5. Also, Roland Totheroh recalled that Toraichi Kono, Chaplin's valet, told him that Chaplin nearly committed suicide. Kono told Totheroh: 'I grabbed him. He was gonna jump out of that window.' Roland Totheroh in a 1964 interview with his family.

24. *New York Times*, 23 August 1927 section 1 page 1. According to David Robinson, the Lita Grey divorce settlement was 'the largest such settlement in American legal history to that time'. David Robinson, *Chaplin: His Life and Art* (London: Collins, 1985), 378.

25. Chaplin and Totheroh had to prepare two negatives (which were made on two cameras) for domestic and international release. An additional two negatives were created as back-ups should the primary negatives wear out.

26. Jerry Epstein, *Remembering Charlie* (New York: Doubleday, 1989), 23. Epstein assisted Chaplin with the 1970 reissue of *The Circus*. In an interview in London, England shortly before his death in 1991, Epstein told the author that, owing to the Lita Grey divorce, Chaplin could not look at the film objectively. It is for this reason that Chaplin dismissed *The Circus* and not because he thought it a minor work.

27. Ed Sullivan, *Chaplin vs. Chaplin*. Foreword by Walter E. Hurst and Frank Bacon (Los Angeles: Marvin Miller Enterprises, 1965), 13.

28. Alexander Bakshy, 'A Knight-Errant', *Dial* Volume 84 Number 5 (May 1928): 413–414.

29. Fred Karno (1866–1941), the English music-hall performer, producer and manager, was born Frederick Westcott. Chaplin joined Karno's Speechless Comedians in 1908 as a comedian and pantomimist and performed in such pantomime comedies as *The Football Match*, *The Mumming Birds*, *Skating* and *Jimmy the Fearless*. Chaplin left Karno for Keystone and a career in films in 1913. Chaplin's elder half-brother, Sydney, had joined Karno in 1906. Another famous Karno alumnus, Arthur Stanley Jefferson (Stan Laurel), accompanied Chaplin on the 1910 and 1912 Karno tours of the United States. Chaplin learned much about comic pacing, the introduction of pathos into laughter and the use of elegant music in counterpoint to comic action from Karno.

30. See Frederick James Smith, 'The Tragic Comedian: An Interview Study of Charlie Chaplin' *Shadowland* Volume 5 Number 3 November 1921 page 51 for Chaplin's fear of returning to the stage.

31. 'What Chaplin Thinks' *New York Times* 7 October 1923 section 9 page 4. According to Lita Grey Chaplin, Chaplin did not think himself physically attractive. He felt that his fame and wealth made him alluring to women. Interview with Lita Grey Chaplin, August 1993.

32. 'Chaplin Among Clowns' *New York Times* 1 January 1928 section 8 page 5.

33. M. Willson Disher, *Clowns and Pantomimes* (1925; reprint edition, New York: Benjamin Blom, Inc., 1968), 34.

34. Chaplin must have also seen Max Linder's last picture, *Der Zirkuskonig* (The King of the Circus, 1924). The second half of the film concerns Max, in love with a circus rider, becoming an animal trainer.

35. The Charles Chaplin Film Corporation daily production report of 23 August 1926 notes: 'Shooting Tiger Sequence. Tigers and Mr. Chaplin in scenes'.

36. Charles Chaplin Film Corporation daily production report (20 August 1926).

37. Documentation in the Chaplin archives indicates that the average running time of *The Circus* is one hour ten minutes, with a running speed of 90 feet per minute (which is sound speed of 24 frames per second). Gillian Anderson, for her concert performances, has the film projected at 20 frames per second. Anderson believes this is the film's original speed, necessary for synchronisation with the film's original accompaniment. This is not supported by the documentation in the Chaplin archives. Indeed, Chaplin recommended *The Circus* be projected at 26 frames per second for the 1928 Berlin premiere engagement. Ms. Anderson's point of view, however, is compellingly put forth in her article 'The Music for *The Circus*,' *Library of Congress Information Bulletin* Volume 52, Number 17 September 20, 1993 pages 341–348.

38. L'Estrange Fawcett, *Films: Facts and Forecasts* (London: Geoffrey Bles, 1930) and L'Estrange Fawcett, 'Chaplin at Work on Comic Scenes Described by British Journalist', *New York Times* 5 September 1926 section 7 page 5.

39. L'Estrange Fawcett, 'Chaplin at Work on Comic Scenes Described by British Journalist', *New York Times*, 5 September 1926 section 7 page 5.

40. Ibid.

41. Ibid.

42. David Robinson, *Chaplin: His Life and Art* (London: Collins, 1985), 369.

43. Harry Crocker, 'A Tribute to Charlie', *Academy Leader*, 1 (April 1972), 15. The article is drawn from the manuscript *Charlie Chaplin: Man and Mime* written by Crocker and deposited in the Harry Crocker collection, Academy of Motion Picture Arts and Sciences, Margaret Herrick Library.

44. L'Estrange Fawcett, 'Chaplin at Work on Comic Scenes Described by British Journalist', *New York Times* 5 September 1926 section 7 page 5.

45. Charles Chaplin, *My Life in Pictures* (London: The Bodley Head, 1974), 233.

46. David Robinson, *Chaplin: His Life and Art* (London: Collins, 1985), 365.

47. Harry Crocker, 'A Tribute to Charlie', *Academy Leader*, 1 (April 1972), 13.

48. Charles Chaplin, *My Life in Pictures* (London: The Bodley Head, 1974), 233.

49. Theodore Huff, *Charlie Chaplin* (New York: Henry Schuman, 1951), 211.

50. David Robinson, *Chaplin: His Life and Art* (London: Collins, 1985), 380–381.

51. L'Estrange Fawcett, *Films: Facts and Forecasts* (London: Geoffrey Bles, 1930), 153.

52. See Edward Rothstein 'The Little Tramp to a Different Tune' *New York Times* 28 February 1994 section C page 11 and Edward Rothstein 'A Night at the Opera (Sans Song)' *New York Times* 13 March 1994 section 2 page 29 for reviews of the film with the 1928 score.

53. Telephone interview with Gillian Anderson, 5 May 1993.

54. Although Chaplin began work on the reissue version of *The Circus* in 1968, the year of its official reissue is 1970. According to Pamela Paumier of Roy Export Company Establishment, Roy Export signed an agreement in December 1969 with United Artists for distribution of the film with the Chaplin score. This agreement was for worldwide rights with the exception of the USA, Canada and the then so-called 'Iron Curtain' countries. It was therefore shown in most countries of the world in 1970. Mo Rothman took over the distribution rights in 1973 for all the countries in the world. Pamela Paumier/Roy Export Company Establishment in letter to the author, 20 July 1994.

Film History, Volume 8, pp. 209–218, 1996. Copyright © John Libbey & Company
ISSN: 0892-2160. Printed in Australia

'It seems that everything looks good nowadays, as long as it is in the flesh & brownskin'

The assertion of cultural difference at Atlanta's 81 Theatre, 1934–1937

Randy Gue

'It seems that everything [vaudeville] looks good nowadays, as long as it is in the flesh and brownskin'.
Gordon DeLeighbor,
Atlanta Daily World, 28 March 1934

In her essay '"The Finest Outside the Loop": Motion Picture Exhibition in Chicago's Black Metropolis, 1905–1928', Mary Carbine argues that motion picture exhibition venues were the site of a unique cultural space for African-American Chicagoans during the silent film era.[1] Carbine concludes that the conversion to sound and the impact of the Great Depression altered the conditions for the construction of this space. An examination of Atlanta's 81 Theatre during the years 1934–37 reveals a similar phenomenon occurring after the coming of sound and in the middle of the Depression. This suggests the need to expand upon Carbine's original argument, adapting it to different conditions in different historical periods and geographical areas.

Scrutinising the local African-American paper, the *Atlanta Daily World*, for the discourses sur-

rounding the motion picture exhibition experience reveals the multifaceted manner in which the Bailey Amusement Company, owner of the 81 Theatre, targeted the black spectators and the ways in which the black press (and by extension, the theatre's patrons) constructed a theatrical experience that was relevant to Atlanta's African-American community. My reliance on the *Daily World*, Atlanta's only black paper during the Depression, was necessary because Atlanta was a segregated city where the activities of the African-American community were poorly documented in the white press. Other local media such as the *Atlanta Constitution* and the *Atlanta Journal* paid scant attention to black Atlanta in general and rarely mentioned African-American leisure activities or entertainment other than to designate the Bailey theatres as 'Colored Theatres' on the entertainment page.

There were three methods of transformation

Randy Gue is a Ph. D. candidate in the Graduate Institute of Liberal Arts at Emory University. Address correspondence to 7585 Chaparral Drive, Atlanta, GA 30350, USA.

that aided the expression of cultural differentiation at the 81. These techniques are manifest in both advertisements and articles in the *Daily World*. For example, the white-owned 81 Theatre booked both Hollywood and race films for extended runs. The stories in the *Daily World* clearly distinguished the race films from the theatre's standard Hollywood product. A chief component in the theatre's construction of a culturally affirming experience involved emphasising facets of Hollywood films which addressed the concerns of the audience, demonstrating a process of selective appropriation of Hollywood films. In addition to showing race films, the main process of expressing cultural differentiation at the 81 during the Depression was its presentation of live stage shows. The variety shows which featured only African-American performers altered the context of the audience's reception of the Hollywood film which followed the shows.

These methods of transformation evolved during the early 1930s as the Bailey Amusement Company responded to the changes produced by the coming of sound and the Depression. The demise of the Theatre Owners Booking Association (TOBA) vaudeville circuit in June 1930 removed an important component of the 81's bills. The TOBA had supplied weekly vaudeville acts featuring popular African-American performers to the 81 since the 1920s. After the death of the circuit, the 81 tried unsuccessfully during 1930 and 1931 to substitute locally produced vaudeville for the TOBA shows. The failure of this policy led to a dearth of stage shows during 1932 and 1933. However, 1934 witnessed a profitable resurgence in live acts at the 81 which continued through 1936. Similarly, the same years evinced the regular booking of race films at the 81. By the end of 1937 the circumstances shifted again. The booking of stage shows and race films diminished in 1937 and disappeared completely the next year. By examining the years 1934–37 at the 81 it is possible to expand Carbine's thesis beyond the silent era and discern a different set of considerations which contributed to the creation of a distinctive cultural space for Atlanta's African-Americans.

The 81 Theatre was located south east of Five Points at 81 Decatur Street between Courtland and Ivy. The 1,500 seat theatre was erected in 1909 by Charles P. Bailey and L.D. Joel as the 81 Decatur

Theatre.[2] There is no information to ascertain if the theatre served Atlanta's black community from its inception, but in 1911 the theatre changed its name to The Arcade Theatre and the *Atlanta City Directory* listed it as 'coloured'.[3] In 1919 The Arcade reverted to the original name, The 81 Theatre. Charles Bailey bought Joel out in the early 1910s and he owned the theatre until his death in 1928 or 1929. His brother, G. Tom Bailey, headed the Bailey Amusement Company following Charles' death. During the Depression the Bailey Amusement Company ran several theatres which served black Atlanta.[4] As Mary Carbine and Dan Streible note, white ownership of theatres which targeted African-Americans audiences was not unique to Atlanta.[5] The 81 Theatre occupied the position of the 'first run' theatre for Atlanta's black theatres. Films appeared at the 81 and then usually circulated to other Bailey theatres or to Meyer Schaine's rival chain of black theatres. The 81 occupied an important position within Atlanta's African-American community. *Daily World* columnist I.P. Reynolds declared, 'the 81 Theatre [is] known from coast to coast and [is] where Atlanta Negroes got their first taste of going in a theatre in the front door and occupying a box seat'.[6] During the Depression the 81 Theatre was also the only theatre in Atlanta in which black audiences could enjoy stage shows without being relegated to the Jim Crow balcony seats. It's history is part of the considerable evidence that films and the theatrical experience were important to the black community in Atlanta during the Depression.

An examination of the *Daily World* quickly reveals the importance of movies to the community. The *Daily World* published summaries of films playing in the city almost daily. In its Sunday edition, it featured an entire page devoted almost exclusively to films. By 1935 the paper employed a film reporter with a small daily column called, 'The Movie Reporter', which was a smaller version of the Sunday entertainment page. At times when stage shows were booked at the 81, the *Daily World* featured articles about the performances.

The most revealing sign of the importance of movies during the Depression is the fact that the number of theatres which catered to black patrons constantly increased during the Depression. Bailey's Atlanta empire alone increased exponentially during a period when most exhibitor's suffered. In

1931 the Bailey Amusement Company purchased the old Paramount Theatre on Auburn Avenue, converted it to sound and rechristened it The Royal Theatre.[7] Bailey opened the Ashby Theatre at West Hunter and Ashby Streets (on Atlanta's burgeoning West Side) on 29 October 1934. The following summer the Royal was completely renovated.[8] In February 1937 Bailey became the proprietor of the Ritz Theatre in Decatur.[9] Two months after the acquisition of the Ritz the Bailey Amusement Company opened the Lenox Theatre at 408 Mitchell Street. Meyer Schaine's two theatres, The New Lincoln Theatre which opened Thanksgiving Day 1933 and The New Harlem, also served Atlanta's black film spectators. Other Atlanta theatres, such as the segregated Capital, attempted to reach the African-American audience by advertising regularly in the *Daily World*. Contrary to Carbine's conclusion that Chicago's black population's 'influence as movie consumers diminished during the Depression', Atlanta's African-American community supported a large and lively film business during this period.[10]

Within this competitive environment, the Bailey Amusement Company employed a multifarious approach to the booking of entertainment at the 81 Theatre in order to appeal to potential customers. The 81 Theatre was the only black theatre in Atlanta which offered live shows during the Depression. Musical and vaudeville shorts featuring popular black performers supplemented the bill in a similar manner in between stage shows. Although the 81 Theatre's main fare was standard Hollywood films, race films were frequently presented for extended runs. This booking strategy presented Atlanta's African-American community with the opportunity to find entertainment at the 81 on a regular basis that addressed their interests as a community.

Part of the theatre's strategy to attract patrons consisted of the booking of race productions. As Carbine notes in Chicago, race films were marketed separately from the typical Hollywood fare. Carbine emphasised that the race films 'were described in opposition to standard Hollywood products as featuring black performers and as referring to the everyday lives and struggles of a black, rather than white, audience'.[11] This pattern holds true for the 81. The run of a race film at the 81 was usually heralded by an article in the *Daily World*. Typical headlines for these articles, such as 'All-Colored

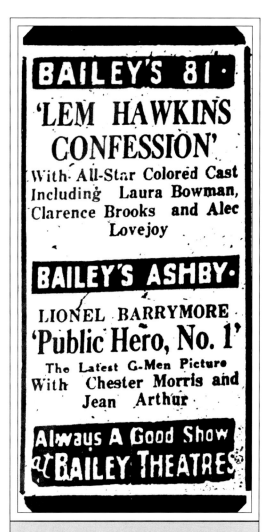

Fig. 1. Advertisement for the August 1935 run of Oscar Micheaux's *Lem Hawkins' Confession*. During 1934–37 all race films at the 81 were promoted in a similar manner. [*Atlanta Daily World*, 12 August 1935.]

Drama Holds Interest Three Days At The 81 Theatre' and 'Cast of Race's Greatest Stars in 81 Thriller', emphasised their all-black casts.[12] The advertisements the Bailey Amusement Company supplied to the paper carried similar lines, such as 'An All-Colored Stellar Cast' or 'All-Colored Film' (Fig. 1). The bookings included films produced by white-financed companies that targeted black audiences and black productions.

The years 1934–36 presented a particularly heavy concentration of race films. In May 1934 the 81 booked Lincoln Pictures' *Harlem Is Heaven* (1932) starring Bill 'Bojangles' Robinson for four days. In April 1935 it showed Southland Pictures Corporation's only film, a satire of Marcus Garvey called *The Black King* (1932). Paul Robeson's *Emperor Jones* (United Artists, 1933) was booked for three days in 1935. Besides films from these white-financed production companies, the 81 featured race films created by black companies. Oscar Micheaux's *Lem Hawkins' Confession* (1935) received its 'Southern Premier' at the 81 Theatre in August 1935. The film ran for four days. Micheaux had an exhibition deal with the Bailey Amusement Company. In 1934 the *Daily World* reported that Micheaux was in town to talk about his new film, *Harlem After Midnight* (1934), as a guest of 'Percy L. Taylor of the Bailey Theatres'.[13] The 81 Theatre also hosted the self proclaimed 'first showing in the South' of Cramerly Picture's *The Vicious Circle* in November 1936. In June 1936, an all-black production called *The Black Network* featuring the Nicholas Brothers and Nina Mae McKinney was billed with a black short entitled '13 Hours By Air'.[14]

One interesting pattern which surrounded the race films shown at the 81 is that the *Daily World*'s reporters never called attention to the low production values of the films. In this regard the films were never compared to Hollywood films, but instead the articles concentrated on the all-black cast. Almost every article about the race films featured a variation of the line 'Boasting the best cast of coloured players ever assembled in one picture'.[15] Although during the period surveyed Bailey booked a number of these films, race films constituted a small minority at a theatre which usually changed its bill three times a week. The infrequency of the bookings did not diminish the importance of the films to the community.

Hollywood films usually dominated the bill at the 81 Theatre. In fact Bailey's advertisements and the *Daily World*'s stories specifically emphasise the Bailey Theatres' policy of booking first-run studio product. The *Daily World*'s entertainment page regularly featured articles with such headlines as 'Nothing But Best Booked in April [at Bailey Theatres]' and 'Bailey Theatres Promise Banner Year for 1937; Carnival of Hits Will Be Shown'.[16]

A 1937 Bailey Amusement Company advertisement also stressed, 'An important message from Bailey Theatres. We take great pleasure in announcing contracts with all the leading studios for the entire year of 1937. NO OTHER THEATRE IN ATLANTA have [sic] the same selections of big pictures we do.'[17] Exploitation of these Hollywood products was often geared to address the specific concerns of Atlanta's African-American audience. Both the *Daily World* and the 81's promotional material reflected this process. For example, Stepin Fetchit in *Helldorado* (Fox, 1935) and *36 Hours to Kill* (Twentieth Century-Fox, 1936) received top billing although he played secondary characters in the films.[18] Another example of this sort of appropriation of Hollywood films occurs with the Paramount musical *The Big Broadcast of 1936* (1935). An article which accompanied the film's last day at the 81 detailed: 'There are some big name stars in 'Big Broadcast of 1936' the musical film playing last times today at Bailey's 81 Theatre, but to the packed audiences that have viewed the picture during the past three days, the Nicholas Brothers, sensational young dancing duo outstrips them all'.[19] The 81's advertisement for the film reflects this trend. The portion of the ad presumably provided by Paramount does not mention the Nicholas Brothers. It concentrates on stars such as Jack Oakie, Bing Crosby and Burns and Allen. The Bailey Amusement Company added the heading 'Nicholas Brothers in' to the promotion placed in the *Daily World* (Fig. 2). The most illuminating example of this practice involves the 1934 Universal film *Imitation of Life*, which was booked at the 81 from 5–10 May 1935. A story accompanying first day of the film's run states, 'Claudette Colbert, Warren William and Rochelle Hudson, not to mention Ned Sparks, supply the background for the unusual picture'.[20] A still photo from the film on the entertainment page carried a caption which also demonstrates this technique of appropriation: 'Claudette Colbert and Warren William have supporting roles'. The publicity material for the film supplied by the Bailey Amusement Company employed selective promotion. The advertisement featured a large picture of Colbert but the tag line read, 'Louise Beavers, Fredi Washington, Dorothy Black in Fannie Hurst's *Imitation of Life*' (Fig. 3). The focus on minority performers in certain Hollywood films emphasised aspects of

Fig. 2. An example of selective promotion of minority performers from Paramount's *The Big Broadcast of 1936*. [*Atlanta Daily World*, 1 January 1936.]

those films that might appeal to local audiences and played an important role in the creation of a culturally affirming space at the white-owned 81 Theatre.

The main procedure for constructing a specifically black cultural space occurred at live stage shows which the 81 booked. Mary Carbine documents the importance of both music and live performance to Chicago's African-American community. Carbine states that within the motion picture exhibition context 'jazz performed during the exhibition of films offered black spectators a lively demonstration of ethnic difference and inventions, quite separate from the entertainment on the screen'.[21] As Carbine ascertained, the conversion to sound eliminated live accompaniment to films and this, combined with the Great Depression, permanently

altered the nature of the theatrical stage shows at movie theatres. With the introduction of sound the major studios filmed popular vaudeville performers as a substitute for live performances thus eliminating a large operating expense for exhibitors. Even a *Variety* vaudeville critic acknowledged, 'Dropping of the stage show immediately eliminates a large slice of a theatre's overhead ...'[22] However, 1933 and 1934 witnessed a profitable resurgence in black vaudeville. The revival of touring vaudeville acts was part of a larger interest and resurgence in all forms of African-American entertainment.[23] In 1934 the 81 Theatre began consistently to present stage shows again. The Bailey Amusement Company used live acts to draw black audiences to Hollywood films. The live stage shows, which featured African-American performers, reconfigured

Fig. 3. Advertisement for *Imitation of Life*.
[*Atlanta Daily World*, 5 May 1935.]

the context of reception for the films which followed. Through the performance the theatre became a site for the assertion of cultural difference and racial pride.

The stage shows presented at the 81 reflected the diversity of black vaudeville. From 1934–37 the 81 Theatre hosted traditional vaudeville revues (Butterbeans & Susie, The Whitman Sisters); curiosity acts such as 'Freckles' the chimpanzee from the Tarzan films; and personal appearances of popular performers like the radio stars, the Cabin Kids. The stage shows usually preceded the showing of the film program. A piece about the Georgia Minstrels' appearance at the 81 detailed the schedule for a stage show: 'During the engagement there will be three performances of the Georgia Minstrels given daily and [these] will be run in conjunction with the regular theatre program of pictures, giving you a three hour show for one price of admission'.[24] A typical touring show would begin the week's engagement with a midnight ramble on Sunday night. The vaudeville shows usually contained a series of

acts and a jazz orchestra featuring a piano, several horns, a banjo and drums. The list of performers would include comedians, burlesque dancers, blues singers, a soubret, tap dancers, a chorus line and a master of ceremonies.[25] The shows were usually booked between January and May allowing the performers to escape the New York and Chicago winters. In 1934 the 81 Theatre featured Irving Miller's 'Brown Skin Models of 1934' for runs in January and a return engagement in April and Butterbeans and Susie's 'Frolics of 1934'. 1935 began in the same manner with a flurry of bookings through the spring months, but the stage shows continued throughout the year. That year featured some of the more exotic shows such as 'Freckles' the chimpanzee and the "Durso" Midnight Spook Show' on Friday 13 September. Adelaide Hall, the noted Cotton Club chanteuse, graced the 81's stage for two days in April 1935. The stage shows continued regularly through 1936 at the 81. The list of stage programs during 1936 included the Georgia Minstrels, Irving Miller's 'Harlem Broadcast', Miller and Slayter's 'Truckin' on Down' and finally the return of Irving Miller's 'Brown Skin Models' in November. Stage bookings became more sporadic in 1937 but the 81 still featured Butterbeans and Susie in May and the Whitman Sister's '1937 Swing Time Review' during July.

The importance of these stage shows to Atlanta's African-American community is mirrored in the reporting about the shows in the *Daily World*. The Bailey Amusement Company's promotional material announcing the stage shows dwarfs the title of the day's feature film. In the advertisement for Irving Miller's 'Brown Skin Models of 1934' return engagement in April 1934, the title of the feature *Hell and High Water* (Paramount, 1933) is buried at the bottom of the ad in small type (Fig. 4).[26] This also holds true for Adelaide Hall's appearance (Fig. 5). Similar to the race films, both the advertisements and the *Daily World*'s stories about the stage shows emphasised the African-American performers. The stories and advertising sometimes drew an explicit connection to Harlem, the capital of African-American culture and entertainment at the time, with such lines as 'Hotcha and Hot from Harlem' or 'The Sensational Harlem Extravaganza' (Fig. 6).[27]

The arrival of Irving C. Miller's 'Brownskin

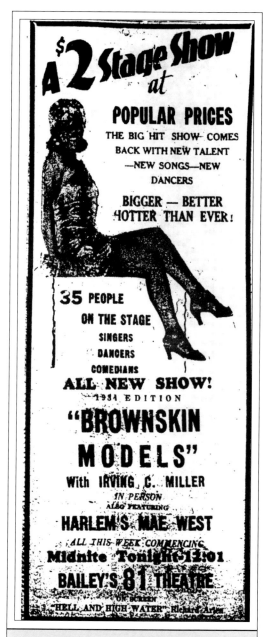

Fig. 4. Advertisement for the April 1934 engagement of Irving Miller's 'Brownskin Models'. The name of the feature film which accompanied the stage show is buried at the bottom of the ad. [*Atlanta Daily World*, 11 April 1934.]

years'[28] The run generated four features and five citations within the *Daily World*'s various columns during the show's week long run. Clifford MacKay's page one review of the show's opening night mid-night ramble described the packed theatre and the audience's reaction. Since it was one of the only articles to give a detailed recounting of the audience's reaction to a stage show it is worth quoting in detail:

> It [rhythm] pervaded the boards and circulated among the 2000 who jammed and crammed every available inch of space in the Decatur street [sic] house made famous years ago by one Charles Bailey. It swept upward to the balcony where sat a throng, not so cultured and therefore suffering from no inhibitions about the free release of their emotions. They

Fig. 5. Advertisement for Adelaide Hall's 1935 appearance at the 81. [*Atlanta Daily World*, 2 April 1935.]

Models of 1934' represented an important event at the 81 Theatre. The revue was championed as 'Atlanta's first sip of red-hot sepia vaudeville in several

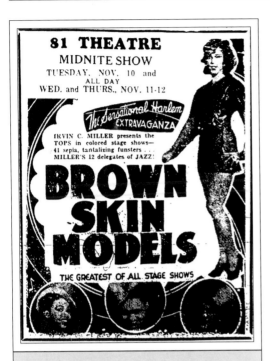

Fig. 6. Irving Miller's 'Brownskin Models of 1936' drew an explicit connection to Harlem. [*Atlanta Daily World*, 8 November 1936.]

shouted, whistled, screamed and stomped ... In other words everybody enjoyed themselves, even if a portion of the audience did get slightly out of control at times. It was an occasion and they meant to celebrate it.[29]

The well-attended shows must have generated profits for the 81 because it continued to book stage shows and especially Miller's stage show well into 1937. The success of the show was also reflected by the fact that the revue returned in April for another engagement.[30] The Bailey Amusement Company used Miller's and other live acts to draw black audiences to Hollywood films. In fact, from 1934–37 no stage show coincided with the showing of a race film.

Stage shows presented black Atlantans with space to assert their cultural difference within a white-owned theatre. Like the race films, the stage shows explicitly drew a connection to ethnicity. An article previewing Adelaide Hall's 1935 appearance noted that the performances were an arena for the expression of cultural difference:

The chief superiority of the coloured show and the thing that distinguishes it from its Broadway competitors, is the dancing. Everybody who has seen many shows on both sides of the colour line have remarked [about] this great difference ... Miss Hall has been quoted as saying that Negroes have a finer sense of rhythm. They catch on to a new step easily and naturally. Dancing is in them, the pride of Harlem declared. They're great in synchronising and they are indefatigable workers, added the little torch singer.[31]

Besides asserting cultural difference, the stage shows also constituted a point of race pride. I.P. Reynolds wrote in his daily column about Butterbeans and Susie's 'Frolics of 1934':

It made this writer feel proud of the fact that he was listening to his people once more after so long a time and after all, my people were the originators of the minstrel show which [was] comprised of blackface comedians, singing and dancing girls, blues singers and like from which came the high priced, high class comedians such as Eddie Cantor who on the stage works under burnt cork and radio singers who sing jazz which was given its birth by such coloured men as [W.C.] Handy.[32]

Reynolds concludes his column with, 'I guess that I'll see the show everyday this week. I can't help it'.[33] The importance of black musicians and performers in the context of the 81 is further demonstrated in the booking of shorts when stage shows were not running.

Since the booking of live acts at the 81 was not a consistent policy, musical and vaudeville shorts helped fill in the gaps. The musical shorts usually featured popular African-American jazz musicians and performers such as Duke Ellington, Cab Calloway and Bill 'Bojangles' Robinson. For example, two months after her show in Atlanta, Adelaide Hall's musical short 'On the Air and Off' and another short entitled 'Hot Pepper' were booked at the 81 with a large amount of publicity. An article announced the beginning of the run of the short and stated, 'Adelaide Hall Tops Huge Offering At Eighty-One'.[34] The feature film *Midnight Alibi* (Warner Bros., 1934), starring Richard Barthelmess, ranked a distant second behind the musical short. Accordingly the advertisements for the 81 Theatre promoted the short at the same size or sometimes larger than the feature film. The musical shorts even became a frame of cultural reference. Gordon De-Leighbor's review of Butterbeans and Susie's show states, 'Atlantans will remember the dance done by the team in Duke Ellington's film short "Black and Tan".'[35] The musical short featuring popular black performers functioned as another component of the cultural affirmation that took place at the 81 similar to the live stage show.

An examination of the *Atlanta Daily World* reveals that films and theatrical experiences in general were important to Atlanta's African-American community during the Depression. Black Atlantans created a unique space for the expression of cultural difference within Bailey's 81 Theatre. The showing of race films presented alternatives to the standard Hollywood fare that the 81 predominantly booked. Both the stories and advertising in the *Daily World* emphasised this difference in terms of all-black casts. Another technique employed was the selective promotion of black performers appearing in Hollywood products. This was a means of emphasising certain aspects of the films which spoke to the interests of the spectators and with which they might be able to identify. The main way of expressing cultural difference, however, was through the live shows which featured African-American performers. The live shows transformed the context of viewing Hollywood films and became the means of an assertion of cultural difference and race pride. Unlike Carbine's conclusion about Depression-era Chicago, the African-American community in Atlanta continued to create a lively cultural space after the coming of sound and during the Depression.✣

Notes

1. Mary Carbine, 'The Finest Outside the Loop': Motion Picture Exhibition in Chicago's Black Metropolis, 1905–1928,' *Camera Obscura* 23 (1991): 31–32.

2. *1910 Atlanta City Directory* (Atlanta: Atlanta City Directory Co., 1909): 1772. L.D. Joel, 'Old Timers Club', [*Atlanta*] *Weekly Film Review* 4 February 1930, 10.

3. *1911 Atlanta City Directory* (Atlanta: Atlanta City Directory Co., 1910): 1772.

4. In 1935 *The Atlanta Daily World* reported that Bailey owned twenty-eight theatres throughout the South, but there was no hint of the ethnicity of the audience outside the Atlanta area. Cliff MacKay, 'Auburn Avenue to Get Brand New Royal; Work Starts Soon', *Atlanta Daily World*, 30 June 1935, 1.

5. Carbine, 18. Dan Streible, 'The Harlem Theatre: Black Film Exhibition in Austin Texas: 1920–1973', *Black American Cinema*, ed. Manthia Diawara (New York: Routledge, 1992) 225.

6. I.P. Reynolds, 'What Sam of Auburn Avenue Says', *Atlanta Daily World* 26 February 1934, 6.

7. Tobie Grant, 'Royal Theatre Will Be Used for Benefit Show', *Atlanta Daily World* 13 December 1931, 1. Cliff MacKay, 'Auburn Avenue to Get Brand New Royal; Work Starts Soon', 1.

8. Gordon DeLeighbor, 'Royal Is the South's Finest', *Atlanta Daily World*, 1 September 1935, 7.

9. 'Bailey Amusement Company Takes Ritz Theatre Under Its Wing Monday', *Atlanta Daily World* 31 January 1937, 7.

10. Carbine, 32.

11. Ibid., 20.

12. 'All-Colored Drama Holds Interest Three Days at the 81 Theatre', *Atlanta Daily World* 29 November 1936, 4. 'Cast of Race's Greatest Stars in 81 Thriller', *Atlanta Daily World*, 11 August 1935, 7.

13. 'Negro Films Have Good Future', *Atlanta Daily World*, 7 May 1934, 1. Taylor, The manager of Bailey's Royal Theatre, worked for Micheaux's film company in 1928.

14. Sheppard O'Neal, 'Ashby, Eighty-One, Royal Theatres Brimming Over With Colored Pictures', *Atlanta Daily World*, 14 June 1936, 7.

15. 'Fetchit, Muse Star in 81's Sepia Film', *Atlanta Daily World*, 13 October 1935, 7.

16. 'Nothing But Best Booked in April', *Atlanta Daily World*, 7 April 1935: sec. 2: 4. Sheppard O'Neal, 'Bailey Theatres Promise Banner Year for 1937; Carnival of Hits Will Be Shown', *Atlanta Daily World*, 31 January 1937, 7.

17. Advertisement for Bailey Theatres, *Atlanta Daily World*, 31 January 1937, 7. Emphasis in original.

18. *The American Film Institute Catalogue of Motion Pictures Produced in the United States: Feature Films, 1931–40* does not mention the Fetchit char-

acters in its plot synopses of the films. This reflects the marginal position African-American characters were relegated to in Hollywood films of the period.

19. 'Nicholas Brothers Steal Show at 81', *Atlanta Daily World*, 1 January 1936, 2.

20. 'Beloved Stars Depict Stellar Drama at the 81', *Atlanta Daily World*, 5 May 1935, 5.

21. Carbine, 34.

22. Joe Bigelow, 'Outlook of Vaudeville', *Variety*, 2 January 1934, 45.

23. Thomas R. Cripps, 'The Myth of the Southern Box Office: A Factor in Racial Stereotyping in American Movies, 1929–40', *The Black Experience in America: Selected Essays*, ed. James C. and Lewis L. Gould (Austin: University of Texas Press, 1973): 135 and 138. Cliff MacKay, 'Along Amusement Alley', *Atlanta Daily World*, 21 January 1934, 5.

24. 'Broomfield and Greely, Famous Dance Team, Featured in Cast at '81 Midnight Tonite', *Atlanta Daily World*, 25 February 1936, 4.

25. Cliff MacKay, '"Models of '34' Is Plenty Good", *Atlanta Daily World*, 16 January 1934, 1. Cliff MacKay, '"Brownskin Models"' Much Better Show', *Atlanta Daily World*, 17 April 1934, 1.

26. Advertisement for Bailey's 81, *Atlanta Daily World*, 11 April 1934, 3.

27. Advertisement for Bailey's 81, *Atlanta Daily World*, 7 January 1934, 3. Advertisement for Bailey's 81, *Atlanta Daily World*, 8 November 1936, 7.

28. Lucius Jones, 'Society Slants', *Atlanta Daily World*, 12 January 1934, 3.

29. Cliff MacKay, 'Models of "34" Is Plenty Good', 1.

30. 'Brown Skin Models' Return to 81 Theatre at Sunday Midnight', *Atlanta Daily World*, 11 April 1934, 3.

31. 'Adelaide Hall Is En Route to the 81', *Atlanta Daily World*, 31 March 1935, 7.

32. I.P. Reynolds, 'What Sam of Auburn Avenue Says: Butterbeans, Susie and "Reubens" Orchestra', *Atlanta Daily World*, 27 March 1934, 6.

33. Ibid.

34. 'Adelaide Hall Tops Huge Offering at Eighty-One', *Atlanta Daily World*, 4 July 1935, 2.

35. Gordon DeLeighbor, 'DeLeighbor Finds Good Show at 81', *Atlanta Daily World*, 28 March 1934, 4.

Film History, Volume 8, pp. 219–236, 1996. Copyright © John Libbey & Company
ISSN: 0892-2160. Printed in Australia

Nostalgia, ambivalence, irony: Song of the South and race relations in 1946 Atlanta

Matthew Bernstein

At the suggestion of the Junior League and the Uncle Remus Memorial Association of Atlanta, Georgia, Walt Disney and RKO Pictures agreed to hold the world premiere of Song of the South in Atlanta in the fall of 1946. The Disney film was of course based on the Uncle Remus stories, which Atlanta Constitution editor and reporter Joel Chandler Harris (c. 1848–1908) had published in the paper and in a series of books from 1880 through 1918. Harris had heard the tales as a youth while working on a plantation in rural Georgia; they were told to him by slaves whom he amalgamated into the figure of Remus.

No doubt inspired by the glittering premiere of Gone with the Wind seven years earlier, which the Junior League had also sponsored, Atlanta's white elite expected a comparable social event on the night of Tuesday, 12 November 1946.[1] The League's half of the proceeds (estimated at between $5,000 and $12,000) would benefit the Egleston Children's Hospital and the League's Speech School; the Uncle Remus Association's half would be spent on refurbishing the Wren's Nest, Harris' west side residence.[2] The premiere was a gala event, attended by city leaders, its social elite and covered by forty newspapers from around the south.

This essay contrasts the responses of white and black Atlantans to Song of the South, as represented in its two major white dailies (the Atlanta Constitution and the Atlanta Journal) and its only black (owned and operated) daily, the Atlanta Daily World. That their reactions to the film were distinctly different is no surprise, but the ways in which they differ are. Where the white papers gave the premiere plenty of space, the Atlanta Daily World's coverage was minimal. In addition, the Atlanta Daily World's only commentary on the film was highly ambivalent: it displayed neither the unabashed enthusiasm of the white papers for the film

Matthew Bernstein is the author of Walter Wanger, Hollywood Independent (University of California Press, 1994). With Gaylyn Studlar, he has co-edited Visions of the East: Orientalism in Film (Rutgers University Press, forthcoming). He and Professor Dana White of Emory University are currently at work on a history of black filmgoing in Atlanta. Address correspondance to Film Studies Program, Emory University, Atlanta, Georgia, 30322, USA.

as in one Atlantan's phrase, 'waking a nostalgia for a gentle way of life lost in the rush of years', nor the critical tone of black civic leaders and of the liberal white newsweeklies and Northern newspapers, which viewed *Song of the South* as, in *New Yorker* critic John McCarten's phrase, 'the purest sheepdip about happy days on the old plantation'.[3]

I will argue that both black and white reactions to the film in Atlanta were shaped by several factors, such as the element of home town pride in Harris' achievement, the shared heritage of the tales themselves and by what was viewed as appealing aspects of the film. Yet home town pride and selective admiration for *Song of the South* were themselves affected by the historical context in which the film appeared that November, in particular, by several racist incidents that had recently occurred in and around the city. Just four months prior to the premiere, a black man, his wife and two in-laws were ceremoniously lined up and shot on a back road less than forty miles east of Atlanta. The incident re-galvanised a neo-Nazi group within Atlanta called the Columbians. Then, roughly one week prior to *Song of the South*'s premiere, Georgia's gubernatorial race was won by former Governor Eugene Talmadge, who campaigned in part with the promise that no black Georgian would be permitted to vote in the state's primary elections. These events only confirmed the suspicions of the black national leadership and Atlanta's black upper middle class that postwar America could fail to build upon the social gains made by African Americans during the anti-Fascist effort. It was in this tense and expectant period that Atlanta's different communities turned to the festivities surrounding Disney's film.

National response

Song of the South is a dubious achievement by many standards, so much so that it is the one feature-length film in the company's library that has not been released domestically to theatres or on video since the mid-1980s (it can only be seen on Japanese laserdisc).[4] Thomas Cripps has characterised the film as a prime example of what he calls Hollywood's post-World War II 'Thermidor' after the heat of its wartime efforts to move forward in its depiction of African-Americans onscreen. Disney's film repre-

sents 'the cooling of ardor that has followed every era of disquiet from the French Revolution onward, the moment when order seems to matter more than liberty, sameness more than novelty', an exception to the virtual disappearance of antebellum Southern movies.[5] The live action of the film dwelt on a young couple's unhappy separation, their son's misadventures on his grandmother's farm outside Atlanta in the late 1800s and in particular the strength the son draws from plantation hand Uncle Remus' tales of the Brers Rabbit, Fox and Bear (the briarpatch, the tar baby and the laughing place), all of which are told in animated cartoons. Cripps documents how Disney resisted all suggestions – be they from Alaine Locke of Howard University; Walter White, executive director of the NAACP and an Atlanta native; screenwriter Maurice Rapf; and even a member of the Breen Office – to give the Uncle Remus and African-American characters of the live-action sequences some humanity, depth and a sense of the pain of their existence in the antebellum South. Instead, Disney opted for a cinematically-coded evocation of the plantation setting that sought to smooth over any such considerations in a nostalgic haze (with the arch-conservative Disney suggesting that some of the Cassandras he heard from had Communist backgrounds).[6]

In 1946, *Song of the South* successfully dazzled uncritical audiences with the technological 'attraction' of integrating cartoon characters with live action – and this emerged as one of its primary appeals.[7] The film's technical achievement and regressive politics could have called forth a splitting of the aesthetic from the ideological, as was the case for *The Birth of a Nation* (1915), which was highly celebrated for its aesthetic achievements and denounced for its racism. Indeed, as Cripps has documented, African-American leadership in the immediate postwar period sought the opportunity 'to work out a postwar formula [in Hollywood films] to replace that which the war had induced, a formula in which otherness might be redefined as a normative part of a larger polity'. Protesting a major film might provide an opportunity for defining that formula and *Song of the South* might provide that opportunity.[8]

Disney's film, however, was clearly a different case from Griffith's film. Many viewers and critics were ambivalent, torn between *Song of the South*'s

Fig. 1. The Disney Version: Walt Disney reads Uncle Remus stories to the film's child co-stars, Luanna Patten (left) and Bobby Driscoll. [Photo courtesy of Walt Disney Productions.]

regressive recreation of the atmosphere of happy darkies on the plantation on the one hand and the appealing animation sequences and especially the very charismatic performance of James Baskett (a vaudevillian and the voice of Gabby in the Amos 'n' Andy radio show), on the other. In Cripps's words, Baskett:

> ... managed to give black viewers a tolerable dignity while playing to whites with a reading so densely packed with ancient props and manners that he transported them into a rose-coloured past ... As a result of Baskette's [sic] charm, not one group of organised blacks mounted a coherent campaign against Disney's movie.

The NAACP leadership was internally divided over the film and ultimately determined that it was not worthy of a major protest movement.

Some ambivalence is apparent in Walter White's statement of December 1946, wherein he publicly acknowledged the artistry of the film but regretted:

> ... that in an effort neither to offend audiences in the North or South, the production helps to perpetuate a dangerously glorified picture of slavery. Making use of the beautiful Uncle Remus folklore, *Song of the South* unfortunately gives the impression of an idyllic master-slave relationship which is a distortion of the facts.[10]

Within two weeks, White proposed the creation of a NAACP 'censoring office', noting that outside of Memphis, 'the vast majority of Southerners would have no objection to films that treated the Negro as an ordinary person' as did Warner Bros.' *In This Our Life* (1942).[11]

Other groups were less conciliatory than White. In New York city, the National Negro Congress bluntly characterised the film as 'an insult to the Negro people because it uses offensive dialect; it portrays the Negro as a low, inferior servant; it glorifies slavery and it damages the fight for equal representations'.[12] Several weeks later, New York's Local 27 of the American Federation of Teachers denounced the film because 'the negro is presented treacherously and slyly in the conventional stereotypes ...'. Baskett's excellent performance was 'hampered by having to portray the fixed conception of the Negro – a lazy, hat-in-hand, spiritual-singing, inferior 'old rascal'.' The teacher's union also objected to the portrayal of 'the theme of "the Negro in service to white people, the Negro apparently whose only thought is to help solve the problems of the white people" instead of picturing blacks as artisans and business people'.[13]

These protests by watchdog groups came shortly after the film's openings around the country. It is striking to note that to some extent, their objections were voiced by the newsweeklies' movie critics, who displayed a sensitivity to racial matters on the screen that, as Eric Smoodin has observed, was unthinkable before World War II.[14] Reviewers were virtually unanimous in criticising the film for too little cartoon footage and too much live action.[15] But they also agreed that Disney's anachronistic vision in this film (portraying a postbellum plantation as if it were of the antebellum period) rendered its setting, in Manny Farber's phrase, as 'a paradise for lucky slaves'. Bosley Crowther was particularly vehement in condemning the film in both his regular review and in a Sunday thinkpiece: 'You've committed a peculiarly gauche offense', he wrote in the latter, which he framed as a spanking to Walt Disney:

> ... in putting out such a story in this troubled day and age. For no matter how much one argues that it's all childish fiction, anyhow, the master-and-slave relation is so lovingly regarded in your yarn, with the Negroes bowing and scraping and singing spirituals in the night, that one might almost imagine that you figure Abe Lincoln made a mistake. Put down that mint julep, Mr. Disney![16]

Similarly, *Time*'s reviewer wrote that:

> ... 'tattered ol' Uncle Remus, who cheerfully 'knew his place' in the easygoing world of late 19th Century Georgia (Author Harris, in accepted Southern fashion, always omitted the capital from the word 'Negro'), is a character bound to enrage all educated Negroes and a number of damnyankees.[17]

Where Crowther assumed all viewers would find the film offensive, *Time*, as Smoodin observes, 'assured its readers that a black audience's sensitivity to racial issues was in fact a function of class privilege, as only 'educated' blacks would take offense. Poor blacks, apparently, would not be bothered'.[18]

Subsequent critics have agreed on the film's paternalistic gloss on post-Civil War plantation life. Donald Bogle has noted that Baskett's Remus is 'a sugary paragon of contentment, domesticity and servility', whose desexualised portrayal refutes the film's hints that he and Aunt Ginny (Hattie McDaniel) might be courting.[19] The late James Snead has written the most insightful analysis of the film. Noting the conventional wisdom that cartoons are the epitome of Hollywood's harmless entertainment, geared as they are toward innocent viewers, Snead has also commented on how Disney copied Harris' fantasy of harmonious relations between blacks and whites, but expanded the frame tale that Harris minimised. In Disney's film, the cartoons illustrate Uncle Remus' tales and hence represent a 'black narrative voice'; live action is associated with little white Johnny's adventures on the plantation and therefore with a white narrative voice: 'The result of expanding the context and shrinking the text of the Uncle Remus tales is, quite simply, to remove the black narrator Uncle Remus and his Afro-American narratives from "the centre of the stage"'. This process is only magnified at the end of the film, when the white boy Johnny – who when recovering from an accident has deliriously called out for Remus rather than his own father – proves capable of conjuring the animal characters without Remus's help – 'Uncle Remus has, in effect, made himself redundant'.[20] As Snead's analysis demonstrates, Disney's attempt to provide a cheerful gloss on troubling matters resulted in complex and disturbing textual dynamics.

The Walton county lynchings

In its review, *Time* had predicted that 'the movie's success in the South, which unabashedly dotes on the good old days, is already assured'.[21] In November 1946, Georgian politics were at an ugly enough stage to heighten most people's nostalgia for the past. The Klu Klux Klan had become highly visible once again in the spring of the year. More dramatically, the lynching of Roger and Dorothy Malcom and George and Mae Dorsey in Walton County, Georgia the previous July was a reminder of more than 3,900 lynchings that occurred in the South between 1880 and 1930 and one of six that had occurred since war's end.[22]

It was committed by residents of a rural white population that resented changes in the economic health of the cotton industry and the initial undermining of the segregation laws that had previously prevailed.[23] The contribution of black soldiers and civilians to the anti-Fascist fight made Jim Crow segregation laws seem hypocritical to Americans outside the south and to many African-Americans within it. The 1944 Supreme Court Smith v. Allwright ruling struck down the system of white primary elections by which blacks could only vote for candidates pre-selected by whites; in 1946 an Atlanta Federal court specified Georgia's compliance. The latter ruling inspired Georgia's African-Americans to increased participation in the vote: in the summer preceding *Song of the South*'s premiere, 100,000 citizens had registered statewide and 18,000 new names appeared in Atlanta.[24] But gubernatorial candidate Eugene Talmadge had promised not to follow the Supreme

Fig. 2. The Uncle Remus Look: James Baskett (centre) in the torn and tattered costume of the plantation slave. Also depicted Luanna Patten, Bobby Driscoll, and Glenn Leedy (right). [Photo courtesy of Walt Disney Productions.]

Court ruling and told supporters, 'I was raised among niggers and I understand them. I want to see them treated fairly and I want them to have justice in the courts. But I want to deal with the nigger in this way: he must come to my back door, take off his hat and say, "Yes, sir".'[25]

The Monroe County lynching was in retaliation for a black fieldhand's stabbing of a white farmer. It was done down a backroad, not publicly, as many lynchings had been done through the 1930s. A dispute had arisen between the black couple Roger and Dorothy Malcom and Barnette Hester, Jr., a son of the Malcoms' white landlord (the Malcoms lived in a tenant shack owned by the Hesters). After a fight with his wife, a drunken Roger had followed Dorothy to the home of the Hester's where he and Barney got into a heated dispute. Roger Malcom stabbed him and Barney was rushed to the hospital. The Walton County sheriff took Roger Malcom into custody that night, after rescuing him from a group of ten white men who had bound and beaten him until he was bloody. Groups tried to lynch Malcom nightly. Two days after Malcom's arrest, blacks in Walton county turned out in record numbers to vote against racist Eugene Talmadge in the gubernatorial elections; Talmadge won anyway.

One week later, Dorothy Malcom's brother, George Dorsey, persuaded the farmer for whom he worked as a sharecropper to pay Roger's bail; the farmer, Dorothy Malcom, her brother George Dorsey and his wife Mae Dorsey retrieved Roger Malcom from jail. Returning home at sundown (after a convenient three-hour delay), the farmer went down a back road where a mob met them, pulled the blacks out of the car and shot all of them with three volleys (the women were killed because they heard one of the white men say another's name). Among the lynchers were apparently several deputy sheriffs. George Dorsey, one of the victims, was a decorated veteran who had served five years in the Army Air Force and had seen action in the Pacific.

Unlike their rural counterparts, the middle and upper class residents of Monroe (the county seat of Walton) were appalled by the lynching, but not enough to cooperate with the Georgia and Federal Bureaus of Investigation. 2500 people interviewed would not name names.[26] On 8 November, four days before the premiere of Song of the South, sitting Georgia Governor Ellis Arnall[27] informed the press that investigators knew the identities of up to 17 members of the mob who had killed the Malcoms and the Dorseys; but they were having trouble finding evidence to prove it.[28] Without hard evidence, the killers went unpunished after an unsuccessful grand jury hearing in December 1946.

Vice-President Henry A. Wallace in mid-September called the Walton County lynching 'not merely the most unwarranted, brutal act of mob violence in the United States in recent years; it was also an illustration of the kind of prejudice that makes war [sic] inevitable', a comment that explicitly linked the lynching with European fascism.[29]

The *Atlanta Daily World* commented that 'nothing more dastardly has happened in the memory of Georgians to disgrace the name of the state'.[30] In January 1947, the *Atlanta Daily World* would report that 95 blacks had been killed in Georgia during the past year, compared to ten whites, a ratio that had previously prevailed only before the war. There had been six lynchings in the South since the end of the war: all the victims were black and 'nearly all' of them veterans. The paper's editorial staff well understood these murders' significance: 'There appears to have been a pattern to this brutal lawlessness – a pattern designed to strike terror in the hearts of men who have returned from their war service with a determination to share in the freedom and the human rights they fought to preserve'.[31]

The investigation of the Walton County murders was continuing in early November when Song of the South came to Atlanta and both white papers and the *Atlanta Daily World* continued to cover it. Racists were also acting up within the city itself, however. A 22-year old white motorman for the Georgia Power company was calmly dismissed from a hearing for shooting outright and killing a black resident, a former member of the Army, after a verbal dispute; one observer at the hearing noted that the murderer 'did not appear to be concerned about the outcome of the trial' and the outraged cry of 'Again! And Again! And Again!' appeared in the headline in the *Atlanta Daily World* story.[32]

Even more harrowing, throughout the fall, a group of poor white, racist and anti-semitic men, largely lower class millworkers, banded together as neo-Nazi 'Columbians'. Their most visible aim was to prevent the integration of any city neighbourhoods. In September, a black woman was stopped from unloading her belongings from a truck on Sells Avenue by several white men who told her not to bother to move in to the predominantly white neighbourhood.[33] *Atlanta Constitution* liberal editor Ralph McGill told his readers that the Columbian leadership consisted of rapists and wife deserters, that their numbers never reached beyond thirty (against their publicly bruited count of 1000) and that their ranks were filled with ignorant working class men who wanted to blame others for their misfortunes and who had not been trained to become better citizens. Yet the Columbians were obviously a force to be reckoned with.[34]

The Columbians divided the city into zones and monitored attempts by African Americans to move into mostly white neighbourhoods. When placed on trial by the city in February 1947, Atlanta residents learned that:

> ... the men who were patrolling these neighbourhoods were also instructed to beat up Negroes seen in the areas and that if they had to kill them, to make certain to plant a knife on their person or drag them on the porch of some white resident, ostensibly to show that they were attempting to rob the home.[35]

With leadership that had been active in the German-American Bund, the Columbians amassed enough ammunition 'to blow the Negroes up in Atlanta' and aspired to take over the US government 'Hitler style'.[36] One week before the premiere of *Song of the South*, the Atlanta police finally arrested four of their leaders – as the *Atlanta Daily World* noted, their arrest prevented an inevitable race riot, because they would sooner or later pick on a black citizen who would fight back. 'The marvel is that such pogroms have been permitted to run so long unchecked, in the capital city of Georgia ...'[37] In early 1947, the state would revoke the Columbians' charter.

Papers like the liberal *Atlanta Constitution*, the *Atlanta Journal* and the *Atlanta Daily World* reported on the Walton County lynchings and the Columbians with outrage and disgust, albeit to differing degrees. Where did the premiere of *The Song of the South* sit amidst this evidence of reactionary sentiment in the city's environs? In what ways did audiences link the film to the neo-Fascists in their

Fig. 3. A Technical Achievement: The 'integration' of live-action and animated characters.
[Photo courtesy of Walt Disney Productions.]

midst, if at all? After all, anyone who read the papers during the *Song of the South* festivities had to be aware of the Columbians' activities and the Walton County probe. McGill published his exposé of the Columbians on the day after the premiere. The responses we find in Atlanta's news reports and reviews are interesting for this reason; and also because they were spontaneous; whatever Atlanta critics and audiences made of the film, they did so without the guidance or influence of northern critics or black activists who had yet to see the film.

Preparations for the premiere

In the white press, the stories on the film and its premiere multiplied as senior editors and writers at the *Atlanta Constitution* recollected details of former editor and reporter Joel Chandler Harris' life. Ralph McGill and many other editors and writers there and at the *Atlanta Journal* weighed in a month before the preview, informing readers that the film was perfect and that it was something the Harris family could be proud of; indeed Harris' granddaughter announced that the film 'had everything' (i.e. humour, pathos, music and James Baskett). While Atlanta's hometown pride was boundless, these writers' approval of *Song of the South* was significant; Disney had run the risk of contradicting how Uncle Remus and the Br'er animals appeared in Atlantans' imaginations (especially since Disney made no effort to imitate A.B. Frost's illustrations which had accompanied Harris' books) and he had apparently run it successfully. Only one local reporter, Wright Bryan of the *Atlanta Journal*, expressed any misgivings at all about the film and he did that after the premiere: he too wished Disney had provided more animated sequences of the tales and less of the frame story.[38]

White Atlanta rose to the occasion of the premiere. Store windows up and down Peachtree Street had Br'er Rabbit displays and Rich's, the hometown department store, took out a full page newspaper ad of sketches from the stories for the occasion. The *Atlanta Journal* devoted its Sunday magazine cover story to the film.[39] Articles in both papers reported on how Pinto Colvig, the voice of Dopey and Pluto and Clarence Nash, the voice of Donald Duck, visited schools and the Egleston Children's Hospital in the city. Additional front page articles reported on the Armistice Day parade the day before the premiere; here the Hollywood group joined the Georgia infantry for a march down Peachtree Street, accompanied by planes from the nearby Naval Air Base and watched by an estimated 300,000 people, among whom were children excused from school by the Atlanta Board of Education.[40] Disney and his wife led the proceedings, followed by child stars Luana Patten and Bobby Driscoll, Ruth Warrick, Colvig, Nash and Adriana Casselotti (the voice of Snow White). None of the black actors – James Baskett, Hattie McDaniel and Glenn Leedy – attended the preliminaries or the premiere; their absence, especially Baskett's, was noted but never explained in the papers.

The reporters interviewed the actors who did come to Atlanta, doting especially on the two child stars. Warrick, who had played Emily in *Citizen Kane* (1941), told them about her decision not to use a southern dialect and wanted to reassure Atlantans that she was not as heartless as her character in the film, who forbids her son to visit Uncle Remus and thus creates much of the film's conflict and unhappiness. 'Neither do I think that is the way Southern women behave all the time. But it was necessary to the story and', Miss Warrick smiled disarmingly, 'besides, the man told me to do it'.[41] Other articles carried interviews with major executives from distributor RKO's New York and Hollywood headquarters, such as RKO president Ned Depinet, who told the papers, 'This is the most enthusiastic crowd of people I have ever seen. It's no wonder that all Hollywood stars are eager to visit Atlanta.'[42] Other articles reported on how Disney was feted throughout the day, including a tea at Harris' Wren's Nest, where he was photographed with the new backyard cabin and Joe McElroy, the 95-year-old Uncle Remus figure hired to tell stories to visiting children (white only; the Wren's Nest was not open to the black community until the 1970s). When considered alongside the looming newspaper ads for the film – featuring a horse and carriage and a white couple in front of a large *Gone With the Wind*-type plantation mansion as the Br'er animals look on – it is fair to say that the festivities and the premiere were given heavy coverage for the three days before, during and after the inaugural screening.[43]

The black press

The *Atlanta Daily World* by contrast, covered none of these events. Published by a family of ministers for a circulation of 30,000 nationwide, 17,000 (of the estimated 150,000 African Americans) in Atlanta and 13,000 rural Georgians, the paper addressed itself to a black middle and upper-middle class, high school and college educated readership – precisely the 'educated' blacks whom *Time* imagined would take offence at *Song of the South*.[44] And judging from the paper's coverage, the literate and civic-minded members of the African-American community were most concerned with the state of civil rights in the postwar era. Front page articles were given over not to the Armistice Day parade

Fig. 4. Br'er Rabbit. [Photo courtesy of Walt Disney Productions.]

and Disney's arrival, but to whether or not national leaders like President Truman would back federal anti-lynching legislation and whether Congress would censure figures like Theodore Bilbo, a Mississippi senator and proud Klu Klux Klan leader. Encouraged by the 1944 Supreme Court ruling and the gains associated with the black contribution to the war effort, the *Atlanta Daily World* in the postwar period espoused a gradualist, as opposed to a radical, position toward ameliorating blacks' political and social rights. Even as it witnessed miscarriages of justice, the election of Talmadge and the flourishing of undisguised racists, the paper's editorials affirmed that black civil rights would inevitably be achieved through changes in national sentiment and through established government channels, but that this would take time.

In fact, the *Atlanta Daily World* had much to cover – watching the gradual unfolding of the Columbians' schemes, reporting on the occasional murder of black citizens in cold blood and headlining

the lack of progress in the Walton county slayings – and few reporters and very little space (a typical issue ran six pages).[45] Besides highlighting federal and state news, its pages carried installments of serialised novels and lists of church sermons and social club activities. It ran a weekly column on the New York's theatre scene, keeping its readers in touch with the latest developments there.

Although the local segregated (and white-owned) Bailey's theatre chain advertised daily in the paper, the *Atlanta Daily World* was giving its programs no attention. This policy differed from the extensive coverage (publicity and reviews) of the mid-1930s when Bailey's showed films such as *Imitation of Life*,[46] or in December 1939, when the paper published front page articles on the Ebenezer Baptist Choir's performance at the Junior League's white-only *Gone With the Wind* Ball at the City Auditorium.[47] The *Song of the South* premiere, by contrast, was clearly not an event that the black community was invited to celebrate and having to

Fig. 5. The Plantation Ad, from the *Atlanta Constitution*, 11 November 1946, 15.

lum costumes and selling souvenir programs. The crowd took their seats or stood, in the 5000 seat orientalist Fox movie palace and were serenaded by the theatre's organ player. At 9 p.m. Parks Johnson (an Atlanta native) and Warren Hull, hosts of the 'Vox Pop' radio show, introduced Disney animators and voice artists Nash, Caselotti, Colvig, Cliff Edwards (the voice of Jiminy Crickett) and Disney himself, who greeted the audience in his Mickey Mouse voice, with 'How are you-all?' Joel Chandler Harris, Jr. came on stage and reminisced about his father; two six-year old Atlanta girls each told their favourite Uncle Remus story; and RKO stars Bill Williams and his wife Barbara Hale (not part of the cast of the film, but asked to show up for the hype anyway) participated in an audience contest. The proceedings were broadcast coast to coast over CBS radio and included the winning contestants in the Mutual Broadcasting Network's *Queen for a Day*, ABC's *Bride and Groom* and CBS' *Art Linkletter's House Party*.[49] This clearly was not in the same league with the huge rally on Peachtree Street that greeted Margaret Mitchell and the stars of *Gone With the Wind*, but it was exciting enough.

Song of the South itself began at 9:30 p.m. As *Time* predicted, the film evoked a nostalgic reverie for many of its white viewers. We have a fairly detailed account of that first public screening of the film in the *Atlanta Constitution*, in an article sarcastically titled 'Disney Puts "Tough Crowd" in His Pocket'; apparently the predominantly white audience found the film an exhilarating experience and displayed no awareness of the racist elements of the film. The *Constitution* writer reported that the premiere crowd met 'each new character with a spontaneous burst of applause that swept the house from the gallery [the review's only reference to the African-Americans in the audience] to the orchestra pit' (about fifteen times in all).[50] She continued, 'Deep sighs and appreciative long-drawn "Ah's" greeted' the opening carriage ride in the Georgia

choose between Harlem/Broadway and Hollywood or between real and immediate racism and Hollywood racism, the *Atlanta Daily World* devoted not a single article to Disney's visit or the film, even in the two months prior to the premiere. It would, however, carry news wire stories of Walter White and the AFT union's denunciations of the film in the weeks following the opening night.[48]

The premiere

The premiere itself was a full evening's entertainment. Tickets sold at anywhere from $1.25 to $7.50, adding up to a $30,000 gross, while scalpers took $25 a seat. After waiting outside the theatre in chilly, forty-degree temperatures, audiences were greeted at 7:30 in the lobby by thirty members of the Junior League, dressed in antebel-

countryside; as well as the first appearance of Hattie McDaniel, 'who will ever be identified locally as "Mammy" of *Gone with the Wind* fame'. A 'roar of laughter' came after the young black character's comment, 'Uncle Remus, you is the best story-teller in the whole 'N'united States of Gawgia!' The first instance of live action and animation together received an ovation. When the film ended Mayor William B. Hartsfield called Disney back and Disney introduced Ruth Warrick, Bobby Driscoll and Luana Patten from the film to overwhelming applause. Hartsfield hailed the film and James Baskett's performance as Uncle Remus as an outstanding bit of work; when he asked Disney to send Baskett a wire of congratulations, 'the house roared with applause'. The next day's papers would carry the superlatives uttered by leading politicians and social leaders, such as Governor Arnall's wife, who felt that Baskett's acting was the best element in the film.[51]

Atlanta's recent racist disturbances were bracketed out of this appreciation of the film; the racial issues the film evoked were 'invisible'.[52] One reporter wrote:

> [The crowd] looked far beyond the red velvet carpet, uniformed doormen, the blazing oriental decor of the Fox Theatre and saw the honest red dirt of Georgia, the weathered cabins that huddle on friendly mounds under tall pines, the dusty shabby old servitors of a kindlier day, focused richly amid the magic wrought from the homely philosophy of Joel Chandler Harris and moulded into reality in the facile fingers of Walt Disney and his crew ... It was everybody's picture. Grandmother, seeing it, could remember the golden days of yesterday. Her daughter, beside her, reached for snatches of tales long sleeping and the modern ones realised restively that much has gone from life that could ill be spared.[53]

The crow's nest

But if this was a film for everybody, not everybody saw it the same way. Having paid 60 cents for their tickets, interested African-Americans could watch the festivities in the theatre from the gallery or the 'Crow's Nest', the ten rows of seats at the very top of the Fox Theater's balcony. In order to get to these seats, black patrons had to go into the theatre at the separate entrance at the side of building and climb several stories of stairs. The Crow's Nest was separated from the rest of the balcony by a three foot wall.

It was from here that the *Atlanta Daily World*'s reviewer, William A. Fowlkes, a ten year veteran columnist and reporter, watched the film. His review, titled 'Baskett Supreme in *Song of the South*', affirms that the audience loved the film. But from the perspective of the gallery with the other black patrons (it appears Fowlkes was not 'invited' to the premiere), the film and the screening had distinctly different meanings. Where the *Constitution* attributed the audience's appreciation to the film's re-creation of rural Georgia, the *World*'s critic suggested that the audience was moved just as much by the spirit of racial harmony the film presented:

> Perhaps the first applause in the film came when Glenn Leedy, as the plantation coloured boy 'assigned' to take care of Bobby Driscoll, the little boy and his charge, began to play as natural children about the place. There was a reluctant but sure applause as those below the gallery apparently remembered days proceeding this Klan-Columbian era when children played more together 'as children'.

The racist incidents occurring beyond the theatre's doors were not far from Fowlkes' mind and this fact meant the film's rendering of interracial harmony among children was hopeful. The film, Fowlkes wrote in his very first paragraph, 'is destined to bring a new warmth and spirit of tolerance and understanding between the races in America's tense melting pot, if future audiences react as did the 5,000 who crowded the Fox Theater ...'[54]

Fowlkes raised the kinds of objections that Walter White and other groups would voice as the film opened nationwide, but noted them only to qualify them by invoking Baskett's performance. He observed that the setting of a 'Southern plantation, antiquated locale' was 'somewhat obnoxious to the aspirations of a race getting away from slavery time settings', yet 'the film brought tears and laughter alike from Negroes and whites who thrilled to the superb performance of James Baskett as Uncle

Fig. 6. Glenn Leedy and Bobby Driscoll (with James Baskett) won applause for the natural playfulness of their relationship. [Photo courtesy of Walt Disney Productions.]

Remus'. Baskett's absence from the opening night festivities 'sort of chilled us at first. But Baskett got the glory and the recognition as soon as his bearded and glowing brown face was first shone on the screen.' The animated sequences were so wonderful that 'we forgot momentarily the influence of an outmoded dialect and Old South way of life'.

In short, *The Daily World* review is more thoroughly ambivalent about the film than any other account, finding solace in a performance that outstrips it and reading the audience as hopefully as the film for signs that Georgia's racist backlash would soon end. Of course, the Fox audience that watched the film was a far cry from the Columbians and Walton County lynchers; and yet the film would play to enthusiastic audiences all around the state, some of whom would include viewers sympathetic to turning back the clock of race relations.[55]

The stark contrast between the *Atlanta Daily World*'s ambivalent reception of *Song of the South* and white Atlanta's whole-hearted embrace of the film is to be expected; but the difference between

the reservations voiced by northern film critics and the denunciations of national black activist groups on the one hand and the *Atlanta Daily World*'s qualified admiration for the film on the other, is surprising.

There were of course grounds for denouncing the film, both those related to the film itself and more forcefully, the unhappy events unfolding in and around Atlanta. The *Atlanta Daily World* was not intimidated by the Columbians nor by the slow progress in the Walton County lynching investigations – the paper's outrage over these events was evident in its headlines, yet there were many reasons not to make an issue of *Song of the South*. The *Atlanta Daily World* editors (and that portion of their readership that shared their views and values) felt enough pride in Joel Chandler Harris' stories and Harris himself as a city institution to downplay its abhorrence of regressive stereotypes; the 'harmlessness' of its animated sequences and the heartwarming aura of Baskett's performance outweighed the film's drawbacks. Had the NAACP organised a protest

Fig. 7. Song of the South: 'De best movie I've seed lately'. [Photo courtesy of Walt Disney Productions.]

at the premiere, of course, the review of the film would not have been so sanguine. Even in the face of the appalling events in recent Atlanta and Georgia history, the paper could affirm its gradualist stance by reading potential progress for race relations in the film's scenes of children playing together. Judging from the premiere audience, nostalgia could be an effective tool for raising white consciousness and making the plight of post-war African-Americans more visible to the city's responsible and humane white citizens.

A white account of black response

So could parody. One additional surprise in the white newspaper coverage of *Song of the South*'s premiere shows a reporter investigating the response of one black viewer and it demonstrates once more how multifaceted white and black responses to the film could be, even in Atlanta. Tom Ham, a reporter for the *Atlanta Journal*, arranged

for Joe McElroy – the 95 year-old former slave whom the Uncle Remus Memorial Association hired to be 'Uncle Remus' and tell stories at the Wren's Nest – to have a special seat at the front of the Fox Theater gallery; Ham sat just in front of the wall separating black and white viewers and much as Fowlkes had watched the white audience, watched the old man as he watched the film.

The resulting article, 'Atlanta's "Uncle Remus" Takes "Song" in Stride', reads like a parody of the superlatives the white 'carriage trade' and civic leaders had heaped on the film in the paper's other pages and on the city and the culture's adoration for the Uncle Remus figure.[56] While acknowledging that McElroy was impressed and delighted by *Song of the South* (even though McElroy informed him that he could not hear all the dialogue), Ham framed his article as a futile attempt to get the old man to gush over the film in Uncle Remus' (i.e. dialect) style, scratching his head and exclaiming, as Ham envisioned it, 'Lawd [sic], Lawd, Lawd, cap'n whitefolks marster – ef dat ain't plumb de beatn'est thing Ah ever seed in all mah bawn days!'

Ham described his expectations of McElroy's response to be one of profound emotion:

> The tears should have been coursing down his grizzled old face, covered as it was with close-cropped hoary whiskers bearing the frost of his 95 years. He should have been completely, touchingly, reverently, overawed.

> What he did was to say, 'Hit was fine', and then start telling us about a picture he'd seen some time ago at the Harlem Theater on McDaniel Street, half a block from where he lives.

> Hence the Fox Theater was no more memorable or impressive to McElory than one of the segregated theatres in the city's black neighbourhood (and it certainly was harder to enter for an African-American viewer).

On the drive home, Ham reported, McElroy told him:

> 'Hit was – [sic] hit was de bes' thing – ' he groped for words and I waited breathlessly. Here, at last, came the superlative I had been trying to worm out of him since the picture started.

> 'Hit was the bes' thing', Uncle Joe said, 'de best movie I've seed lately'.

Ham concluded the piece by characterising McElroy's remark that he didn't fall asleep once during the film as 'the loftiest tribute' the elderly man could pay to Disney, whom he had been photographed with earlier in the day.[57]

Clearly the article and the evening was a set-up. Ham like other white reporters made no mention of the racist troubles occurring in Atlanta as a factor in how one would view the film. In McElroy, Ham had a near centenarian of remarkable lucidity who probably would never have complained about the film he had been taken to see by a white reporter. Yet Ham's interest in a black viewer's response – a viewer singled out as a citizen of Harris' era – reflects a certain scepticism on the part of the *Atlanta Journal* (and by extension, of some white Atlantans) toward the Disney film and the city's festivities surrounding it. This sensibility contrasts with the *Atlanta Constitution*'s whole-hearted and unanimous embrace of the proceedings and of the film (and its disinterest in black responses to it) and complicates any effort to generalise about what white Atlanta thought of the film. Not every white Atlantan was totally in thrall to *Song of the South*. By framing the piece in terms of an ironic, self-mocking quest for black affirmation of Uncle Remus' cultural authenticity and of Disney's portrait, Ham illustrated the conventionality of such representations and the absurdities of such expectations.

White Atlanta's response to *Song of the South* was ultimately more complex than *Time* magazine or anyone else could have anticipated. The whole-hearted embrace of the film by certain white reporters, the ambivalence of the *Atlanta Daily World's* reviewer and the irony of the *Atlanta Journal* reporter testify yet again to the value of local histories for nuancing our understanding of how a film played out upon its release – particularly in Atlanta, where the views of northern film critics and black activists had not yet been expressed – and it opens up for us a range of more specific issues affecting a film's reception beyond the basic question of how the film depicted race and race relations. If in the context of virulent racism, viewer nostalgia could be read as a sign of hope for better inter-racial relations in the South, viewer irony could prove an effective antidote to the codes of black subordination in Hollywood films of the postwar era. Atlanta's reactions to *Song of the South* encompassed both these attitudes, as well as responses that resided ambivalently between them.✤

Acknowledgements: My thanks to Lance McCready and Todd Wright for research assistance, to Professor Dana White for corrections and to John Belton for his editorial acumen and encouragement. The research in this essay was supported in part by the University Research Committee of Emory University.

Notes

1. *Song of the South* was the sixth premiere to take place in Atlanta; earlier premieres included *Who Killed Aunt Maggie* (1940), *Parachute Battalion* (1941) and *Wilson* (1943). Bob McKee, '"Remus" Premiere is Fifth for City', *Atlanta Journal*, 13 November 1946: 6. The premiere of King Vidor's Civil War melodrama *So Red the Rose* in November 1935 had been forgotten in the aftermath of

GWTW. *Atlanta Constitution,* 10 November 1935: 15A

2. 'Wren's Nest, Well-Featured by Premiere, To Get Face Lifting', *Atlanta Constitution,* 10 November 1946: 14A. The president of the Uncle Remus Memorial Association was married to the owner (William M. Jenkins) of the palatial Fox Theater, where *Song of the South* premiered. Paul Jones, 'Disney's Contingent Honored at Reception', *Atlanta Constitution,* 13 November 1946: 3. The Wren's Nest is still maintained in Atlanta's west side and still offers storytelling sessions to weekend visitors.

3. Harold H. Martin, *Atlanta and Environs: A Chronicle of Its People and Events, Vol. 3* (Athens: University of Georgia Press, 1987): 126; John McCarten, 'Films in Review', *The New Yorker,* 30 November 1946: 88.

4. Critics typically remark that *Song of the South* was a commercial success for Disney but actual figures are hard to come by. *Motion Picture Herald* reported a gross of $920,500 as of 1 March 1947, four and a half months after its Atlanta premiere.

5. Thomas Cripps, in *Making Movies Black* (New York: Oxford University Press, 1993), 175.

6. Cripps, 188–190. Lawrence W. Levine has discussed the appeals and meanings of the trickster tales for African-Americans in *Black Culture and Black Consciousness* (New York: Oxford University Press, 1977).

    Peter Noble recounts how reporter Frederic Mullally asked Disney at a press conference if educated blacks were protesting the film's Uncle Remus as a 'not very subtle attempt to confirm the white American's argument that the Negro was a much more likeable fellow when, like Uncle Remus, he "knew his place" and had no impertinent political or social aspirations'. Disney denied there would be any real antagonism towards the film, went on to assert that the criticism came from the radicals ... [and later] declared that the time had not yet come when Negro susceptibilities could be treated with as much delicacy as Hollywood reserves for, say, the American Catholics!'. See *The Negro in Films* (rpt. New York: Arno Press & The New York Times, 1970): 219.

    Disney told the Atlanta papers he obtained the rights to the stories from the Harris family in 1940 and considered *The Song of the South* the first of several folktale films he planned (one on Pecos Bill and one on Irish leprechauns). This is recounted in Rebecca Franklin, '5,000 Give Ovation to Remus Premiere', *Atlanta Journal,* 13 November 1946: 1, 6. It is possible but unlikely that Disney's agreement with the Harris family stipulated what the treatment of plantation life should be.

7. I use the term 'attraction' in Sergei Eisenstein and Tom Gunning's sense; see Eisenstein's 'The Montage of Attractions' in *Selected Works, Volume I, Writings, 1922–1934,* trans. and ed. Richard Taylor (Bloomington: Indiana University Press, 1988), 33–38; and Tom Gunning, 'The Cinema of Attraction: Early Film, Its Spectator and the Avant-Garde', *Wide Angle* 8, no. 3–4 (1986): 63–70.

8. Cripps, 187.

9. Cripps, 190–191.

10. 'White Regrets Film', *The New York Times,* 28 November 1946, 40.

11. 'Film Censoring Bureau Planned', Atlanta *Daily World,* 12 December 1946, 2. Citing a scene in *In This Our Life* in which a black secondary character tells Bette Davis he wants to attend law school so he can work for the betterment of black people, White commented: 'Since I am light enough to pass as a white, I attended exhibitions of this film in Richmond, Atlanta and Houston – and in every instance, a preponderance of the white audience applauded the statement'.

12. '*Song of the South* Picketed', *The New York Times,* 14 December 1946, 18. Thanks to Todd Wright for bringing this to my attention.

13. 'Teachers Union Raps *Song of the South*', *Atlanta Daily World,* 12 January 1946, 7.

14. Eric Smoodin, *Animating Culture: Hollywood Cartoons from the Sound Era* (New Brunswick: Rutgers University Press, 1993), 107–108.

15. Only Philip Hartung of *Commonweal* appreciated Disney's handling of the frame tale that surrounded Disney's retelling of Joel Chandler Harris' Uncle Remus tales with animation. John McCarten, 88; Bosley Crowther, 'The Screen', *The New York Times,* 28 November 1946, 40; Bosley Crowther, 'Spanking Disney: Walt Is Chastised for *Song of the South*' *The New York Times,* 8 December 1946, Sec. 2: 1; 'The New Pictures', *Time* 18 November 1946, 101; 'Disney's Uncle Remus', *Newsweek,* 2 December 1946, 109; Philip T. Hartung, 'Look Away Look Away', *The Commonweal,* 6 December 1946, 202; and Manny Farber, 'Dixie Corn', *The New Republic,* 23 November 1946, 879.

    By contrast, to Bosley Crowther, the film showed that 'the Disney wonderworkers are just a lot of conventional hacks when it comes to telling a story with actors instead of cartoons' (28 November 1946). Though the film script tried to weave the tales and the frame story together – whereby little Johnnie

(Bobby Driscoll) learns a lesson from the tales about how to handle his own trivial troubles – Crowther felt the animated and live action sequences did not fit in together well at all (8 December 1946).

16. Crowther, 'Spanking Disney ...'

17. 'The New Pictures', *Time* 18 November 1946, 101; cited in Eric Smoodin, 107–108.

18. Smoodin, 107.

19. Donald Bogle, *Toms, Coons, Mulattoes, Mammies and Bucks*, 3rd. ed. (New York: Continuum, 1994), 198.

20. James Snead, *White Screens, Black Images* (New York: Routledge, 1994, 84–88, 96–97. Cripps makes similar points about Remus' position in the film, 192.

I would argue that the film is more contradictory than such criticisms suggest, at least until its conclusion. Remus is rendered unnecessary by Bobby's mastery of storytelling at the film's end, but until that point, the film has placed all of its excitement and emotion with Remus, who demonstrates the power and magic of storytelling, albeit with the overtones of menace that Snead describes (see page 92). It is not difficult to see how Disney and his scriptwriters created in Remus (and the way he is placed in particular shots) an ideal image of the storyteller/animator – best appreciated by children, misunderstood by cultural guardians and deeply wounded by the circumscribed nature of their endeavours.

Similarly, the narrative of *The Song of the South* brings the white family into harmonious healing once again. (Jonathan Rosenbaum has pointed out the resonance of Bobby's absent father for American families during World War II; see his *Moving Places* (Berkeley: UC Press, 1995) pp. 153–154). But until that time, however reactionary and regrettable the portrayal of Remus, Aunt Ginny and the black workers on the plantation as pseudo servants are, they are far more appealing as characters than any of the whites. Bobby's mother Sally (Ruth Warrick) is a haughty, cold, shrill, totally uncomprehending mother, whose prohibitions against Bobby's consorting with Remus obliviously and inexplicably deny the child the only comforts he can find at his grandmother's house. And while Ginny, Bobby's po' white trash neighbour, is also appealing, her big brothers, who threaten to drown her favourite puppy, extend the film's negative portrayal of whites across class and families. The film gives very compelling reasons why any new arrival in *that* community would prefer the company of African-Americans.

21. 'The New Pictures'.

22. Wallace H. Warren, 'The Best People in Town Won't Talk: The Moore's Ford Lynching of 1946 and Its Cover-Up', in John C. Inscoe, ed. *Georgia in Black and White: Explorations in the Race Relations of a Southern State, 1865–1950* (Athens: University of Georgia Press, 1994), 266.

23. The lessening importance of cotton to local industry, combined with new federal wage laws, meant that white landowners' profits from the exploited poor whites and blacks could no longer continue. See Warren for an excellent discussion of this economic background.

24. Warren, 268; Jacqueline Jones, *Labor of Love, Labor of Sorrow: Black Women, Work and the Family from Slavery to the Present* (New York: Basic Books, 1985), 267.

25. Quoted in Warren, 268.

26. Warren describes the investigation, 278–282.

27. Arnall subsequently lead Hollywood's Society of Independent Motion Picture Producers.

28. '15 to 17 In Lynching Mob Known, Governor Says', *Atlanta Constitution*, 8 November 1946, 1.

29. 'Wallace Blasts Monroe Lynching As Prejudice Making For Warfare; Says Cost of Peace Must Be of Heart Value', *Atlanta Daily World*, 18 September 1946, 1.

30. 'With Our Regrets', *Atlanta Daily World*, 24 December 1946, 6.

31. Claude L. Weaver, 'Negro Homicides In '46 Outnumber Whites 10 To One', *The Daily World*, 1 January 1947, 1; and 'There's A Difference', *The Daily World*, 1 January 1947, 6.

32. 'Georgia Power Motorman Freed in Negro Slaying', *The Daily World*, 17 October 1946, 1.

33. 'Atlanta's Tension Spots', *Atlanta Daily World*, 17 September 1946, 6.

34. Ralph McGill, 'A Failure and the Blame', *Atlanta Constitution*, 13 November 1946, 8.

35. 'Even-Handed Justice', *Atlanta Daily World*, 25 February 1947, 6.

36. 'Columbians Confess Terrorism; Fantastic Scheming Uncovered', *Atlanta Daily World*, 11 December 1946, 1.

37. 'Atlanta's Hate-Peddlers', *Atlanta Daily World*, 5 November 1946, 6.

38. Paul Jones, 'News Writers Enjoy "Uncle Remus"

Film', *Atlanta Constitution*, 13 October 1946, 11-B; Bessie S. Stafford, 'Harris, Painfully shy, Dodged T.R.'s Reception Line', *Atlanta Constitution*, 12 November 1946, 12. Ernest Rogers, '"Enchanting" Is Word for *Song of the South*', *Atlanta Journal*, 3 November 1946, 19A; Ralph McGill, "Critter Company" To Arrive Today To Kindle Light of Remus Stories', *Atlanta Constitution*, 10 November 1946, 14A. Ralph McGill praised Baskett for not indulging in stereotype and caricature and making 'something genuine of it'; McGill's sentiments were typical:

The light of the Uncle Remus stories had grown dim with the passing of the years ... So the windows of the world – windows that Joel Chandler Harris' great genius could not reach, will blaze with the light of that genius and the far reaches and forgotten corners of the world will laugh and grow misty of eye as they see on the screens of their countries the sassy arrogance of Br'er Rabbit, the frustrated plots of Br'er Fox and his lumbering aid, Br'er Bear.

Wright Bryan's dissent appears as 'Brer Rabbit Returns to His Briar Patch', *Atlanta Journal*, 13 November 1946, 14.

39. Full page ad, *Atlanta Constitution*, 11 November 1946, 13.

40. Bob Collins, 'Thousands Watch Armistice Parade', *Atlanta Journal*, 10 November 1946, 1; 'RKO Launches *Song of the South*', *Motion Picture Herald*, 16 November 1946, 54.

41. Celestine Sibley, 'If Atlanta Likes Song of the South, So Will World, Disney Feels', *Atlanta Constitution*, 11 November 1946, 1, 12.

42. Paul Jones, 'Eager Autograph Hounds Flock About Film Stars', *Atlanta Constitution*, 12 November 1946, 6.

43. The *Atlanta Constitution*, probably because of its historical association with Joel Chandler Harris, gave the events more coverage than the *Atlanta Journal*, but even the latter gave the festivities a considerable amount of space.

44. The *Atlanta Daily World* was founded as a weekly in 1928 by W.A. Scott and went daily four years later. Scott's successor, his brother C.A., was active in the Ebenezer Baptist Church where Martin Luther King, Sr. preached. On the Scott-King connection, see Taylor Branch, *Parting the Waters: America in the King Years, 1954–1963* (New York: Simon & Schuster, 1988), 287. The paper is still published today by the Scott family.

Atlanta's black population of roughly 150,000 in the mid-1940s boasted the largest professional class of blacks in the South. Although black neighbourhoods remained concentrated in the south and west of the city and although a definite colour line was described in a 1922 zoning ordinance, the black population of Atlanta, thirty per cent of the city's total population, had never been confined to a ghetto as such. Howard L. Preston discusses residential patterns in Atlanta in the 1920s and 1930s in his *Automobile Age Atlanta* (Athens: University of Georgia Press, 1979), 96–112. This is surprising, given the city's infamous race riot of 1906 and the 1915 renewal of the Klu Klux Klan at nearby Stone Mountain, Georgia, roughly ten miles outside the city.

Atlanta also boasted historically black colleges which make up the Atlanta University Centre (which Martin Luther King, Jr. and many other business and political leaders attended; King studied at Morehouse College). The city had an extensive number of black private businesses; outstanding among these was Heman E. Perry's Standard Life Insurance company and the Citizen's Trust Company, the first black owned bank to join the Federal Reserve system and the source of many a mortgage for black middle and upper-middle class homes in the city. Many of these concerns thrived by catering to African-Americans in the Jim Crow South and concentrated most notably along 'Sweet Auburn Avenue', which was a core middle-class neighbourhood. The *Atlanta Daily World* was one of these businesses. See Robert J. Alexander, 'Negro Businesses in Atlanta (1894–1950)', *Southern Economic Journal* 17 (April 1951): 451–461.

45. William A. Fowlkes, who penned the review of *Song of the South* I will be discussing, has recalled, 'We were so busy covering so many things. The *World*'s coverage at that time was limited to a great degree. We had in 1946 a city editor and a city newsreporter and we used to alternate day and night shifts. We just couldn't get around to everything.' Telephone interview with William A. Fowlkes, 24 January 1996.

46. See Randy Gue, '"It Seems That Everything Looks Good Nowadays, as Long as It Is in the Flesh and Brownskin": The Assertion of Cultural Difference at Atlanta's 81 Theatre, 1934–1937', elsewhere in this issue, for a detailed description of the *Atlanta Daily World*'s coverage of movies in the mid-1930s. The policy of not giving over significant space to movies predates the city of Atlanta's February 1945 ordinance calling for segregation of the races in all public spaces.

47. 'Ebenezer Choir Scores at Gala "GWTW" Ball', *Atlanta Daily World*, 15 December 1939, 1; 'Atlanta Back to Normalcy As Stars Depart', 16 December 1939, 1. See Taylor Branch, 54–55, for an account of the political rows Martin Luther King, Sr.

faced for allowing his choir to participate in this white-only, 'sinful' event.

48. 'Considers "Uncle Remus" Dangerous', *Atlanta Daily World*, 6 December 1946, 1; 'Teachers Union Raps *Song of the South*', *The Daily World*, 12 January 1946, 7.

49. '3 Networks to Spotlight *Song of the South* Premiere', *Atlanta Constitution*, 10 November 1946, 12-C.

50. Celestine Sibley, 'Disney Puts "Tough Audience" in his Pocket', *Atlanta Constitution*, 13 November 1946, 1; Rebecca Franklin, '5,000 Give Ovation to Remus Premiere', *Atlanta Journal*, 13 November 1946, 1.

51. For example, Paul Jones, 'Disney's Great "Remus" Film Hailed for Abundance of Humor, Pathos', *Atlanta Constitution*, 13 November 1946, 14.

52. See Joel Williamson, *The Crucible of Race: Black-White Relations in the American South Since Emancipation* (New York: Oxford University Press, 1984), 459–510, for a discussion of the dynamics of black 'invisibility' at the turn of the century.

53. Doris Lockerman, 'Atlanta Welcomes Uncle Remus Back in Golden Film of Old South's Glory', *Atlanta Constitution*, 13 November 1946, 1.

54. William A. Fowlkes, 'Baskett Supreme in *Song of the South*,' *The Daily World*, 14 November 1946, 1.

55. *Motion Picture Herald*'s 'What the Picture Did for Me' column reflects unanimous success for the film in small towns within and outside of Georgia for a year after the Atlanta premiere. After a two-day run, the Gray Theater manager of Gray, Georgia reported, 'This is tops in entertainment. Being a Georgia picture and being true to Southern tradition, the crowds turned out en masse ... Everyone will profit by playing this' (1 March 1947, 43; and again 29 November 1947, 36); a theatre manager from Dahlonega, Georgia agreed (19 April 1947, 45). Similar sentiments were published from south Miami (26 April 1947, 48); Loveland, Ohio (10 May 1947, 49); Milan, Indiana (31 May 1947, 42); Danville, Indiana and Dewey, Oklahoma (14 June 1947, 41); Rivesville, West Virginia (9 August 1947, 49); Galena, Illinois (25 October 1947, 38); Inverness, Mississippi (13 December 1947, 41); Homer, Louisiana (3 January 1948, 37).

56. Tom Ham, 'Atlanta's "Uncle Remus" Takes "Song" in Stride', *Atlanta Journal*, 13 November 1946, 11.

57. Bill Boring, 'Dedicates Log Cabin at Snapbean Farm', *Atlanta Constitution*, 12 November 1946, 8.

Film History, Volume 8, pp.237–248 1996. Copyright © John Libbey & Company
ISSN: 0892-2160. Printed in Australia

A conversation with writer and director Kevin Smith

Clinton Duritz, Jr.

The following interview with writer and director Kevin Smith took place on Friday, 13 October 1995 at the offices of Smith's View Askew Productions in Red Bank, New Jersey. In 1993, Smith and his friends produced *Clerks* (1994) for less than thirty thousand dollars and in less than thirty days. A week before his second film *Mallrats* (1995) was due to be released, Smith took some time out in order to discuss filmmaking, the production of *Clerks* and why he detests certain aspects of film theory.

* * *

cdj: So,. How old are you anyway?
Smith: 25.
cdj: Did you graduate high school?
Smith: I graduated in '88.
cdj: And what were you planning on doing?
Smith: I wanted to make it to '89. That was my deepest ambition at that point. Right after high school I went to college in New York. Basically, I wanted to be a writer ... So I went to the New School for Social Research and skipped the first semester. I stayed until May but I just couldn't stand the city; the sound of horns in the morning, the smell of Chinese food everywhere. Plus, I got in trouble once for throwing water balloons from our 8th floor room. The school caught on and I got busted. They sent two notes home to my parents! (laughs) I was in college, that was the thing that infuriated me! ... So I decided it wasn't for me, I came back home and ended up at the local community college.
cdj: Brookdale?
Smith: Yeah, I tried doing that on and off for two

or three years and that didn't really pan out. The only thing I knew I was really good at was writing. But I just didn't know what I could do. I figured if I was lucky I could get a job at a paper or something, but is that the kind of writing I would want to do? I couldn't imagine ever getting into writing books or just finding that niche. I didn't really know how to enter that world.
cdj: Were you always interested in writing even when you were younger?
Smith: Yeah, the dream in high school was to write for *Saturday Night Live*.
cdj: Really?
Smith: Yeah, well the dream is dead.
cdj: Were you confident in your writing?
Smith: It's never me, I'm one of these people that waits for a reaction. So the first thing I wrote was a story about my relatives. I let my brother read it and he was just laughing, so that made me feel good. The more people I hung out with and respected their opinions ... I would usually write stuff about them and let them read it. Then they would laugh and tell me it was pretty good so that helped. I mean I could always turn a phrase but it's still embarrassing to read the stuff I wrote in high school; how overwritten and [redundant] it was, it's just painful. But it was there, at least it was all of something. Then it gets

An excerpt from this interview was originally published in the November 1995 issue of Smug Magazine. **Clinton Duritz, Jr.** is in fact Shai Halperin, Senior Film Editor of Smug Magazine. Please address correspondence to Shai Halperin, 32 Gloucester Ct., East Brunswick, NJ 08816, USA.

trimmed down to become what the style eventually is.

cdj: So what kind of classes were you studying at Brookdale?

Smith: For one year, me and a friend took all these Criminology courses.

cdj: Why?

Smith: No reason. Secretly, we thought we could turn into hard core vigilante detectives, we'd just need a place to store the car. But it was just for the hell of it.

cdj: So where did film come in?

Smith: Well, film was a two step process. I was working at this video store for a couple of years and this guy, Vincent, was the mop boy. He would come in every night for four or five months and we would never talk. And then one night we just started talking about *Twin Peaks* for some reason. Suddenly we realised that we both liked movies. But at this point I wasn't into film, I just watched movies galore.

cdj: Did you really watch movies galore though?

Smith: Oh galore, galore! Yeah I watched a lot. So after hanging out we found mutual interests in terms of 'everything sucks, this sucks! All these movies suck'. And we got into the idea of people making better movies or cut-above movies. The ones that were widely accessible to us were by people like Martin Scorsese, David Lynch or Spike Lee. But then we started getting into independent film and we started going into the city (NYC) to see movies, a concept which was totally mind-bending to my friends. I mean, why would you drive over an hour away to see a movie? But they were running movies around there that they just don't run around here.

cdj: Doesn't that suck about New Jersey?

Smith: Absolutely. There's no art house. The closest one is the Angelika Theatre. They do one at Rutgers but that's a one-shot screening months after it's over. So we were introduced to the Angelika and one week we read this review in *The Village Voice* about *Slacker* (1991). The review was really good and the movie just sounded 'whacked'. Finally, on the night of my 21st birthday I had nothing better to do, so we went up to New York to see the movie and that was the moment. That was the key moment: Watching that movie and finding it amusing and different. I thought, 'How could someone make a movie like this? There's no plot.' And then hearing the audience just go nuts around us, I found

it funny, but just not as funny as they were. It was strange. So, it's cliché by now because I always say it, but it's a mixture of awe and arrogance. It's like you sit there and say, 'This movie is amazing, it's truly amazing'. And then on the other hand it's like, 'I could make a better movie. If they think this is funny, I could really make them laugh'. So based on that night I decided 'that's what I want to do with my life'. I looked around and saw this ad for the Vancouver Film School. It was a cheap program and the phone call was free so I enrolled. All of my friends weren't really condescending but they just thought I would go there and drop out ... which I did four months later but that's where I met Scott (Mosier, producer) and David (Klein, Director of Photography).

Film school

cdj: What was bad about the school? What were you learning there?

Smith: Well, we hit this four month mark where you could cancel the second half of the tuition and I was just weighing the pros and cons: 'What have I learned? Nothing. I've learned that I hate film school. I've met some good people but I haven't learned anything about the craft'.

cdj: What were they teaching you?

Smith: They promised no theory and they spent the first two months doing theory before you even touched any equipment. Then when we got to hands-on experience it was Hi-8 video, so me and Scott made a documentary. We had this idea to document this female who was going to have a sex-change operation and our idea was chosen as one of the four that the class would work on. Well, being chosen was a great feeling but now we had to actually do it. Then, the woman backed out and we were stuck. Our crew, which was made up of people whose projects hadn't been picked to begin with, just hated us because they thought it was our fault. So, the school was going to pull the plug on our project but we asked them if we could make a documentary about how our documentary fell apart. So, they gave us three days and we did it. Me and Scott just put together this really tongue and cheek piece. We had ourselves back-lit so it was just our silhouettes and we were all ashamed of our failure. Everyone else was all serious and their work was like a manifesto for why they should pass the class. For us, we just wanted to have something done, but it wound up being really well received. Now it's funny because they show that to every class considering we went on to make *Clerks* and *Mallrats* (1995) and we're in the business, so to speak. But I dropped out and went home. The plan was that David, Scott and I would all start writing and whoever finished first, the other two would come down and help. So, I was first out of the gates.

cdj: If I could backtrack for a second, since I notice the Kristin Thompson book on your shelf … (Smith turns back, confused.) You didn't even know you had it?

Smith: Oh, that's a gift from my lawyer. (laughs) There's a little post-it note on the page where 'Smith' should be saying, 'You'll be here next year'.

cdj: You say you dropped out because they were teaching film theory. Were you always one of those film viewers who, when someone interpreted it and analysed it, was like, 'Shut up, it's just a movie!'

Smith: Exactly! That was it. It was a matter of somebody else giving you their idea of what that movie was about. It's like the only one you could ever listen to is the filmmaker himself. You produce the filmmaker and let him tell me what it's about and I'll believe him! But, you've got a teacher in Vancouver translating what this film was, it just doesn't wash! And it's just that talking about movies was not what the school was supposed to be about. It was supposed to be hands-on filmmaking … Because, in the end, it depends what you want to do. I wanted to write, I didn't even necessarily want to direct. The only reason I wanted to direct was to maintain what I wrote. For example, I recently did this rewrite for Caravan Pictures. I mean, this was an abysmal fucking terrible script. All they did was buy it for the concept and it read like shit. So, I thought it would be an interesting challenge to rewrite it. And, I just destroyed the script and rebuilt it until it was something totally different. And then Caravan sold the script to New Line and they hired this director to do it. So I'm supposed to be working with this director on the script and for the first time something I've written is

Fig. 1. An interview with Kevin Smith. [Photo by Dennis Kleiman.]

going to be directed by someone else. But since the script, if you read it, it reeks of me and it reeks of my style and characters; it just smells like my movie. I don't know if he's working from the position of actually believing his notes are valid or from the position that 'I have to instill some sense of authorship on this project because in the end I'll make this movie and people won't even know I made it'. But going through these notes, I'm reading it and totally disagreeing with everything he's saying! He wants to take out characters that are fresh and original and replace them with stock characters. On one hand you just want to take the guy and shake him but you can't do that. So, ultimately it just reinforced the idea that I had always worked on in theory which is, 'I only want to direct because I don't want to write a script and then have some asshole change it'. Now I can speak from experience that I never want to write a script where I have something emotionally invested in it and then have some asshole translating it. That's why I want to direct, but going back to the original point about film school, if you want to do what I'm doing, if you want to write and be a writer/director, either you can write or you can't write. And if you can write, nine times out of ten you can direct. Because you've written it and you know exactly how it should sound and look or feel and … who better than you to translate that? I mean, in the end people ask, 'Well what about lenses and stuff, what about all the technical shit?' (Forcefully) Well surround yourself with people who know that stuff! Filmmaking is a collaborative process! It's like, you could put a lens in front of me and I couldn't even tell you what it was. And people say, 'Spielberg knows all his lenses'. Well that's all fine and good, maybe I don't know but David, the cinematographer, does. And so, I put all my trust in David. I'll tell him basically what I want in the shot, what the framing should be and he'll light it any way he wants.

cdj: So you're not involved in lighting but you do have ideas of how you want to frame the shot when you go into it.

Smith: Pretty much. In *Mallrats*, there were a few scenes where I wanted them lit a certain way. Some shots I know exactly how they should be. But with *Mallrats*, it's a studio movie right? So you have to do 'coverage' because the rationale is basically: when we shot *Clerks*, it was all master shots and the audience was going to pick what they want to look at. Sometimes they would look at the guy who's talking, sometimes …

cdj: … They would look at the porno mags in the background.

Smith: Yeah, sometimes they would look at the scenery. When you're shooting 'coverage' basically what you're saying is', You, the audience, are idiots and this is what you have to look at when we tell you to look at it'.

Film school dropout

cdj: So, how did the studio express to you that you had to or it was preferred that you, use this kind of method?

Smith: Oh, point blank! I mean they watched *Clerks* and they were just like …

cdj: … 'You can't do this'.

Smith: Yeah, exactly. It's like, 'if you think you're going to do this movie in "masters", you're insane'.

cdj: And you didn't respond badly to that? I mean, you took that?

Smith: Well, yeah. It was one of those things that, going into *Mallrats*, we knew it was a commercial movie, we knew there were certain things we had to adhere to and adapt to make a commercial movie or a mainstream movie and that was just one of them. But even though we shot coverage doesn't mean we had to use it, so there are an inordinate amount of master shots in *Mallrats* for a mainstream movie; especially for a mainstream movie directed straight at the 15–30 year old young males, because their attention span is supposed to be the shortest and you're supposed to be cutting back and forth to keep them there. But there are master shots that we hold on to for three or four minutes. I don't think you always have to dictate what the audience is looking at. But, again back to film school, yeah I dropped out. I already knew how to write, they weren't going to teach me how to do that. And as far as directing, that's not something that can really be taught, that's something you can kind of learn from watching movies. If you talk to everybody, listen to people that do it; Martin Scorsese, he's a film library, he just watches so many movies. You basically combine so many elements to create whatever style it is you have. And it was funny, the first piece ever written about *Clerks* was by Amy Taubin in *The Village Voice* and it was after the IFFM (Independent Feature Film Market) in 1993 where it was screened for the first time. She was like, 'His style, is that he has no style'. And I always thought that was really funny but it's true. It's a conscious effort to not do something wacky. The music video I directed for *Mallrats* is like that and it's a parody of that style. So, I can do that if I want to but I just don't like it. That's not the kind of film I like to watch. I like to watch stuff in masters, I don't like to be told what to look at … So, if you want to be the sound guy, if you want to be a cinematographer, there's a craft there to be learned; it's very technical. But if you want to direct, I'm sure a lot of people would disagree with me, but you absolutely do not have to know all that stuff.

cdj: So, would you say that the most important thing is to meet people in film school that would take up these roles?

Smith: Exactly.

cdj: You said that David and Scott also wrote up

scripts. Was it agreed that whoever finished first was going to direct it or you were going to direct no matter what?

Smith: Oh, No. Nobody goes to film school wanting to be a producer or a DP (Director of Photography). Everyone goes to film school with the idea that they want to direct a feature. So, it's just bizarre how the roles laid out. David knew the most about the camera and he was very interested in directing photography. I'm sure he does want to direct some day, but right now all he's interested in is the camera. Scott, in film school, wanted to write and direct and still wants to write and direct and I know he will. But right now he's taken on this role of producer, which he's brilliant at. I mean, he's a fantastic organiser and he can keep shit in line and … I find it so hard, I don't care if it's *Clerks*, the music video or just Q and A after a screening, I find it so hard and I don't know if I could do it if he was not standing right there. It's weird, he's just an enabling type of personality. And people are always like, 'What does the producer do?' Well, we've met a bunch of them and the roles vary, but to me a producer is somebody who enables you to make whatever it is you're trying to make … So, after film school, if Scott came up with a script, he would have directed it. If Dave came up with a script that everyone agreed on, he would have directed it.

cdj: So he would have been Director of Photography too?

Smith: Probably not, he would have gotten someone else to do it. A perfect example is this movie *Drawing Flies* (work in progress) that my friends Malcolm and Matt shot in Vancouver. Malcolm writes for *Film Threat* and he showed me this script. I was really into it so I said, 'If you want, if you can make this movie for thirty thousand then I'll put up the budget'. And he wound up getting so much of the *Mallrats* cast in it which is funny … But Malcolm and Matt know nothing about directing; they know as little as I do or did. So since we were shooting up in Vancouver (Scott knows the area) and since we both went to film school up there, it was so easy to find a support base to surround them with so they were fully taken care of. All they had to do, since they wrote the script, was concentrate on the performances and setting up shots so to speak. But because of that incredible technical staff, they didn't have to know everything about camera and light-

Fig. 2. Collaboration: Cinematographer David Klein (top) frames a shot for director Kevin Smith (bottom). [Photo courtesy of Miramax.]

ing. And I think there's something certainly liberating about that. I don't knock certain directors that do know that stuff, I'm sure it's invaluable, but there's something very liberating where all you have to worry about is performance. Or rather, for a certain period all you think about is the script and then all you think about is performance. And it comes down to, you can have some of the most brilliant visual shots, but can you elicit a performance from an actor? Do you have that kind of presence that you can actually make somebody flesh a character out and make it believable? Because actors, not always, but in most cases will blow it out and make it much larger than real life and sometimes that works and sometimes it absolutely does not. So can you tone them down? Can you craft a performance?

cdj: But you personally didn't have any acting experience and you said at the first *Mallrats* screening that you don't like to act. So when you're working with these actors, don't you have trouble communicating with them in relation to their craft?

Smith: Not really. I think it comes from the fact that I wrote it, so I know how it should sound. I know where all the inflections should be.

cdj: Going back to film theory … In school, were they screening a lot of movies and analysing them?

Smith: Yes.

cdj: What were they showing you and what bothered you? Were they screening Godard or what?

Smith: No, that's a brilliant question because, if you're in this particular film school … if you're at NYU or UCLA, they could show you big movies because that's basically what you're aiming for. But in a film school like Vancouver, no one has enough money to attend the big schools. The thing they should be pushing on you is independent and guerrilla filmmaking; over and over again. They should show you nothing but independent films because these are the films that you can conceivably make first time out of the gate. Because we can't all be John Singleton. John Singleton goes to USC or UCLA, I think it was USC [Singleton studied film as an undergraduate at USC – ed] and when he graduates, immediately the first thing he does is make *Boyz N the Hood* (1991). That doesn't happen all the time! So the most sensible thing is 16 mm film. And so you would figure they would show you stuff like *Slacker*. They were showing *Silence of the Lambs* (1991)! Number one: who in that class could make *Silence of the Lambs*?! And number two: who would even have the opportunity to make something close to it their first time out? Second time out? Even third time out? It's like, if you're good enough one day to be making the calibre of film like *Silence of the Lambs* and have the resources to do it, then, shit man! You've been around! Because no one is going to come out of the VFS [Vancouver Film School] and have somebody be like, 'Here's a bunch of money, go make something like *Silence of the Lambs*'. It just wouldn't happen. So that was infuriating. And then you watch it and they're breaking it down and all. They're telling you, 'Demme's all into the close-up'. And they're telling you really obvious shit. I mean, you watch the movie and of course he's really into the close-up. Look at it, the camera's in the face of every actor! But again, using that as an example of filmmaking … that we could possibly approach in a class full of total neophytes! It just wasn't washing.

And then they tell you to bring in video clips of your own and talk about why you like them. I'd bring in stuff like *Do the Right Thing* (1989) which is conceivable. *Do the Right Thing* was made for about six million dollars. Conceivably, one could make that movie if you had a script that powerful. And I'd bring in stuff like *Stranger than Paradise* (1984), Jim Jarmusch's first film. He made it for what was rock bottom at the time, one hundred and fifty thousand or so; an unheard of price at that time. Now the average mean is like thirty thousand dollars, so it got lower for some reason. But I'd bring in that and most of the class is bored. But the people that aren't bored are the people you know you're going to identify with. And the teacher would be like, 'Why don't you bring in something else'. So, in the end it just did not mesh, film school and I; particularly that one. I mean, if you're going to go to film school, especially a nine month program like that, you should be showing nothing but independent films and do it for like a week. Be like, 'These are the people, here's your equipment go out and make a movie'.

cdj: It seems like there are two extremes of independent filmmaking: one extreme is, 'To hell with analysing and interpretation. Let's take a practical approach to making films. People will take what they want out of it but it'll still be a film.' Then there's the other extreme in that you put a lot of thought into it and try to organise all the formal aspects of it (lighting, editing, framing) to work with the story. Do you think that one is succeeding more than the other? Do you think that independent filmmakers that are more 'artsy' are having trouble because people just aren't accepting any of it?

Smith: Well, the year we were out on the festival circuit, at Sundance, there was a movie like us. There was *Clerks* and there was a movie called *Suture* (1993). Did you ever see it?

cdj: No.

Smith: I think it's out on video now. It was a first time film, shot in 35 mm black and white; Luscious! And it's 2.35, wide screen, with actual stars. It cost one million to make. And then there was *Clerks*. And *Clerks* was scrappy, nobody's in it and it was made for twenty-seven grand. You've heard of *Clerks*, but you haven't heard of *Suture*. Why is that? That movie looked polished, it looked good. It owed a huge debt to Hitchcock; it was riveting, not in its subject matter, but in its theme. And it was kind of 'heady', it was very 'artsy'. So nothing ever happened. It just got a really small distribution. And then ours, which is really down and dirty, is everywhere. So what works, what doesn't? But then there's stuff like *Sex, Lies and Videotape* (1989) which was made, again, for about one million. And it is polished and it is clean; there are stars and it's real smooth, but it's a first film. The movie [ends up making] twenty-seven million dollars and creates *Sundance* as it is known today. *Reservoir Dogs* (1992), first feature; polished looking film. Scrappy in content, but certainly not scrappy the way it was made and it's got stars. We out-grossed *Reservoir Dogs* when it first came out. *Reservoir Dogs* first made two million, *Clerks* made three point one. So, it's just so hard to judge ... Then you have something like *Brothers McMullen* (1995) down and dirty made but no edge whatsoever! It's just like every mainstream romance comedy you've ever seen and it makes ten million. And just because it doesn't look as good as any other Hollywood movies, people will assume, 'that's independent film'. And who's to say that it's not? But I'll sit here and I'll decry it 'till the day I die that it is not an independent movie. It's a Hollywood movie without the budget. But people will just say, 'Oh no, that's alternative'. The category of independent film is just so bizarre right now because in a world where *Pulp Fiction* (1994) is an independent film ... and *Mallrats* was made for six million and was bought by Gramercy, an independent distributor ... the lines are hazy. To me, what do I consider an independent film? It's a movie that's made by any means necessary ... But in the last five years things have so dramatically changed in the independent field in terms of: Miramax used to be a self-run company and they're still self-run, but it was two guys (Harvey and Bob Weinstein) who built that company from nowhere and then Disney turns around and buys it. Now they're still autonomous, they still make all their decisions, but there's more money coming in from the parent company ... Then New Line Cinema starts making Freddy Krueger films and Ted Turner buys them. It's still independent but it's getting a lot of money from the parent company. The true small distributors are like October Films and Samuel Goldwyn; nobody owns them. Gramercy is a key example, it's owned by two companies: Universal and Polygram. And

so, you've got fat money coming in from two of the biggest conglomerates in the business. And this is their art house label. So how does it actually work? Universal [gives] six million dollars to Gramercy and Gramercy in turn gives it to our production company (View Askew) to make the movie. And then it's about distancing yourself so you can buy the movie back when it's done. When it's done, they can 'buy' it but they've already bought it; they paid for it. It's [called] a negative pick-up.

cdj: So has the business side of it tainted anything?

Smith: No. The business side, if anything, is fun. It's nice when you sit around and field phone calls all day. Some days, you just come in and that's all you do is call people back. And that's kind of nice because when I look at the message board, [I remember how] two years ago somebody told me I'd have these messages. It doesn't [taint any of it] as long as you have a clear vision of what it is you're doing. With *Mallrats* [the business side] never bothered us because we knew exactly what we wanted to do; we were going to make a commercial film so we knew what we were in for.

cdj: You said that a few years ago it really bothered you when you saw movies of poor quality. Weren't you of the opinion that the people (and the business) behind these movies were just disgraceful?

Smith: Well, it's like when you go to a theatre and you're watching a 'comedy'. The people around you are laughing and you know in your heart of hearts, 'this is not funny, it's terrible'. You don't knock the filmmaker, you knock the audience. They'll watch anything! They're so starved for entertainment. It's funny. Now I still hate so many movies and can't believe that they get made. But now, going into the second film, where all of a sudden I'm going to be judged again; and I'm going to be judged against the first movie. Suddenly, you tend to censor yourself, you don't want to say shit any more because ... I can't remember how many times I've said ... every Spike Lee movie that came out after *Do The Right Thing*, 'It's great, but it's not *Do The Right Thing*'. And now people are going to say that in droves about *Mallrats*: 'It's funny, but it's not *Clerks*'.

cdj: Did you see *Clockers* (1995)?

Smith: Yeah.

cdj: What did you think?

Smith: Oh I like it a lot. I thought the signature stuff

Fig. 3. Guerrilla Filmmaking: Jeff Anderson (left) and Brian O'Halloran (right) in a scene from *Clerks*. [Photo courtesy of Miramax.]

was really great like the walking camera when people stand on the platforms …

cdj: … and the shot in the eye?

Smith: Yeah. Shit like that was amazing. And the beautiful thing about Spike Lee is, no matter what film he's making or who he's making it for, he's making an independent film because he's got a singular vision.

cdj: So, he went through NYU, he survived it and I'm sure he learned a lot of theory. Did that serve him well or was it a distraction?

Smith: No. In that respect, I think it did him well. But then again, if he hadn't gone through that experience, would he still be a filmmaker today? I think so. There's something in you that pushes you and makes you want to do it.

cdj: In terms of motivation: when you started doing *Clerks*, did you plan on budgeting the film on credit cards to begin with?

Smith: No, it was pretty much by accident. It was never about, 'Yeah, one day I'm going to need all these credit cards!' It was all about [a friend] and I

ran this contest to see who could get the most credit cards. We both had nothing jobs, so we would just fill out all these applications … By the time it was all over, each of us had about ten or twelve credit cards.

cdj: So when it got to the point that you wanted to make a movie, did you think, 'Hmmm, where am I going to get all this money? Oh wait I have all these credit cards!'

Smith: It wasn't even that. I knew I had all these credit cards and I [was] reading so much about independent film and how important credit cards were. So we said, 'Well, there's our budget'.

cdj: How much of a risk is that?

Smith: It's huge. And it's something that you don't think about until a certain point. I didn't. I mean, you cruise on the volition of the project. You've got the momentum and the passion that's driving you and you can't stop to think about things like that. As long as you're just paying the monthly minimum for some credit cards then you're okay. But it wasn't until after the film sold at Sundance: When we went to Sundance, we exploded, the film sold, I came back to Jersey and started going through all my bills. The budget of the film was twenty seven thousand, five hundred dollars. But that doesn't include interest or living costs. So, when all was said and done it was a forty thousand dollar debt. I had a forty thousand dollar debt looming over my head! I knew the film was already bought, I knew I had a fat check coming, but I just got these sudden shivers! It was like, 'What would have happened? What would have fuckin' happened if this movie didn't sell?' ... And we were never so confident in the film to think, 'This will get sold'. We never thought about Sundance because it always seemed to be a polished film festival.

cdj: So when you finally sat there and wrote the actual checks that erased this debt, was it empowering?

Smith: Well, dealing in a sum that large is kind of mind bending. Knowing that you've never had, even on a really great month, more than a thousand dollars in the bank. Suddenly, to be handed a hundred and twenty seven thousand dollar check, you're just like, 'What do I do?' So, the first thing you do is pay off your debts. Then, you write checks for the people who put time into the movie ... And then [the sum] shrinks down and it's time to get another job.

cdj: So you get a check for a hundred and twenty seven thousand and the film makes 3.1 million.

Smith: You don't see any of that money. See, we made the movie for thirty thousand. They paid us two hundred and twenty thousand for it, which to me is a lot of money, but then you hear about people who get a lot more for their first film. But to us, it was never about the check. It was always a question of, 'This movie would be better served by whom? Miramax'. So, they gave us two hundred and twenty thousand and a hundred thousand of that was allotted to getting the film up to 35 mm specifications: blow-up costs, re-mix and stuff like that. That's why the myth of the thirty thousand dollar movie is immediately gone ... Yeah, that's the movie that Miramax did see and buy. But the viewing public, when it went out on its commercial run, did not see a twenty seven thousand dollar movie. They saw a hundred and twenty thousand dollar movie. It's just like Robert Rodriguez with *El Mariachi* (1992), the seven thousand dollar movie. Nobody ever saw the seven

thousand dollar movie except the studio executives that bought that! He shot it on film and edited on video. Then he handed out video tapes and someone was smart enough to buy it. So he makes it into the Guinness book for having the world's cheapest movie. But nobody ever saw that movie! The viewing public at a festival never saw that movie because, believe me, they had to pump in a lot more money than we did into *Clerks* to get it up to 35 mm specifications.

cdj: During the shooting of *Clerks*, was it a fairly relaxed process or was there a lot of stress working within that low-budget framework?

Smith: With *Clerks*, there was stress only because the schedule was so fucked. I would work in the store from six in the morning to ten or eleven. Then my boss, Mrs. Topper, would come in and I would go home and sleep until about four. After that, I would come in again and work until ten thirty at night. So, from ten thirty to six in the morning we shot the film. If there was any stress it was from sleep deprivation.

cdj: Were you adding any material from that day at work while you were shooting?

Smith: No, I can't stand improvisation. For me, the script is the map. If you follow the map, you complete the journey. So, I'm a real weird dictator when it comes to people asking, 'Can I do something like ...' 'No! Do what's in the script, that's it'. And I think that comes from ... not being comfortable enough or considering myself a visual director. The only reason I really consider myself a director is because of the writing and the performance that I can elicit from the writing.

cdj: So while you were working at the store, you just had David take care of the camera and the film stock? And he would just bring it every night?

Smith: It was almost exactly like that. David would give Scott a list of everything he needed and we'd budget for it. So David submits this long list and we said, 'We can do the camera. That's about it'. He wanted all these light packages but we had no choice, we had to shoot under the fluorescents with a couple of sidelights. I'm sure David until this day watches *Clerks* and hangs his head thinking, 'I could have made it look so much better if we had more money'. But we didn't have the money to spend. That's why *Mallrats* was important for him because he got to showcase [his talents].

cdj: You're working now on the screenplay for your

third film, *Chasing Amy*. When proposing an idea for a screenplay, don't Hollywood producers want a 'hook?' If *Chasing Amy* is about a guy who falls in love with a lesbian, what would be the 'hook?'

Smith: Yeah, they all speak like that. They always want to know if there's a 'hook'.

cdj: Would the guy lose the girl to another girl or would the guy get the girl ...?

Smith: No, no. He'll never wind up with her! This is a return to independent film and not mainstream. If he wound up with her I'd probably crucify myself. But, I'm not a firm believer in that 'hook' [concept]. So far, I haven't made a movie where you can do one of those quick pitches. I mean, *Clerks* is about two guys who sit in a store and talk a lot, but nothing really happens.

cdj: So do you think nothing happens in *Clerks*?

Smith: I think so much happens but there's no real 'hook'. In *Mallrats* it's the same thing ... It's not complicated but you can't sum it up in one sentence. I don't think I've [written a screenplay] yet that has a 'hook'. And what it comes down to is that there has to be dialogue in there and that dialogue has to speak to the audience. With *Mallrats*, the dialogue speaks to a very specific audience and with *Clerks* it spoke to a much broader audience. So, it just depends on what you have to say. For example, *Sex, Lies and Videotape*. What was it about? A guy tapes [women] talking about sex and [masturbates] to them. On paper it doesn't sound like much but there's something in that movie. *Reservoir Dogs*, I guess, had a 'hook': 'Bank heist goes wrong'. But it was more about the dialogue than anything else because how many 'Bank heist gone wrong' movies have there been? ... I mean, in the end it's about ... what do you have to say? Do you have anything to say? I think that's the key.

cdj: So returning once more to film theory; If you have something to say and you want to present some of those ideas as sub-text, is it worth knowing theory and understanding what formal devices are at your disposal?

Smith: See, going into *Clerks* I was of the firm belief that: I'm going to make a movie that's about absolutely nothing and I want to see what people think it's about. And what was funny was when the critics started looking at the film and dissecting it, analysing it and coming up with shit that in a million years I never thought of.

cdj: So when you read that does it make you laugh or do you think, 'Wait a minute, there's something to that?'

Smith: Sometimes it makes you laugh but it makes you laugh because it's like, 'Wow! Who would put in this much time to figure this out?' And, 'They got that? That's interesting, maybe it's true'. It's never that they're so off the mark, but everyone is going to see it exactly as they want to see it. So going into it, it's never about establishing a particular sub-text. It's just what you have to say at that particular moment. With *Chasing Amy*, there is a sub-text, if you would call it that and it's about art vs. commerce.

cdj: So *Clerks* was about nothing and you didn't want to have a sub-text ...

Smith: ... But it wound up having it.

cdj: Okay, so what about *Mallrats*?

Smith: Well *Mallrats* I think is about way less than *Clerks*!

cdj: Okay, what about *Star Wars* (1977).

Smith: With *Star Wars* you're dealing with classic mythological characters.

cdj: If you consider the idea of parody, which I think you do really well in *Mallrats*, (digression) ... which leads me to ask: Who composed the *Star Wars*-like musical score?

Smith: Ira Newborn. He's a composer. He did all the scores for a lot of those John Hughes movies. He also worked a little on *The Blues Brothers* (1980). He's just amazing. He's the king of the comic score ... While writing the movie, I realised that you needed that *Batman*-like music and I immediately thought of him. So, there's sub-text there and it's in the music. But again, it's such a collaborative process! And that's why I can't stand these [directors] that write, 'A film by ...' And lately I've been seeing it everywhere. I think there are very few people in the business today who could really get away with it. 'A film by Martin Scorsese'. That's fine, the guy's earned it. 'A film by Spike Lee'. The guy's earned it. It's really such a slap in the face to everyone that helped you make that movie. On the poster, when it says 'Written and Directed by Kevin Smith', I can handle that because that was my job. But saying, 'A film by' [would imply] that I took care of everything and all these people were just helping out.

cdj: This ties in with the long standing question of authorship. It seems as if your stance is that there are many people involved in the process and it

Fig. 4. Silent Bob (Kevin Smith, left) and Jay (Jason Mewes) in a scene from *Mallrats*. [Photo courtesy of Gramercy Pictures.]

shouldn't be, 'A film by ...' When you have a certain director whose personality becomes so much larger than the film itself it becomes a problem. Do you see that happening to Quentin Tarantino? As a personality, when you see him on interviews you see that he's kind of ... he's got something to him that's sort of ...

Smith: ... Problems.

cdj: Yes.

Smith: Big problems.

cdj: So in that case, the personality of the director overwhelms the film and who knows who operated the camera in *Pulp Fiction*? You won't hear of anyone else who was involved in *Pulp Fiction* except for Tarantino and the stars. But I don't know how much Tarantino himself had to do with that. He's not at fault completely.

Smith: Well, it depends on whether you're willing to accept that. It comes down to ... you're given a choice. You can shun that or you can embrace it. I shun it, Quentin embraced it. We met Quentin in Cannes that year when *Clerks* was in Cannes and then me and Brian hung out with him in Germany. And this was before *Pulp* was 'Pulp'; in Cannes

particularly because it was before the first screening ever. He was pretty down to earth and very approachable; just like a film geek. And we thought it was funny how he was so into it. But Quentin's personality just embraced what was thrown at him and accepted the title of 'Second Coming'; he ran with it and exploited it. And that's something I could never feel comfortable doing; never in a million years if it was thrown at me.

cdj: But it was thrown hard at him; really hard.

Smith: It was thrown hard.

cdj: What kind of reaction could you have to that? Maybe it was the way he was brought up as a 'film geek'. Perhaps he grew up revering these filmmakers the same way.

Smith: I think he bought into the celebrity. He loved the celebrity aspect of it. Still does. I mean, I like seeing my name in print, don't get me wrong. But I could never feel that seriously about what it is I do. In the end it's just a job and in the end it's like: You look at *Clerks* and it's a fine film. I like it a lot. And *Mallrats*, I think, is a great movie. It's just fun to watch. But I'm not curing cancer. I'm not reinventing the wheel.

cdj: As a writer though, you have an affinity for creating art. And let's say someone was tossing these titles at you. Let's say you were being put up on a pedestal by the media and you respond by saying, 'It's just a job'. But you chose this job for a reason. It's art and you want to do something artistic right? (Smith agrees) You don't want to work at a desk?

Smith: Right …'he says from behind his desk'.

cdj: So is it more acceptable in art to admire the person or personality or the 'vision?' If it all stems from the writing, from the dialogue, is it appropriate to admire it as art and recognise the individual for his ideas and how he/she brings them out?

Smith: People do. There are certainly people that do. I don't know if people are going to look at *Mallrats* and say, 'It's art'. But art is a term that I've had so much trouble adapting to. It just sounds [pretentious]. I love to be self-deprecating about both the [films], but there is way more going on in *Clerks* than [obscene] jokes. It's like there's something going on there. But I just feel uncomfortable [thinking], 'Am I an artist?' I mean, by definition, yes. I work in the field of the arts but …

cdj: … You're sitting behind a desk.

Smith: Yeah, it's a weird thing. When all is said and done, the product is up there. You're putting it on display.

cdj: Film as an art is extremely industry and business oriented.

Smith: Oh yeah.

cdj: So, Tarantino's *Pulp Fiction* was an independent production. *Mallrats* is a studio picture. Had you made your second film independently, how would it have been different?

Smith: It would have been *Dogma* (work in progress). But again, it's the freshman/sophomore thing. On our freshman effort, you would have thought that we did cure cancer. The press was so resoundingly positive. Now, because of that, the sophomore effort is bound to be slammed. It's bound to be slammed.

* * *

This prophetic statement concluded the taped portion of our conversation. *Mallrats* did not do very well at the box office. However, a number of critics, including myself, gave it positive reviews. Kevin Smith's third film, *Chasing Amy*, will be produced independently as will *Dogma*, an ambitious project dealing with a truly unique vision of Catholicism. Perhaps personality traits do in fact translate onto the film frame.❖

Film History, Volume 8, pp. 249–253, 1996. Copyright © John Libbey & Company
ISSN: 0892-2160. Printed in Australia

William K. Everson

The editors of *Film History* each had their own experience of William K. Everson, the teacher, archivist, and historian who died earlier this year at the age of 67. The following pages offer their varied perspectives on an extraordinarily dedicated and wonderful life.

At his death on 14 April, the *New York Times* wrote that William K. Everson's place in the America cinema was comparable to that of Henri Langlois in France. There certainly are few other candidates. Operating from his crowded west side apartment, Everson brought together an entire generation of critics, scholars, filmmakers and buffs. His collection and the endless cycles of screenings he spun out of it, really was the New York equivalent of the Cinémathèque in its glory days.

But while they may have shared the same passion for films, it would be hard to think of two more different human beings. If Langlois was the dragon guarding his treasure (a typical collector's posture), Everson was open, amicable and generous to the point of embarrassment. The following story may be extreme, but it's hardly atypical: one evening in his apartment after an all-night screening session he overheard me discussing a rarely-seen silent classic with a friend whom he had never met before, but whose enthusiasm was obviously genuine. The screening room area, which must have originally served as the apartment's foyer and living room, was lined with piles of film cans and boxes four or five feet deep. Everson reached out his right hand and from the top of the nearest pile plucked a 16 mm negative of this very title and handed it over. 'Just return it when you're finished with it', he said.

I saw such acts of spontaneous generosity many times over the years and I came to understand that what was happening was very different than, say, the borrowing of a book. Everson was proselytising, the way some people hand out Bibles in airports. He wasn't simply running a film exchange, he was spreading the faith, like Johnny Appleseed with a sackful of 16 mm prints.

While those who knew him personally have endless stocks of anecdotes like this, it was not just Everson's personal generosity that made him so formidable a figure, especially during the crucial years of the 1960s and 1970s. At a moment when an unprecedented hunger for Ford, Walsh, Hawks, Lang or Murnau collided with the realities of print availability, Everson had the stuff.

The most memorable evening in my career as a graduate cinema student was 17 December 1969, when William K. Everson appeared for his 'American Cinema' class, right off the plane from Hollywood, cradling a print of Murnau's *City Girl*. Depending on what source you read, this film was either (a) never completed, (b) never released or (c) entirely reshot by others. Word had gotten around and the back of the room was filled with visitors like Andrew Sarris and Herman G. Weinberg. Everson explained that the film had been misfiled in the vaults, shelved with Fox's 1938 *City Girl*, which we learned had starred Phyllis Brooks and was in no way connected to this version.

The New York premiere of *City Girl* was magic – a 1960s equivalent of the opening of King Tut's tomb. I walked out into the cold East Village air with the sense of having participated in something astonishing and the expectation of more revelations to come. Everson didn't disappoint; two months later he had *Hello, Sister!* and I had a dissertation topic.

Everson's collection survives him, of course and he wasn't alone in digging out rarities and sharing them with eager audiences. With a little good fortune, students will still be able to see *Blanche Fury* and *One More River* and *A Kiss for Cinderella*. But they'll have to be *really* lucky to find someone like Bill Everson to share the treasure with them.

Richard Koszarski

ill Everson's life and work had an impact on me long before I met him for the first time. It all started in the mid-seventies, during my early days at the Cineteca Griffith in Genoa, while I was working with Angelo R. Humouda for the development of what should have become the leading private film archive in Italy. With his typical, relentless energy Angelo would spend hours telling stories about the expanding galaxy of collectors and the first signs of interest for the resurrection of the silent motion picture heritage: The Brighton Conference of 1978; a then-mysterious acronym (FIAF) for a no less secretive International Federation of Film Archives; legendary names such as those of Eileen Bowser, George Pratt, Jay Leyda, Raymond Rohauer, Kevin Brownlow; the restoration of Abel Gance's *Napoleon.* Bill's name was often at the top of the list and it didn't take much to understand why. Very much like Angelo, who was born in Palestine, Bill was an emigré of sorts. A more relevant similarity between their projects was a truly independent attitude towards the institutional and academic community. The conflicts arising from such perspective were instrumental in shaping my own awareness of the need of a closer cooperation between collectors, archivists and film scholarship.

A much debated, revealing case in point involved the rediscovery of *A Kiss for Cinderella* (1926). At the time its preservation became an object of debate I was barely aware of the director's name, Herbert Brenon; most importantly, I knew very little about the fact that most films produced during the so-called silent era were distributed in tinted or toned copies. My acquaintance with film history had started in a black and white world, where the uneven quality of late-generation 16 mm prints was the rule and the term nitrate was little more than an abstraction. One has to start somewhere, though and my initiation to the colour of 'nitrate' coincided with Bill's passionate claim for the supremacy of the tinted and toned version of *Kiss for Cinderella* against its monochrome version. That was quite a rough beginning, for I abruptly learned why collecting and preserving film are the *Yin* and *Yan* of film culture and why the two extremes could so easily get into collision. Whenever Bill's biography will be written (it ought to; but I can't figure out who might take the challenge), the details and circumstances of his approach to film preservation might reveal the inherent complexity of the issues laying behind the well-known catchphrase, 'nitrate won't wait'.

Now that Bill's gone, however, something else appears to me as of much greater importance. As far as I can tell, his personal history is the best argument against those who believe that film collectors use films as a substitute for an emotional life. I have known Bill for little more than ten years; long enough, though, to witness the intensity and beauty of the love between him and Karen. At her side, he had found the kind of happiness without which cinema is nothing but moving shadows.

Paolo Cherchi Usai

---

first met Bill Everson in 1970 when I moved back to New York City from Cambridge, MA. A couple of my friends were graduate students in the Cinema Studies program at NYU. I went with them to screenings for Everson's classes. I particularly remember the semester he devoted to the films of John Ford, when I saw *Cameo Kirby, Three Bad Men, Four Sons, Pilgrimage* and *The World Moves On* for the first time. Though not a regular, I went six or eight times to the Theodore Huff Society, a film society run by Everson, to see rare James Whale, Howard Hawks and Frank Borzage films. I frequented his lecture/screenings at the New School. I went to the Saturday (or was it Sunday?) afternoon triple features for NYU students in a building on Second Ave. I even recall going to his apartment once with Adam Reilly for a screening of *Blessed Event.*

I was a product of the film society movement. I've taught film for more than 25 years, but I've never taken a film course. My first serious exposure to the cinema was through a film society in Cleveland Heights when I was a high school student. As a graduate student living in Cambridge, I went three or four times a week to film society screenings at Harvard and MIT. Everson was the leading figure in the film society movement in New York. His screenings were my graduate school education in film.

If you were interested in films, New York was a great place to be in the 1960s and 1970s. Bill Everson played a major role in making New York a centre for film culture during this period. He screened films that were – and still are – hard to see. Though his passion for the cinema tended to centre on films made before 1953, his interest in the films of this period was eclectic and wide-ranging, embracing almost everything. And he worked hard to share his passion, his interests and his film collection with others, even to the point of flying to film festivals in Europe with film cans on his lap.

During the last four or five years, Bill Everson

and I were colleagues on the National Film Preservation Board. Everson educated us on the board about neglected films such as *Hell's Hinges, The Italian, Poor Little Rich Girl* and *Where are My Children?*, titles which were eventually placed on the Registry. At the same time, Everson worked hard to help develop a national plan for film preservation. In a letter noting his achievements, Associate Librarian of Congress, Winston Tabb, wrote that 'Bill's greatest role quite possibly was that of film rescuer, saving films far before the time it became fashionable to do so' and that 'few persons have meant more to the preservation and exhibition of film than Bill Everson'.

I don't think that the explosion of interest in the cinema that occurred in the 1960s and 1970s could have taken place without people like Bill Everson, who provided the films to fuel it and the passion and energy to keep it going. We will all miss him.

John Belton

Reminiscing about William Everson, long-time colleague Charles Turner recently recalled the time that the film historian was on his way to give a lecture in California. While crossing the street, Everson was struck by a car and thrown a considerable distance. Friends urged him to seek medical attention, but he insisted on fulfilling his commitment. Only after the film screening and lecture could he be persuaded to go to hospital and be treated for broken ribs.

This was typical behaviour of the man that Charles Silver of the Museum of Modern Art Study Centre characterised as 'a giver, not a taker'. William Everson was one of the last survivors of a group that popularised serious study of film in North America after World War II. Everson was there at the first screening of The Film Circle on 8 February 1952 (in the august company of Theodore Huff, Charles Turner, Robert Youngson, Seymour Stern, Herman Weinberg, Henry Hart, Joseph Cornell,

John Griggs, Gerald McDonnell, Parker Tyler, Mary Ellen Bute, William Kenly and Amos Vogel) and remained at the heart of the film community from that day on.

Everson's scholarship was characterised by an encyclopedic knowledge and a willingness to give serious consideration to all forms of cinema, from the work of W.C. Fields to the films of Victor Sjostrom. His contribution to the discipline included books like the first study of the Western to be published in the English language and a valuable survey of silent cinema. For many years he contributed to journals including *Film in Review* with the results of his primary investigations of areas that later would be explored by those of us who followed in his footsteps. As a faculty member of New York University, Everson's lectures on silent cinema, the western and other topics educated class after class of film students.

The William Everson that I will remember was the fellow who lived opposite my building on West

79th Street in New York when I was a student in the early 1970s. I knew him only by reputation as patron saint of the FOOFS (Friends of Old Films) and dean of the local film collectors. One day, it was suggested to me that a film I needed to see for a research project was in the Everson collection. I called him up to ask under what terms might the film be available. There were no terms at all. Everson suggested that I drop over at the end of the week.

Days later, I nervously entered the Everson apartment to meet the great man. Although his looks were somewhat reminiscent of Donald Pleasence, Everson exuded the affability and decency of Roger Livesey. I was immediately put to ease by his courtesy and gentlemanly demeanour. His trust in people was implicit. Although he never laid eyes on me before, he handed me several reels and asked for their return whenever I found it convenient. I later discovered that this was a typical gesture. By run-

ning what amounted to the best private lending library of films in the days before videotape, William Everson was probably the greatest single contributor to film education of his time. His collection was the bedrock of courses at NYU. Thousands over the years attended screening of his films at the Huff Society, the New School, the Museum of Modern Art or even in the privacy of his home. His munificence was fundamental to the development of generations of scholars, archivists, editors and programmers.

Concerning W.S. Hart, whom he greatly admired, Everson once wrote that Hart brought stature and poetry to work which he approached with passion and devotion. No better epitaph than this could be written for William Everson.

Mark Langer

My fondest memory of Bill Everson is of him, David Bordwell and me eating banana splits in Pordenone in 1987, during a rare moment of calm between screenings at the 'Le Giornate del Cinema Muto' festival. That was the year he received the Jean Mitry Award for his archival work. This image seems appropriate, in that Bill's interests continue to be reflected in the festival's programs – e.g. this year's Herbert Brenon retrospective. In some ways, Bill's book American Silent Film (1978), took a traditional enthusiast's approach. During the 1970s, however, he was also one of the pioneers who brought forward obscure figures that are now thought of as mainstream. How many earlier synoptic histories would have emphasised Reginald Barker, Brenon and the director in whose honour Bill renamed himself, William K. Howard?

Bill was never interested just in the certified classics. He could find something good in virtually any American film, even cheap Poverty Row items. His catholic tastes reflected what was perhaps his greatest insight: save everything, study everything. His own collection reflected this belief. Only much more recently have other, official archives realised

the point of preserving drive-in cheapies and other previously despised films.

He was enormously generous to this younger generation of historians. In the late 1970s, David Bordwell, Janet Staiger and I set out to define and analyse the 'classical Hollywood cinema' (resulting in The Classical Hollywood Cinema, 1985). As part of our research on ordinary film style, we used a random-number generator to come up with an 'unbiased sample' of 100 features from the era 1915 to 1960. The list was not truly random, because most of the films on the original list were lost or unavailable. To compensate for this difficulty, we generated a much longer list and kept going down it until we located 100 accessible prints which we could analyse in detail.

Naturally we contacted the major American archives – including Bill – in search of prints. More of the titles on our random listing proved to be in his collection than in most of the other archives. This was not because his collection – impressive though it is – was bigger than all the others. But Bill had collected across the spectrum of films. For example, we were able to see the 1949 Lewis R. Foster detective film Manhandled (cast: Dorothy Lamour,

Fig. 1. William K. Everson at home with his RCA projector.

Dan Duryea, Sterling Hayden) because Bill had a print; if he had not, we would probably have had to eliminate it from our list. And if we had had to jettison many more ordinary films like that, we would have ended up with a final sample more heavily biased toward the respectable Hollywood classics. Bill allowed us access to several such prints and helped us to keep our sample closer to a true cross-section of standard American filmmaking. I would like to think that, despite the considerable differences between *American Silent Film* and *The* *Classical Hollywood Cinema*, we shared Bill's respect for the entire range of Hollywood cinema.

Bill's willingness to search beyond Porter and Griffith in his study of silent American film reflected his love for the cinema in general. And those who now routinely preserve and study the lesser-known classics and the ordinary films of Hollywood and other countries are, to a large extent, following in Bill's footsteps.

Kristin Thompson

Chronology of Early Cinema: corrections from Deac Rossell

Several corrections and additions to the chronology of early cinema published as *Film History,* Vol. 7, No. 2, Summer 1995, have turned up in letters to either the editor or myself and I am most grateful to all those who have taken the trouble to write. They are noted here so that readers may update their copies of this issue. Any further corrections, additions or comments are most welcomed.

Corrections are as follows:

1889 10 December: US patent 417, 202 to Henry M Reichenbach.This is the issue date of the patent and not the application date, which was 9 April 1889 and is not so specified.

1890 8 October: DRP 57, 133 to Emil Kohlrausch. Also 9 January 1891 and Index.

Kohlrausch's correct first name is Ernst, not Emil as I call him or Eduard, as he is called in all other modern sources. See my article Lebende Bilder: Die chronophotographen Ottomar Anschütz und Ernst Kohlrausch in Pamela Müller and Suzanne Höbermann, eds, '100 Jahre Filmproduktion in Niedersachsen' (Hanover, 1995: Gesellschaft fur Filmstudien, e.V.), which includes a great deal of previously unknown material on both Anschütz and Kohlrausch, who may have projected his chronophotographs as early as mid-1893.

1895 22 February: Electrotachyscope of Ottomar Anschütz. *Typographical error: text should read, 'the taking for March 1895 amounted to ...'*

1896 4 April: Cinématographe Lumière at the Salone Margherita. *This screening took place in Naples, not in Turin, I am indebted to Luciana Spina of the Museo Nazionale del Cinema for correcting my error.*

1896 13 April: Unidentified screening in Birmingham. *Richard Brown reminds me that the unidentified apparatus was advertised as a Cinematograph, not as a Kinetoscope.*

1896 4 May: Lumière Cinématographe opens in Cardiff.

The date for this show should be 11 May not 4 May. Wholly my own error, as I trusted both John Barnes and Richard Brown rather than new research by David Berry in his Wales and Cinema. I am indebted to all three gentlemen for bringing this to my attention and I am abashed. Correct as well in Citations, where the previously published works of Barnes and Brown are incorrect and Berry is correct, plus my apologies to David for not trusting his careful work.

Page 201. Note 8: from 'If Edison and his collaborators were themselves capable ...'

This is a silly and mistaken comment, as I missed a passage in Hendricks (and Dickson) which clearly shows that Edison changed the whole course of his research into the Kinetoscope based on the Anschütz Electrotachyscope. See the same article noted above.

Typographic errors are as follows:

1896 26 April: Kinétograph of Méliés and Reulos in Berlin: Line 4: Unter den Linden.

P.200, Note 5: Second paragraph, line 13: *application*

P.202, Note 13: First Paragraph, line 1: ... *learned the business practise ...*

P.203, Note 20: line 8 ... *worked out in December 1872* ... (No *the*)

P.203, Note 26: Line 2: Patent title in *italic type*

P.209, Note 62: Line 2: Patent title in *italic type*

P.215, Note 102: last line: ... *supplied* ... (Spelling)

P.223, Bibliography: Aurelio de los Reyes, first entry: *Reyes, Aurelio de los* ... (Spelling; next two are correct)

P.224, Bibliography: Steen, Jürgen, ed., first line: *Eine neue Zeit* ... (Spelling)

Additions are as follows:

1896 2 March: Bioskop of Max Skladanowsky opens at the concert hall in Köthen, Germany, running through 8 March with their Wintergarten program, opening to a sold-out audience. The screenings in Köthen included dissolving lantern slide shows and a demonstration of X-rays, plus special shows for families and schoolchildren. [Joachim Castan: *Max Skladanowsky, oder der begin einer deutschen Filmgeschichte.* (Stuttgart, 1995: Füsslin Verlag), 93–94].

1896 25 March: Unidentified apparatus opens at the Pandora Gallery, King's Road, opposite the West Pier, in Brighton, England, becoming the first regional showing of films outside London, continuing for four weeks with hourly performances. Admission 1 Shilling, children half price. Called a Cinématograph, but probably a Theatrograph of Robert Paul the *Sussex Daily News* though 'In comparison with Professor Rontgen's startling and far-reaching discovery' the showing 'can only occupy a position of secondary importance, though its results are scarcely less astonishing and distinctly more entertaining to the general public'. [*Sussex Daily News*, 25 March 1896; Gareth Monaghan first cited this show in his paper 'Victorian People - Victorian Films' given in Bradford at the conference 'Celebrating 1895'. I am indebted to Richard Brown, Frank Gray and John Barnes for bringing it to my attention.]

UPCOMING ISSUES/
CALL FOR PAPERS

Cinema and Nation, Part Two
edited by Kristin Thompson

International Trends in Film Studies
edited by Paolo Cherchi Usai

Silent Cinema
edited by Richard Koszarski

Non-Fiction Film
edited by Mark Langer

Screenwriters and Screenwriting
edited by John Belton
(deadline for submissions
1 March 1997)

International Cinema of the 1910s
edited by Kristin Thompson
(deadline for submissions
1 June 1997)

FILM HISTORY encourage the submission of manuscripts within the overall scope of the journal. These may correspond to the announced themes of future issues above, but may equally be on any topic relevant to film history.

FILM HISTORY

Back issue and subscription order form

PLEASE SUPPLY:

.... Subscription(s) to *Film History*
at Institutional/Private rate (please specify)
Surface/Air Mail (please specify)
.... Back issues of the following volumes/issues

....
....

I enclose payment of £/US$ ....
Please send me a Pro-forma invoice for: £/US$ ....

Please debit my Access/Master Card/Visa/
American Express/Diner's Club credit card:
Account no..Expiry..........

Name ....
Address ....
....
....
.... Zip/Postcode ....

Signature ....Date ....
(This form may be photocopied)

SUBSCRIPTION RATES & BACK ISSUE PRICES

Institutional Subscription rates:
All countries (except N. America)
Surface mail   £85/A$170 Air mail   £95/A$190
N. America
Surface mail   US$151   Air mail   US$172
*Private Subscription rates (subscribers warrant that
copies are for their PERSONAL use only):*
All countries (except N. America)
Surface mail   £33/A$66 Air mail   £44/A$88
N. America
Surface mail   US$59   Air mail   US$79
Back issues: All issues available – Volumes 1 to 7:
£12/US$20 each number.

JOHN LIBBEY & COMPANY LTD,
Level 10, 15–17 Young Street
Sydney, NSW 2000, Australia
Telephone: +61 (0)2 9251 4099
Fax: +61 (0)2 9251 4428

FILM HISTORY

An International Journal

Aims and Scope

The subject of Film History is the historical development of the motion picture, and the social, technological and economic context in which this has occurred. Its areas of interest range from the technical and entrepreneurial innovations of early and precinema experiments, through all aspects of the production, distribution, exhibition and reception of commercial and non-commercial motion pictures.

In addition to original research in these areas, the journal will survey the paper and film holdings of archives and libraries world-wide, publish selected examples of primary documentation (such as early film scenarios) and report on current publications, exhibitions, conferences and research in progress. Many future issues will be devoted to comprehensive studies of single themes.

Instructions to Authors

Manuscripts will be accepted with the understanding that their content is unpublished and is not being submitted for publication elsewhere. If any part of the paper has been previously published, or is to be published elsewhere, the author must include this information at the time of submittal. Manuscripts should be sent to the Editor-in-Chief:

Richard Koszarski
American Museum of the Moving Image
36–01 35th Avenue
Astoria, New York, NY 11106, USA

excepting for submissions to thematic issues directed by one of the Associate Editors.

The publishers will do everything possible to ensure prompt publication, therefore it is required that each submitted manuscript be in complete form. Please take the time to check all references, figures, tables and text for errors before submission.